SHARED EXPERIENCE
The Psychoanalytic Dialogue

SHARED EXPERIENCE
The Psychoanalytic Dialogue

edited by
Luciana Nissim Momigliano
and
Andreina Robutti

foreword by
Eric Brenman

Karnac Books
London 1992 New York

Translated by:
Cristina Coronelli (chapter six)
Gina Danile (chapters one, two, four, nine)
John Denton (Introduction; introductions to parts one, two, three)
D. E. W. Jones (chapter three)
Mary Rubick (chapter eight)
Scott Staton (chapter seven)

First published in 1992 by
H. Karnac (Books) Ltd.
58 Gloucester Road
London SW7 4QY

Distributed in the United States of America by
Brunner/Mazel, Inc.
19 Union Square West
New York, NY 10003

British Library Cataloguing in Publication Data.

Momigliano, Luciana Nissim
    Shared Experience: The Psychoanalytic Dialogue
    I. Title   II. Robutti, Andreina
    III. Danile, Gina
    150.19

ISBN 1 85575 034 1

Printed in Great Britain by BPCC Wheatons Ltd, Exeter

ACKNOWLEDGEMENTS

Acknowledgements are due to the *Rivista di Psicoanalisi*, in which some chapters of this book originally appeared:

- chapter one is a slightly revised version of ". . . Due persone che parlano in una stanza . . .", *30* (1984), 1: 1–17.
- chapter three is a revised and enlarged version of "A journey through the bipersonal field of analysis. From roleplaying to transformations in the couple", *37* (1991), 1: 4–46.
- chapter four is an updated version of "La fiaba della mano verde o dell'identificazione proiettiva", *29* (1983), 4: 459–475.
- chapter eight is a revised and enlarged version of "Una psicosi di transfert: prospettive cliniche nel lavoro con pazienti border-line", *30* (1984), 1: 55–72.
- chapter nine is a revised version of "Cassandra: un mito per l'ipocondria", in: G. Bartoli Bonaiuto (Ed.), *In Due Dietro il Lettino* (Castrovillari: Teda, 1990).

We also wish to thank Emma Gioia Piccioli, François Michell, and Parthenope Bion Talamo for their precious help in revising the English translations.

Special gratitude is due to Cesare Sacerdoti for giving us both the idea and the opportunity of publishing this book, and to Klara Majthenyi King for her scrupulous and highly competent editing of the whole text.

CONTENTS

PART TWO

The analyst's mind

PART THREE

The clinical field

CONTRIBUTORS

FRANCESCO BARALE: born in Verona; graduated in medicine; is an associate professor of psychiatry at the University of Pavia and an associate member of the Società Psicoanalitica Italiana (SPI).

MICHELE BEZOARI: born in Voghera (Pavia); graduated in medicine and specialized in psychiatry; worked as a psychiatrist at the psychiatric clinic of the University of Pavia until 1988; is an associate member of the SPI and works in private practice in Pavia.

FRANCO DE MASI: born in Airola (Benevento); graduated in medicine and specialized in psychiatry; worked as a psychiatrist at the "Ugo Cerletti" Psychiatric Hospital, Parabiago (Milan) until 1979; is a full member of the SPI and lives and works as a psychoanalyst in Milan.

GIUSEPPE DI CHIARA: born in Palermo; graduated in medicine and specialized in psychiatry; lives and works as a psychoanalyst in Milan and is a full member and training analyst of the SPI.

ANTONINO FERRO: born in Palermo; graduated in medicine and specialized in psychiatry; lives and works as a child- and adult psychoanalyst in Pavia and is a full member of the SPI.

ROSANNA GAGLIARDI GUIDI: born in Marina di Massa; graduated in pedagogy and specialized in clinical psychology; taught at the Catholic University of Milan until 1969, and worked as a psychotherapist at the "Paolo Pini" Psychiatric Hospital in Milan; is a full member and training analyst of the SPI and works as a psychoanalyst in Milan.

LUCIANA NISSIM MOMIGLIANO: born in Turin; graduated in medicine and specialized in paediatrics and psychiatry; lives and works in Milan and is a full member and training analyst of the SPI.

ANDREINA ROBUTTI: born in Milan; graduated in medicine; specialized in neurology and worked at the Clinic for Nervous and Mental Diseases of the University of Milan until 1982; is a full member of the SPI and is in private practice as a psychoanalyst in Milan.

DINA VALLINO MACCIÒ: born in Cagliari; graduated in philosophy and specialized in psychology; worked as a child psychotherapist in public institutions until 1972; is a supervisor in infant observation groups at the University of Milan in the past, and currently for the National Health Service; lives and works in Milan as a child- and adult psychoanalyst and is a full member of the SPI.

FOREWORD

Eric Brenman

Psychoanalysis is an inexhaustible subject—hence its fascination and difficulty. As all science, it has gone through changes, transformations, and developments, particularly in the technique of clinical practice. The constant enquiry as to what is considered to be more important and less important at any given time in the analysis and the technique of reaching another human being's psyche so that optimum meaning is achieved, together with dealing with impairing anxiety, is the science and art of psychoanalysis.

Psychoanalysis, and in particular its practice, is a truly pluralistic art and science. Its very discoveries show the inevitable unfolding of a precise repetition compulsion of basic primitive processes that has already gone through transformation in psychological development; and once again the analysand has to encounter understanding provided by another human being (the analyst). How such encounters are met, as well as the nature of the understanding and experience, determines the quality of further psychological development. The building and storing of this experience becomes part of the new equipment for dealing with the vicissitudes of life, both currently and for the future.

In this volume the contributors from the Milanese Society show themselves to have gone through their own "growing pains" of psychoanalytic development and arrived at their diverse personal ways of getting closer to dealing with what is thought and felt to be most important. They have gone through the struggle of slavish devotion to foreign models of psychoanalytic practice and xenophobic rejection of alien viewpoints; they have arrived at distilling that which they considered most valuable and marrying this to their own thoughtful and intuitive personal understanding.

It is interesting to note that the central theme that emerges in this book is the encounter between analysand and analyst, which they describe as a "two-way affair"—two persons having a living, emotional interaction, observing and influencing each other. Out of this comes the task of reflecting, containing, studying, and deciding the most useful understanding to impart at any point.

They are mindful of the history of the analysand—where he has come from—and the power of the repetition compulsion when faced with critical issues and circumstances. At the same time they apply the same critical rigour to that which goes on in the mind of the analyst, who also has to contend with his own internal world. This process, together with monitoring the unique specific interaction between analyst and analysand, in addition to what is transferred both ways, is regarded as the task of understanding—a task they consider and describe as "on its way" and thus available for further understanding and growth. In this project they share an enterprise with much of the rest of the psychoanalytic world, which, in different ways, has moved in this direction. Their unique contribution is how they arrive at their understanding from their own diverse backgrounds, which they use gainfully to understand "the other".

It is worth noting that this process is valued, if not prized, because in their view it is considered both to heighten the sense of "self" in oneself (whether analyst or analysand) and to promote a respect and concern for the "self" of others, without which no real human understanding or human dignity can properly thrive—a self within a culture and yet a unique individual.

I am very impressed with the work shown in this book, and the ongoing movement that is clearly taking place. I am sure they will go on weathering the storms, the pains, and the inevitable setbacks and take heart from the encouragement of their valuable achievements. I am honoured to play a part in introducing this volume to English-speaking readers, and I look forward to further developments and publications in the future.

Meeting at a cross-roads

Andreina Robutti

T he contributors to this volume do not belong to any specific "school". They are analysts who, following somewhat different paths in the course of their professional life, have come to concur on certain views and to share a certain approach to the psychoanalytic relationship. This book, we might say, is a meeting at a cross-roads.

The authors are all members of the Milanese Centre for Psychoanalysis, a local branch of the Italian Psychoanalytical Society, which was founded by Edoardo Weiss in 1932 and officially recognized by Freud in 1936. Born in an unfavourable cultural environment, dominated by idealistic philosophy on one side and by organicistic psychiatry on the other—as David (1966) puts it, "between Croce and Lombroso"—psychoanalysis was soon banned in Italy by the Fascist government, and the few pioneers of our society were obliged to disperse (Musatti, 1976; Servadio, 1976). A rather ill-starred beginning. It seems that Freud himself was somewhat sceptical about the chances of psychoanalysis taking root in our country. For once, his forecast proved to be wrong. Immediately after the war, contacts between the first few Italian psychoanalysts were resumed. The society, re-founded in 1947, quickly began to grow. Today it is a group of considerable size, and its members, spread out all over the country, have as point of scientific reference nine local "centres", situated in different cities. The Milanese Centre is one of the largest, with very varied scientific viewpoints being held by its members. Followers of different psychoanalytic models live side by side, but there are no official separate groups. Debates and discussions are lively, and while at an individual level the others' points of view can be harshly criticized when not totally rejected, on the whole, at the official level of public discussions, clashes of opinion tend to occur in a climate of mutual respect. In this atmosphere of basic tolerance each member has a chance to develop the way of thinking and working that is most congenial to him, according to his own personality, his vision of the world and of human relationships, and, last but not least, his analytic experience.

It is in this context that, travelling along different paths, the authors of this book have reached the cross-roads where they met.

Before I deal with the ideas contained in this volume, I should like to devote a few words to describing the atmosphere in which they developed, following the thread of my personal memories.

The atmosphere

When I joined the group in the 1970s, I found myself in a very lively and stimulating environment. To my naive mind discussions assumed the Manichaean simplicity of a clash between "Freudians" and "Kleinians". Basically, however, it was a confrontation between imported ideas, to which certain leading Italian analysts were giving their own somewhat personal interpretations. These were the years immediately following the pioneering stage sketched by Nissim Momigliano (chapter one, this volume). Some members had returned from abroad, where they had gone to improve their training, and brought back new ideas, which were received by others with curiosity. Indeed, followers and supporters of the various foreign trends were sometimes accused of xenophilia, as they often appeared to be influenced in their choices by linguistic preferences and personal friendships. Well-defined groups inevitably formed around certain Milanese leaders, but drastic divisions were never created. It was always possible to sympathize with the ideas of one movement and at the same time to pick up the ideas of another, because in Milan the training was, and still is, only one. This encouraged the daily mixing and exchange of ideas among young analysts.

During that period the publishing of psychoanalytic books was greatly intensified. Apart from the complete works of Freud, many other foreign texts were translated, and there was also a considerable increase in original Italian contributions. We owe a great deal to the publishers who encouraged the promotion of psychoanalytic knowledge in Italy. Our *Rivista di Psicoanalisi* has also certainly played a significant role in this development. Founded in 1955, it became a quarterly in 1976, and for the last five years it has been published in an Italian/English version.

In Italy the 1970s were the years of "revolution" in psychiatry, which led to the extreme resolution of abolishing psychiatric hospitals, through an attitude towards mental illness ranging from total denial to a more scientific and responsible understanding of human suffering. It was an upheaval that had, and still has, both positive and negative consequences, and one that created considerable turmoil. Many psychoanalysts working in public institutions were involved with different functions and often conflicting approaches, and results were, on the whole, constructive for both psychiatry and psychoanalysis. The latter, often charged with being better suited to an ivory tower than to the battlefield, nevertheless continued to give its contribution through the many psychoanalysts—both medically qualified and "lay analysts"—who worked and are still working in public and private institutions, in hospitals and universities. In Italy as well as abroad, problems related to indications for analysis and to the possibility of extending psychoanalytic knowledge to the treatment of patients suffering from more serious mental disorders have been developed through the personal contribution of analysts working in psychiatric institutions and dealing with extreme pathologies. What I called the psychiatric "revolution" stemmed from an attitude that, being more oriented towards social dynamics, was basically polemical towards psychoanalysis. However, I tend to believe that, on the contrary, psychoanalysis itself gave this movement a definite impulse, not so much at an official level as through the many psychiatrists who, having had a personal analysis, had radically changed their attitude towards their role, and towards mental illness and its treatment. On the other hand, many psychoanalytic "vocations" sprang up precisely in that period, influenced, I believe, by the "revolution" itself. In the uncertainty of this general state of confusion, the psychoanalytic group appeared to many of us as a point of reference, and as the possible container for a creative research on mental dynamics, offering both the security of a noble tradition and the chance for new developments of thought. This view is certainly debatable. However, as a matter of fact, during those very years the Italian Psychoanalytical Society expanded and became a more cohesive group. National congresses and other kinds of meetings began to be held on a regular basis, and an atmosphere of collaboration was achieved through frequent exchanges of various kinds.

In my view, one of the features of Italian psychoanalysis is the fact that over the last twenty years many centres of thought have been established in places that are geographically very far apart (from Palermo to Turin). The language and ways of thinking may vary considerably from place to place, but the continual occasions for meetings and an overriding desire to communicate prevent the solidification of positions and the formation of over-rigid "family jargons". Communicating among ourselves in Italy is a constant challenge involving mental gymnastics.

While our group was growing larger, contacts with colleagues from other countries became increasingly frequent. In Milan, thanks to the personal initiative of some members, a considerable number of clinical seminars held by foreign analysts were organized. I believe that the fact that our groups are not rigidly divided is also due to the vital contribution of these exchanges, which provided us with the opportunity of meeting and mixing. The style of such seminars, based on the description of the session in detail (a style that we owe mainly to analysts of the Kleinian group), make "in-field" meetings possible, enabling each participant to leave aside for the moment his theoretical approach and to engage in discussions that might otherwise not even be attempted.

The cultural background I am trying to outline was unquestionably deeply influenced by child analysis and by the study of the mother/child relationship carried out through different methodologies: infant observation, as introduced by analysts from the British school (Bick, Harris), as well as contributions coming from neighbouring sciences, such as cognitive psychology (Bordi, Mattagno, & Muscetta, 1982). Constant references to such cultural trends will be found in several chapters of this volume.

I realize that in describing the atmosphere in which our individual thoughts germinated and developed I have referred mainly to historical events or to methods of treatment or research. Something closer to the specific development of psychoanalytic thought, through the work of various schools and individual researchers, should be provided. The cultural frame in which we live is made up of the work of many authors, whose writings should be carefully and repeatedly studied. I am very grateful to those colleagues who periodically carry on for us all the job of weaving threads, creating links, and recognizing lines of thought through an intelligent, detailed work on texts (Bordi, 1985, 1989). But I do not think that I can trace here a line of, so to say, common descent, of a theoretical heredity with which the various authors of this book would agree to identify themselves. I can only say that we consider our common ground to be the line of development running through Freud, Klein, and Bion. However, apart from this, each of us has found inspiration in the authors to whom he feels closest. At times they coincide, at others they do not. This is the reason why I feel that we do not belong to a "school". If, however, by "school" we mean the meeting-place where a common thought may be developed, then it can be said that, at the cross-roads where we have met, a common way of approaching psychoanalysis has been found and may develop further. I personally recognize that I have taken many of the ideas that shape my approach to work at the present time from some of the authors of this book, and that I have many points of agreement with others. Moreover, collecting these writings in book form has been for us a precious opportunity to develop and enrich our thoughts. Now I hope that our work will turn out to be a useful contribution to a dialogue among analysts. Most of our theses have no claim to particular novelty, but ideas and trends in psychoanalysis often arise simultaneously in different places, which are sometimes geographically far apart. They are produced by authors who, belonging to different linguistic worlds, may not even know each other. I think that this phenomenon is both stimulating and reassuring in that the development of analogous trains of thought, which are both original and genetically independent, endows such thoughts with a particular element of "truth".

I shall stop here. As Nissim Momigliano says (chapter one, this volume), fortunately we are still on our way, and this way does not merely lie in contacts among psychoanalysts. The "royal road" of our science is still that strange, peculiar journey that each of us makes in his consulting room, with one travelling companion at a time, who changes several times a day and comes back regularly the day after. And it is essentially there, in that apparently motionless world, that the most interesting part of our adventure takes place.

The contents

The fundamental train of thought, which can be found in every essay of this volume, basically concerns a way of conceiving psychoanalysis as a meeting between two people involved in a relationship from which creative developments are expected. Compared with the early Freudian approach of an uninvolved analyst observing and unveiling the patient to himself, often strenuously combating his defences and resistances, here we have a focusing of attention on both members of the couple, and the relationship that grows up between them becomes the real "object" of their research. In a recent paper, Nissim Momigliano

(1987) has attempted to show how Freud himself often departed, in his clinical practice, from that "objective" attitude which he developed in his theoretical writings. Analogous observations have been made by other authors (Cooper, 1985; Lipton, 1977). I myself like to recall that Freud, as far back as 1903, after rejecting suggestion and hypnosis, defined the analytic session as "a conversation between two people equally awake" (Freud, 1904a, p. 250)—two people, therefore, who consciously meet with a shared aim. We might not be so confident today in defining these two people as "awake". Thanks to Freud himself, to Klein, and to many others, we know a great deal about the many unconscious communications and relations that dominate the psychoanalytic field. Nevertheless, in those two equally awake people I see the origin and the core of formulations that tend nowadays to underline a certain symmetry in the analyst–patient relationship.

There are two main themes developed in the various essays of this book: the analytic dialogue and the study of the analyst's mind. These are also the themes that have guided us in the choice of the contributions to this work. Closely interlinked to each other, they can be traced in the writings of all the contributors.

The study of the analytic dialogue leads us to see the patient's free associations in a way that differs from the traditional approach. It is still true that the patient is supposed to express in the session everything he freely wishes or is able to. Careful attention, however, to the exchange taking place between patient and analyst shows that, in the course of any session, the patient's associations are responses to the analyst's interventions, including silences and non-verbal communications, in a discourse that, for the patient, is not so free as it might be assumed and which develops through a spiral movement. This idea, which, as far as we know, was first formulated by Pichon-Rivière and subsequently described by Bleger (1958), has more recently also been re-proposed by Langs (Nissim Momigliano, chapter one, this volume). Attention to the dialogue between two people who influence each other broadens the field of research. Alongside what is happening in the inner world of the patient, attention must also be paid to what is going on in the analyst's mind. The field of observation becomes far more complex. The analyst, seen as emotionally involved in what is occurring in the session, has the two-fold task of observing and letting himself be observed, of dialoguing and watching the dialogue in which he plays a leading role.

I think that one basic tenet of our common thought hinges on the idea that every human being is from the very beginning in search of the Other, and in the relationship with that Other he constructs what will become his own internal mental contents. This view is based on the object relation theory (Ogden, 1986). The idea may seem very far removed from the theory of drives formulated by Freud. In reality, however, the work of theoretical psychoanalysis, in the course of its development, might also be seen as a gradual working-through on how drives, unconscious phantasies, inborn codes, or preconceptions could be considered as human tendencies that achieve their realization and subsequently their expression in words upon the meeting with the other. This is why we think that everything that is conveyed between patient and analyst in the consulting room is just a reproduction, in a particular setting, of what normally happens in relationships between people, and what happened to us all at the dawn of our existence.

From this standpoint, the aim of psychoanalysis is no longer seen as an unveiling, but rather as a recovery and construction of what could not properly develop in the course of previous relationships. If it is held that both comprehensible (and constructive) exchanges as well as non-receptive or rejecting (and therefore destructive) communications can take place between human beings, then it is clearly fundamental that the analyst should listen and understand the patient, making room for him inside himself (Di Chiara, 1985); but this is not all. It is equally important that he should observe carefully the moments of the dialogue when this understanding fails to occur. The reproduction in the analytic meeting of "alienated" areas, if perceived by the analyst and re-proposed to the patient at the right moment, may be extremely constructive, precisely because what has occurred is eventually overcome. A particular kind of trauma is relived and overcome in the session: the trauma of mental absence, of missing encounters, of what was supposed to occur but did not occur (Winnicott, 1955, 1974).

The present-day situation of psychoanalytic theory may be seen as the continuous meeting or clash between two basic models. the intrapsychic and the interpersonal (Levi & Sharff, 1988; Mitchell, 1988). The followers of the first model attach greater importance to the patient's inner world, which is considered to dominate the psychoanalytic process, while the analyst, through his presence in the setting, is there merely as the container of projections or as the occasional stimulus for the re-emergence of emotions that belong to the patient. The supporters of the second model, on the other hand, attach greater importance to the relationship unfolding in the here and now, and what appears to come from the patient is considered as the exclusive product of the meeting with the analyst. In this book none of us perhaps completely identifies with either of these extreme positions. We move in an area that is closer to the interpersonal position, even if, as the reader will see, in various degrees and to different extents. We all share, however, one very clear basic idea.

Our approach lays considerable emphasis on the interpersonal moment, although it also takes the intrapsychic viewpoint into consideration. We do, however, acknowledge and pay particular attention to the analyst's intrapsychic world, as well as to that of the patient. All those patterns of mental functioning that psychoanalysts have "discovered" in their patients (such as defence mechanisms like splitting and denial, projective identification, compulsion to repeat, unconscious phantasies, and so on), are recognized as being active in the analyst too, and operating in the analyst → patient direction. The analytic encounter, which our interest is focused on, is seen as a complex "two-way affair" in that the analyst is supposed to be capable of a sort of "benign splitting" within himself. The analyst is invested with the capacity and the task of living an emotionally involved and even impassioned relationship with the patient, and at the same time with the ability to have the necessary detachment to withdraw from and observe it, and to assume the patient's angle in observing himself (the analyst) at work. The patient, our best colleague, observes us just as much as we observe him, and our attempt to put ourselves in his place and to assume his point of view enables us to see ourselves, and the relationship that is unfolding, from different angles. This is, in my opinion, one of the most important features of the present stage of our research (Bezoari & Ferro, chapter three this volume).

The attention to what happens in the analyst's mind that we are proposing is not a new model of the mind, but, rather, an approach to existing models from a different perspective, a point of view that might also lead to a rearrangement and perhaps eventually to a certain re-conjunction of different patterns.

The fact of envisaging the analytic relationship as the meeting between two equally involved people increases the analyst's responsibility. These two people who meet in the setting and laboriously try to understand each other and to construct new ways of relating do use their "awake" side, but they must also both continuously come to terms with the vast unconscious areas of their being. We sometimes forget that the unconscious is sheer unconscious (Coltart, 1986), and the analyst who recognizes how much influence his own has in the relationship with the patient, realizes how fearfully difficult his task is. This theme is dealt with by several authors in this book (Bezoari and Ferro, chapter three; Barale and Ferro, chapter seven; Gagliardi Guidi, chapter six; Vallino Macciò, chapter five). Personally I think that this is a subject which will be worth developing, also because, as Winnicott (1962) says, our primary task is "keeping alive, keeping well, keeping awake", and we must therefore take care of our minds at work.

Difficulties for the analyst are manifold, not least the fact that every new way of seeing things, every change of perspective, substantially challenges previous theoretical conceptions, and this also creates pain and insecurity. We must continually re-examine the pillars of our science, without losing faith and identity. This challenge, however, is perhaps one of the most attractive and fascinating aspects of our work.

PART ONE

THE ANALYTIC RELATIONSHIP

The three chapters that make up this first part express from different angles a common approach to psychoanalysis and have many recurrent themes in common. The analytic relationship appears as a meeting between two people trying to understand each other through their common emotional substance (Di Chiara). The progress of the analytic dialogue is very carefully observed, and the patient's only partly "free" associations are interpreted as answers to the analyst's contributions, including silences and non-verbal communications (Nissim Momigliano). Thus in every analysis it is not only the patient but also the analyst who reveals himself through his interventions. Within a "bipersonal field" the characters appearing in the analytic narrative are not considered as aspects or "parts" of the patient, but as "functional aggregates"—a product of elements originating in both participants (Bezoari and Ferro).

From this viewpoint, a number of classical psychoanalytic concepts become open to fresh discussion and possibly even to revision. Here I shall mention only a few of them.

The so-called *analyst's neutrality* is no longer seen as an impartial, objective attitude, but as a making room for the patient within oneself—without, however, losing one's own identity. It is not so much neutrality as interior separateness that is required of the analyst (Di Chiara), separateness with regard to the patient and to one's own internal objects. Such an attitude allows the analyst to take on the patient's perspective in order to observe himself at work (Bezoari and Ferro).

The concept of *transference* is also worked through. Being emotionally involved in the relationship, the analyst no longer takes part in the session simply as a container of projections. He is there in person, and, in his associations, the patient speaks about him and not only about the objects of his own internal world. Thus the analyst is asked to select continually, from the patient's discourse, what belongs to the latter and his internal world, and what belongs to himself and his actual behaviour in the relationship (Nissim Momigliano). There is a tendency in recent psychoanalysis to replace the concept of transference as repetition with that of actual interactive communication. By speaking about himself, the patient is trying to set up a relationship with the analyst (Di Chiara). Going even further, it could even be affirmed that during the analytic process there is an oscillation between two poles, *Transference ↔ Relationship*, the former representing the repetitive moment and the latter the creative moment of a really genuine meeting (Bezoari and Ferro). Thinking about the concept of transference inevitably leads to reconsidering *countertransference*, a subject that is central to the second part of this book.

Within the perspective of a meeting taking place under conditions of bilateral emotional involvement, analysis is seen as a *natural process*, in the sense that it is part of our nature to seek a relation with others. During analysis an emotional developmental process—which previous, insufficiently welcoming relationships may have distorted or blocked—is resumed. A number of concepts, such as "primary narcissism", "physiological autism", and "infantile omnipotence", are challenged. From this approach emerges the idea of *nature* and *culture* as dialectic poles, rather than being in opposition to one another. The idea of analysis as a development of natural tendencies, which is posited by Di Chiara from a theoretical point of view, is illustrated by clinical examples in the chapter by Bezoari and Ferro. Di Chiara deals with the dangers of opposing nature, and, through some clinical vignettes, Bezoari and Ferro show how the patient's new-born thinking (chick, foetus, etc.) can risk being suffocated by the analyst's interpretative intrusiveness. Nissim Momigliano borrows from a Chassidic tale the image of a therapist who reaches the patient where he actually is. The story is about a wise man who, in order to cure the king's son from thinking he was a chicken, joined the boy naked under the table where he was hiding. Nissim Momigliano stops at this point, but the story goes on to tell us that the wise man, in order to convince his "patient" to put on normal clothes, to eat like a human being, and not to isolate himself from others, assures him each time that he will continue to be a "genuine chicken". Is this not a reassurance that his original nature will not be altered? It is essential for the patient not to be misunderstood in his own specific self. He needs an analyst who is free from cultural clichés and who is thus able to reach and respect his nature and facilitate his growth (Di Chiara).

The classical opposites, *narcissism/object relation*, are also considered here in dialectic terms. The natural tendency in human beings towards object relations exists side by side with the inclination to separateness. The innate tendency is probably that of separateness, and not of narcissism. Within the framework of Freudian theory, the latter was seen as a tendency towards libidinal cathexis of the self, which ought to be opposed and directed towards the object by education (and analysis). It is this approach that is under discussion here. In Di Chiara's view, narcissism is the result of a relational failure—a giving-up of seeking responses from outside oneself—rather than the satisfaction of a natural tendency. But the question is, in such a view can we still speak of narcissism? This theme is developed in stricter meta-psychological terms in the second part of this book, where Di Chiara argues that it is confusing to transfer a concept like narcissism, which developed in the context of the structural theory, to the internal object model. Thus narcissism remains an open question, deserving further investigation in the light of more recent models. Nissim Momigliano, albeit indirectly, also alludes to narcissism. Careful attention to the analytic dialogue shows how difficult (if not impossible!) it is for the patient to give up seeking for answers. She notes how much he puts into his efforts to overcome the analyst's reluctance to understand and, finally, how he also has a vocation for treatment.

From this standpoint, *interpretation* takes on specific features and aims too. It is no longer seen as an uncovering but becomes a tool for building up new meanings together with the patient (Di Chiara). The importance of sharing before interpreting is pointed out (Nissim Momigliano), and the model of unsaturated, interlocutory, "weak" interpretation is introduced. Its function is that of an "incubator" for newly born and developing meanings (Bezoari and Ferro). Within the context of a relationship between two people, the interpretative moment also becomes a "two-way affair".

Andreina Robutti

CHAPTER ONE

Two people talking in a room: an investigation on the analytic dialogue

Luciana Nissim Momigliano

Bion describes the psychotherapist's task as being somewhat similar to that of an officer on the battlefield, who carries on thinking with clarity in the midst of an emotional storm. He states that we can expect this only from someone who has become a "feeling person"—someone who is sensitive and therefore capable of sharing the emotional experience that such a storm provokes, because he has had a "real" analysis and training from a "real" institute of psychoanalysis.

When we read this, we, the Italian senior analysts, look at each other and shake our heads. Of course, we think, this is just what we are trying to provide for our young colleagues, even if it implies a strictness that is not universally appreciated. On the other hand, we have to acknowledge that in Italy at the time when we applied to become psychoanalysts, our society was still in its pioneering stages; it welcomed us affectionately without imposing any rigid terms, and therefore without subjecting us to the restrictions of a "real" school. This, I believe, was in its way fortunate, since it encouraged us to seek new opportunities to meet and to read and so find food for thought in the most varied sources. In this way we could not become fossilized on past acquisitions. So we, too, have been engaged on a lengthy march, of which I will not list here the various stages since I hope that we are all still on our way. But how exhausting it is! We must contend continually with our own sincere desire for quiet. Freud had to learn this at his own expense. As Hebbels wrote: "*Er hat an den Frieden der Welt gerührt*" [he has disturbed the peace of the world]. And even after him our world continued to be disturbed. In fact, Melanie Klein first and Bion later have gone on upsetting our peace.

Klein re-examined by Bion might be an effective manner of describing a certain present-day evolution in the understanding and practice of psychoanalysis. But coining slogans, labelling things, putting things into ready-made categories would be as anti-Bionian as possible. . . . Furthermore, it would not be the whole truth: in fact, at least as far as I am concerned, my present understanding of things has been stimulated by multiple and even eclectic sources. To mention a few, there is first of all the experience acquired in my work with patients and the exchanges of ideas with colleagues and candidates in clinical seminars and in supervision. Then there is the acquaintance, in person or through their writings, of the most congenial of authors. Among these, I must say, I find child analysts particularly interesting in their dual guise of therapist and observer of the mother–child relationship.

But if we take time to page through the "family album"— how enthralling our past history is!—we find a wealth of surprises: it is not unusual to discover in the writings of the past authors, possibly differently expressed or only fleetingly mentioned, or maybe opposed and refuted by others, many things that are turning up anew today—Ferenczi, for instance, or, closer to us, Nacht, or even the oft-debated Greenson.

In the course of my readings I have recently become acquainted with Robert Langs (1975, 1980, 1981), whose prolific production has been for the most part translated into Italian. In my opinion, this author, for all his characteristic North American pragmatism and technicality (which, if you like, place him farthest from the complexity and inspiration of an Indo-European like Bion), deserves consideration, both for the originality of some ideas and for the quite novel way in which he develops concepts already proposed by others. Among his numerous contributions I should like to mention briefly, and in my own way, the concept of psychoanalysis as a bi-personal field, and the description of the spiral movement of the analytic dialogue.

The concept of psychoanalysis as a bi-personal field (an idea resumed from an important work by M. and W. Baranger, 1961–62), considers the two components of the analytic couple equally involved in the same dynamic process, so that neither can be understood without the other. Needless to say, the roles are asymmetrical, the analyst having the crucial task of maintaining the setting. All this implies, among other things, that any inattentiveness or infringement on the part of the analyst, above all as concerns the setting, constitutes a stimulus of excessive intensity for the patient, and one that is difficult to metabolize. This generally becomes a sort of "organizing element" (which Langs calls "adaptive context") of the successive communication, which therefore needs to be urgently recognized.

The concept of the spiral movement probably dates back to Pichon-Rivière. Langs takes it up again, and this is how he describes the sequence of events: a communication (usually from the patient, more rarely from the analyst), leads to a formulation/intervention (usually by the analyst, more rarely by the patient), and this elicits a new communication which is a response, and so forth.

Now, we have always been accustomed to listening carefully to this response, to its conscious and unconscious aspects of confirmation/acceptance or refusal of what we have suggested in our intervention, but we are less accustomed to considering the above "sequence", in which every communication is closely linked to the preceding one. If we take this point of view, we can see how the patient, by means of so-called "free" associations, conveys not only characteristic elements of his internal world —what we traditionally call "transference", which activates countertransference in its broad sense—but these free associations are also a message directed at the analyst *within the actuality of the relationship* and a response—generally an in-direct one—both to the analyst's interventions and to his silences. Deep down the patient experiences both the analyst's interventions and his silences as conscious and unconscious communications on the latter's part. This is particularly the case when these interventions contain elements that can be construed to indicate the existence of projective identifications directed towards the patient. Therefore they are experienced as part of the interaction that is taking place between the analyst and the analysand. These phenomena, so to say, occur in both directions (Di Chiara, chapter four, this volume) and accom-pany every intervention by either member of the couple. It is in fact this feed-back from the patient that, as I said before, sup-plies useful elements for the assessment of the extent and the effectiveness of the analyst's intervention and may even be-come an essential indicator of the critical point in the actual situation.

I shall now try to say something more about this dialogue, defined by Bion in his *Brazilian Lectures* as "a conversation . . . that ought to be like real life", as it takes place when two people are in a room, the relationship between these two people being "a two-way affair". This is a conversation dealing with what occurs *between* the two instead of *about* the analyst and the analysand. When this room is a professional consulting room, the "conversation" that takes place has rather "strange" as-pects and the "relationship" that develops is an interpersonal exchange that is much more than and very different from a common "relationship between two people". An environment or space is created in which something emerges of which neither of the two is any longer the master.

A direct consequence of this type of approach is a definite change in the atmosphere of the consulting room. The oracular, sphinx-like, shamanic style of the analyst is toned down and psychoanalytic arrogance disappears—an arrogance that can still be traced in a paper by Viderman (1974), where it is stated that the analyst should deliberately keep up "the stereotyped solemnity of the encounter" (p. 470), in order to favour and establish transference neurosis.

To my mind the author who best expresses the change of attitude I am referring to is Klauber. He states that the aim of analysis nowadays is to aid the patient's development through a process that will accompany him for the long period of his life following his last session. This process will have a better chance of being internalized if the patient "has enjoyed the analytical process" (Klauber, 1980, p. 111)—all the more if both participants have succeeded in establishing a human relationship over and above a professional encounter between the analyst and the patient, working together to solve transference and countertransference problems.

But what happens when the analytic dialogue, with its particular characteristics of verbal and non-verbal, conscious and unconscious communication on the part of both components of the analytic couple, comes up against distortions and misunderstandings, or even runs aground or gets lost? I imagine we have all had this experience. On listening to the report of a seminar, or during supervision, or on re-reading our own notes after a certain lapse of time, at a certain point we may even experience a feeling of almost physical discomfort, a flat note, when we become aware that the couple is no longer talking a common language, but that a divergence is gradually forming that will lead each further and further from the other. In the protocol of the session, as in the actual session, we perceive an echo of lifeless words and a subtle undercurrent sense of hostility and reciprocal reproaches. We must become aware that something has occurred at a certain point of the mutual communication, which far from having been listened to, "confirmed", and integrated, has been ignored, "disqualified", and attacked. It is up to the analyst to realize this, pause, and point it out to the patient, and perhaps also to make the effort to reconstruct what has happened, observing the whole sequence again as "on a movieola", so to speak. This implies recognizing our mistakes (obviously without self-punishment—we should learn tolerance for ourselves as well!) so as to extract something meaningful. At this point the patient, too, may be able to help the analyst by sending messages that, even if distorted by his particular defence system, contain elements of amazing sensitivity and discernment.

Langs worked for a long time with young doctors specializing in psychiatry who were having their first experiences of psychotherapy (an indispensable part of any psychiatric training in the United States). Very young psychotherapists tend to make macroscopic blunders, and Langs listed them in a brief article (1975), in which he attempts a classification of the most typical reactions to the analysts' mistakes. These reactions are derived from a careful observation of the clinical material that emerges following the therapist's error. The author states that various possible types of break-down or disturbances of the therapeutic alliance, such as acting-in, lateness, absences, interruptions, or the appearance of regressive, somatic symptoms and acting out of varying degrees of seriousness, can be considered as an indication that there has been a technical error, above all concerning maintenance of the setting. We already know this, and we are accustomed to questioning ourselves in each instance.

I believe that the novelty consists in the attention Langs pays to the patient's successive associations, both manifest and latent, since these associations may contain recurrent images that not only point out an error, but also sometimes indicate the type of error involved. Accounts of blindness (or deafness, I might add), about situations that have to do with people who are unable to help, to understand, or to be sensitive, or communications concerning being maltreated, frightened, seduced, or attacked must awaken our interest. Langs goes on to say that very frequently the persons these accounts refer to are found among parental figures, such as teachers, doctors, or other characters who in some way represent authority. A clinical vignette from my experience can illustrate this point.

In the course of a supervision I came across a dream that might be an eloquent example. In the dream the analyst was represented as "a doctor in double-breasted suit . . . who examined me and told me that there was nothing wrong with me . . ." . This dream was related by the patient the day after a very dramatic session, in which the ardent young analyst had been very taken aback by material brought in and had only managed to give a vague sort of reassurance in order to show his sympathy.

Such occurrences can be very unpleasant, but we must try not to be too upset. It may not be a great consolation—but there have been illustrious forerunners. In another of his works, for instance, Langs wonders about the Rat Man's last dream, reported in Freud's posthumous notes, published not long ago. Did this dream, in which the patient, Dr. Lorenz, said that the dentist had pulled out the wrong tooth (a dream that in fact perplexed Freud for a while), represent his unconscious reproach to the analyst for his deviation, for his "error", which was to have offered him a snack? Remember Freud's note? "He was hungry and was fed" (Freud, 1909d, p. 303).

Is it really possible to work according to the model that the patient *is our best colleague*? Here is a beautiful passage from one of Bion's seminars held in New York in 1977, which I found in the little volume *Bion in New York and São Paulo* (1978):

> While we are prepared to argue about the various ideas that we have, we are not prepared to argue about what it feels like to be me. I can compare what it feels like to be me with what somebody else says that I am feeling like. The patient knows much more about what it feels like to be him or her than any analyst. So it is important to work on the basis that the best colleague you are ever likely to have—besides yourself—is not an analyst or supervisor or parent, but the patient; that is the one person on whom you can rely with confidence to be in possession of the vital knowledge. Why he doesn't simply make use of it I don't know. The human being is an animal which is dependent on a mate. In analysis it is a temporary mate; when it comes to life itself one would prefer to find somebody not oneself with whom to go through the rest of one's living days. The biological unit is a couple. . . . [p. 104]

The statement "the patient is the best colleague we have" makes the concept of work in common in analysis sound a bit emphatic; perhaps I would not have underlined that if it were not that recently I have noticed this same concept developed, with equal emphasis, in various circumstances. Searles, in the well-known work, *The Patient as Therapist to His Analyst* (1975) expresses the rather extraordinary opinion that ". . . innate among man's most powerful strivings . . . is an essentially psychotherapeutic striving . . .", and "As for the appreciably larger percentage of human beings who become patients in psychoanalysis or psychotherapy I am suggesting here . . . that the patient wants to give therapy to, as well as receive therapy from, his doctor; . . . in transference terms the patient illness expresses his unconscious attempt to cure the doctor" (p. 95). This has almost become a joke: "Bye—says a therapist to a friend of his—I must leave you . . . I'm off to my patient's for treatment. . . ." But I still think it interesting to take note of an attitude that is so different from the traditional one. For tradition has accustomed us to considering and stigmatizing the so-called "psychotherapeutic" aspects of the patient as manifestations of omnipotent wishful thinking, as a pathological vocation for treating that represented a particularly subtle resistance to analysis.

In a seminar held in Rome in 1980, Rosenfeld made certain statements that do not appear so very surprising now, but that at the time made a particular impression on me. He maintained, for example, that we should include in our theory the splits occurring in the analyst's mind, and he added that the patient may be able to perceive these hidden split areas. The aim of the session may then be to restore contact with such split parts, and one of the functions of the patient's dream may be to signal and shed light on this mental situation of the analyst. Similar ideas are developed organically in the fine article, "Some Therapeutic Factors in Psychoanalysis" (1978b), which Rosenfeld read and discussed on that occasion.

* * *

What my lengthy discourse finally leads me up to is the reflection on the ways in which we are already applying some of Bion's clinical concepts in our everyday work, and to what extent these concepts are possibly prevalently derived from some particularly enlightening extracts from his published seminars, rather than from his books (which, even if clinically generous, are sometimes obscure and certainly contain rather ephemeral sections). I shall here refer to the simpler concepts, leaving to the in-depth and especially talented contributions made by Meltzer the understanding and, as it were, the "translation" of the more difficult topics in Bion's thought.

This is what I can say so far:

1

The concepts of "container" and of "maternal reverie" are so frequently used today that it is almost embarrassing to have to use them yet again. Nevertheless they can be very helpful, because they indicate a type of analytic functioning, which is tied up with what a "good-enough mother" does with her baby and also involves her ability to learn from him. When I say the good-enough mother I also include the quality of the original introjected breast, and therefore the type and quality of care received by the single individual (or, as Di Chiara would say, the functioning of the parent's mind)—a point that is nowadays exhaustively considered. Since in the actuality of the transference the patient continues to project into the analyst his internal objects, the quality of the analyst's work becomes essential—that is, his regularity and trustworthiness, his availability to recognize the patient's feelings and to be ready to listen to him, putting himself in the appropriate state of mind so as to contain his anxiety, despair, dejection, even when they are communicated through non-verbal or verbal messages that can be perceived as hostile, arrogant, and perverse. The fact that the analyst takes upon himself the burden of the internal world the patient projects (i.e. he accepts the projections), avoiding rebuffs and respecting the defensive splits for as long as necessary, means that he offers the patient an experience with an object that is both new and different. However, this requires a further effort on the part of the analyst. He must try to discriminate, in the persecution experienced by the patient in that moment, between, on the one hand, what corresponds to a projection in the transference of his original objects, and, on the other, what may more-or-less adequately express his current experience of the analyst's behaviour and/or interventions. These may constitute a persecutory stimulus—for the most part unconscious—in the actuality (for example, certain interpretations that sound accusatory). This discrimination is, of course, essential when the person in analysis presents strong paranoid anxieties or actual persecutory delusions. In such cases interpretations, which too hastily translate in terms of transference what is said (everyday events, anecdotes, childhood memories, etc.) are understood not as such, but, rather, as declarations by the analyst that no credit is due to them, that the patient's words and emotions deserve no consideration —briefly, as a confirmation that he is mad.

2

To see through the eyes of the patient, that is, ". . . I would change my vertex because I cannot see anything very much from where I am observing the patient . . .". This is the second point I would like to examine in greater depth. This may just be a more sophisticated way of saying something already known. The analyst's work requires a physiological splitting, a sort of to-and-fro movement between an experiencing ego, which shares the patient's feelings, and a critical-observing ego, which records, works through, and interprets these vicissitudes. But another nuance is nonetheless worth underlining: this has to do with the recognition of the different quality of the analyst's emotional involvement.

A little Chassidic tale attributed to Nachman from Breslav may be a good example of this:

Once upon a time . . . there was a king's son, who believed he was a chicken. After taking his clothes off, he crawled under a table, refusing to accept any kind of food, only pecking at some corn. The king sent for many doctors and specialists, but no one was able to find a cure. After a few days, a wise man came to the king and said: "I think I can cure the king's son." The king gave him permission to try, and the wise man took off his clothes, crept under the table, and began to peck at the corn. The king's son looked at him suspiciously and asked: "Who are you, and what are you

doing here?" The wise man replied: "Who are *you*, and what
are *you* doing here?" "Me? I'm a chicken", replied the king's
son angrily. "I'm a chicken too", said the wise man very
calmly, and the two of them stayed under the table until
they got used to one another.

The tale goes on until it comes to a happy ending. The king's
son returns to his human status amongst humans. Our results
are not always so brilliant, even if we, too, when thinking about
a patient in analysis, implicitly decide to accept him and to be
his travelling companion in an endeavour to reach him where
he is. This is what people who come to us are probably asking
us to do, and in particular the many who have built up their
personality around especially traumatic infantile events, and
who ask for analysis in order to find someone who will realize at
last what it means to them to be what they are. We were able to
observe various clinical cases in a seminar in which we also
saw how difficult it could be for the analyst to take on this
burden without defending himself in some way from what the
patient insistently asked him to understand: for instance, what
it felt like deep down to be an illegitimate child, or have been
fostered by people outside the family, or to have lost one's
father at an early age, or to have had a baby brother die—but
even to have lived with only one eye because of a childhood
accident, or to be physically disabled. Each of us could certainly add other examples from personal experience.

Even if these and other similar tragedies may be seen in the
classical sense as castration anxieties or may be used venge-
fully by the patient who is trying to obtain impossible compen-
sation, it is doubtful whether knowledge based on "analytic"
interpretations of this sort (even if they are correct and we must
give them) can be of help to a patient in the life that he has to
lead [see also what Bettelheim (1982) has to say on Freud's
humaneness]. It seems more likely that what will really help
him is having shared his particular situation with a travelling
companion (in this case, the analyst) endowed with identifica-
tory, holding and thinking capabilities through which he will be
able to internalize a new way of mental functioning. It is clear, I
believe, that I am not talking about a corrective emotional expe-

rience, nor about mothering, but about what is both an affective and a cognitive experience.

In almost every analysis, we come across particularly dramatic sessions or moments in which we are pressingly requested to bravely sit and observe (and share in) what the patient feels, even when—or because—this is especially painful.

I remember the intense anxiety and almost physical nausea that I felt during a supervision session, on listening to a dreadful tale that patient C had told his analyst about the disinterment of a corpse that he had had to witness. In talking about this, C was expressing both the desire to get rid of it, and the need to make the analyst actually feel horror at the putrefying objects that were being exhumed. But he was also hoping that the analyst would be strong enough to stomach all this and live it through with him.

We are not always capable of this. Every so often it happens that we feel like running away from so much mental pain. Unfortunately we are better at noticing this phenomenon in others than in ourselves. What we may note in ourselves is that we are having a bad time not only with that particular patient, but with all the rest of our work too, and we may find ourselves wondering "who on earth made me choose this job?" In this case, even if we do our best to master such a state of mind and give adequate interpretations, we may not be very successful. The tone of our voice or a slip of the tongue may spell out an ambiguous or rejecting message. The patient immediately picks this up, and more often than not has no hesitation in interpreting that his phantasies are so intolerable that the analyst cannot wait to get rid of them after just four or five minutes, while he is asked to live with them 24 hours a day. At this point he will react with great hostility, and if we become entangled in the game, we will think, in turn, "what an impossible patient! He doesn't take anything in, he doesn't listen to what I am saying! . . ." and so on.

When we are better able to bear both our own anxiety and the inevitable sense of impotence when faced with what we really cannot mend, then we are also able to convey to the patient the possibility of tolerating *his* sense of death and the horror at what he is feeling.

3

If the patient does not resign himself to the fact that the analyst does not understand him, *he will probably keep on trying* to make contact by repeated communications, all of which express in differing ways the problem at stake: what a lot of unanswered entry-phones will appear in his dreams and in his associations, what a lot of useless ringing of telephone bells and door-bells!

> A young analyst who was very enthusiastic about her new patient, a pleasant and athletic-looking young man, tended to gather and interpret all his communications at a genital and sexual level, ignoring repeated remarks about food allergy problems, alluding to a different level of conflicts. One day the patient told her in detail about having had to go abroad to look for special kinds of food that he needed, and he went on for a long time about how the customs people had questioned him at length about the package that he had with him, and then, fully understanding his problem, "had lifted up the barrier and let him through . . .". The analyst finally got the message and let through his infantile and painful parts into the analysis, managing in this way better to differentiate herself from the seductive mother image that was a characteristic of this patient's internal world.

When verbal communication difficulties become too massive, either because the analyst is not permeable enough or because the patient is very ill, the latter may try to express himself through acting-out (I should like to insist once again that, alongside resistance, acting-out does have a communicative value). Or he may use another far more primitive form of *non-verbal communication* which we usually call *projective identification*—a mechanism that is not only finalized to getting rid of intolerable parts of oneself by pushing them into the analyst (according to Melanie Klein's definition) but also to *communicate their charac-*

teristics (Bion), by making us experience them first-hand, so to speak.

This concept, too, may now appear obvious to us, since we have all experienced it at one time or another and we know how powerful—and mysterious—are these phenomena that do something concrete to us and whose communicative value is not always easy to recognize and understand. Nevertheless I think it interesting to remember that, as far back as 1962, Wangh had already described similar phenomena, calling them "evocation of a proxy"—the search for someone else to whom feelings and reactions may be delegated in one's stead. This he linked with the persistence of narcissistic object relations. With a patient of mine we used to call this function "the sherpa".

These observations may lead to the following conclusions: when we do not know what is happening, and the same things keep on appearing, or when the analysis does not seem to be making any headway, and we feel irritated, exhausted, or judgemental, the question that we should ask ourselves is not only "Why is this patient attacking me in this way, why is he defending himself like this?" but also, "What is the matter with me today, what is stopping me from accepting and understanding him?" or, "What does this unbearable attack that I am experiencing represent in the conscious and unconscious intention of the patient? Does he want to attack me, or is he trying to make me understand something that I just cannot grasp?"

I believe it is also useful to pose ourselves some questions when the opposite is true: sometimes, perhaps after years of being in the dark about a particular analytic event, finally one day it suddenly becomes clear and interpretable, to the mutual satisfaction of analyst and patient. What has made this happen? Why has the communication finally got through? And how?

4

Another of Bion's well-known concepts—*the differentiation of the psychotic part from the non-psychotic part of the personality*—deserves a thorough discussion, which I am not yet ready to undertake. This concept has become a basic element of our theoretical and clinical heritage. One of the reasons for my reluctance is that I am wondering whether our study topic may not instead be how it is that the analytic relationship assumes psychotic characteristics.

For the moment I will limit myself to pointing out that very often we come across serious difficulties, obstacles, or misunderstandings in analyst–patient communication. These are not so much a result of what, to be brief, we call the analyst's "impermeability" or his "mistakes"—while he is trying his utmost to keep close to what the patient is saying—or a result of particularly serious obstacles put forward by the patient himself, but, rather, they can be due to the analyst's difficulty in getting in tune with the patient, in reaching him where he is.

When the analyst does not succeed in reaching the particular facet the patient is presenting in that moment of the session, it is as if "he had got the wrong patient". The analyst may give interpretations that would better suit the neurotic part of the patient—which understands what a metaphor is and knows, for example, that a boss at work appearing in the analytic narrative may represent a transferential allusion to the analyst. But he may fail in reaching the part whose "turn" it is on that particular day. This part may not be recognized, presented as it is by the same person, with the same voice, who is lying on the couch at the same time every day. Here the analyst's main task is to use the type of language that can be understood by the part he wants to get through to, first of all by studying the particular meaning the patient is giving even to the most normal words and images that he is using.

5

Bion's famous recommendation to work *without memory and without desire*—a theme that I examined in detail in another paper (Nissim Momigliano, 1981)—represents a fundamental indication to the analyst to experience the situation the patient is experiencing at a given moment together with him so as to actually listen to what is conveyed to him instead of allowing himself to be deafened by the "noise" that theoretic problems, memories, and desires of different kinds are creating in his mind.

* * *

In examining, as I have done so far, these rather simple analytic concepts, nowadays the basic elements of the analyst's mental setting, I intended to illustrate a way in which psychoanalysis can be practised today. This is a model with which we may identify and communicate among ourselves, without being overly influenced by our favourite theories and frames of reference (even if I have not been able to avoid giving my own in this essay). Such a model is based on a progressively more accurate and detailed way of listening to what the patient has to say, both in his spontaneous associations and in his responses to our interpretations—responses that should be considered an indispensable feed-back.

Of course, I realize that the model proposed is somewhat provocative, being based substantially on Bion's statement that the patient is "the best colleague we are ever likely to have" (not because he is our therapist, but because he helps us to understand him). This turns up-side-down both the old Freudian model (which, as we know, included the use of military and surgical metaphors) according to which the patient comes to analysis absolutely determined to oppose and to present strenuous resistance to the analyst's work, and the old Kleinian one which tended above all to insist on underlining the aggressive and envious aspects of the patient's words and behaviour. Naturally things are not as drastic as this, nor are our patients only "little lambs"—and neither do I wish to deny the importance and often massive presence of their omnipotent, destructive, projective, and envious aspects. This model is useful because it requires us, as analysts, to be aware to what extent similar and/or symmetric aspects of our own personalities [see the work of Brenman, 1978, on the narcissism of the analyst] can be unconsciously activated simply by contact with the patient and work furtively within us like a saboteur, hindering the satisfactory development of dialogue and mutual work.

CHAPTER TWO

Meeting, telling, and parting: three basic factors in the psychoanalytic experience

Giuseppe Di Chiara

In meeting, telling, and parting I identify three basic elements, or factors, of any psychoanalytic experience. I believe that the analytic process is the result of their interweaving and interaction and that these elements must always be at work in any experience that is to be considered psychoanalysis. This is, of course, a broad overview and remains to be confirmed by an exchange of experience with other analysts. I reached this formulation through long hours of work in my consulting room and at my desk.

The three factors I have pointed out, which are certainly well known to every analyst, are to be considered a sort of common denominator, an invariable of every analytic experience. Many mental, relational transference–countertransference operations converge there. At the same time a theory about them embraces numerous points of view, models, and theories that have succeeded one another in the course of time. These factors are, in my opinion, the very substance of psychoanalysis rather than an eclectic frame of reference encompassing psychoanalytic theory and practice.

"Parting" refers to those experiences that have to do with the sense of separateness, both in its normal and in its pathological aspects, and with our feeling of being autonomous, separate individuals.

"Telling" covers all experience and theory of narration in analysis, from the most elementary communications to psychoanalytic interpretation in the strict sense of the term, right up to those models that are almost exclusively founded on psychoanalytic narrative.

"Meeting" refers to the psychoanalytic encounter and expresses mental exchange in its most archaic essence: the affective one. Concisely defined as empathy from the beginning, in more recent times the renewed attention of many psychoanalysts, who seem more interested than in the past in the affective matrix of psychoanalysis, has focused on this deep humoral essence of the psychoanalytic experience.

Meeting and the basic emotional elements of the psychoanalytic experience

Our reflections on meeting necessarily take empathy as their starting point. This term, whose historical roots are difficult to trace, has been right from the beginning a basic element of every psychoanalytic route. Empathy is not an entry word in the Laplanche and Pontalis dictionary, which only mentions it in passing in reference to identification (Laplanche & Pontalis, 1967). On the other hand, it is mentioned by Rycroft (1968a) as an important concept in psychoanalysis, but without any reference to its history. Actually, "empathy" is the English translation of the German *Einfühlung*, which Freud uses rarely but significantly and sometimes in inverted commas.

Freud considers empathy as a mental activity directed towards the perception and in-depth understanding of the other person. In *Jokes and their Relation to the Unconscious* empathy is opposed to cathexis of the ego (Freud, 1905c). It is the ability to make "a comparison entirely within the other person". At the same time, when examined from the standpoint of the links between the comic and the preconscious infantile factors, it means becoming children again (Freud, 1905c). The relationship, which I consider essential, between empathy and infantile factors is taken up again in "The Claims of Psycho-Analysis to Scientific Interest", in the paragraph about educational interest in psychoanalysis. Freud ascribes to psychoanalysis the discovery of how we can find our way into the mind of the forgotten and repressed child (Freud, 1913j). In "On Beginning the Treatment", Freud recommends "sympathetic understanding" as an essential element of the analyst's attitude (Freud, 1913c). In *Group Psychology and the Analysis of the Ego*, empathy, we are reminded, is what ". . . plays the largest part in our understanding of what is inherently foreign to our ego in other people" (Freud, 1921c). In this same work in a footnote (page 110), Freud regrets the incompleteness of his research into the nature of identification and underlines the importance of empathy in explaining the relationships with another mental life through the "acknowledgement of the possession of a *common substance*"—a term that is worth stressing (Freud, 1921c, my italics).

In Freud's work empathy is not developed any further than this, above all as concerns the way it works. His interest moved on towards the theory of libido poised between narcissistic cathexis and the effort of overcoming it and moving towards the object, which is always hindered by the tendency towards a reduction of stimuli and by the need for discharge. On the other hand, the most important elements necessary for the achievement of empathy are the affects: and these, too, found little room in the first psychoanalytic models, where they were substituted by drives of which they were considered the manifestations. According to Muscetta (1990), when Freud set up the theoretic models of psychoanalysis, affects did not have a good name in the scientific and psychological field and were even about to disappear from general psychology! More quantitative than qualitative concepts were required, which could be measured and, as it were, manipulated in a mechanistic way. For this reason Darwin's lesson on primitive relationships between human beings through communication of affective states, which Freud approached very closely in the footnote that I mentioned above, was developed no further. (For the place that the affects have in Freud's work see Green, 1977, and Ammanniti & Dazzi, 1990). Yet primitive affective transactions would have revealed many things about the way children function in their relationships with other human beings around them and would certainly have helped approach the problem of putting oneself into another's shoes. In any case, empathy remained a basic element of clinical work, which was and is the real background of psychoanalysis, in the sense that without it there is no fruitful relationship between patient and analyst; and without this fruitful relationship there is no analytic activity. As a consequence something rather extraordinary has come about: the evolution of psychoanalysis has increasingly indicated the importance of affective communication. In this way psychoanalysis has placed affects back on the centre of the stage—as Trevarten points out (1990)—with reference to those psychoanalysts who have most significantly contributed to this shift (such as Melanie Klein, Fairbairn, Winnicott). Among the Italian contributors, I wish to mention Nissim Momigliano (1987, and chapter one, this volume), Bordi (1980, 1985), Bordi et al. (1982), Bonfiglio (1986, 1987), and my own paper on this subject (Di Chiara, 1985).

All this deserves more attention and elicits a reflection on the difference that exists between yesterday's psychoanalysis and that of today, above all as far as theory is concerned. Yesterday's analysis evolved within the precincts of a mechanistic interpretation of natural science, and it tended to develop methods based on laws of repetition. Today's analysis is centred more on the relationship and perfects the strategies of this experience. The cardinal concept of transference follows and marks this evolution. In the original situation transference appeared mainly as repetition; nowadays the importance of interactive communication is being discovered, studied, and developed. This evolution has been brought about by progress in clinical experience and in appropriate theoretic models to represent this experience. Of course there has been controversy: not only between Anna Freud and Melanie Klein, but between psychoanalysts generally, concerning links between relationship and interpretation, between the relevance for the expansion of the ego through interpretation or of introjection and projection, mainly at primitive levels. Gitelson's paper "The Curative Factors in Psychoanalysis: The First Phase of Psychoanalysis" (1962) and Rycroft's "The Nature and Function of the Analyst's Communication to the Patient" (1956) are worth reading to get an idea of the scientific background in which such a dispute developed.

At the time great interest in non-verbal communication had developed in London, partly under the influence of other disciplines. The cultural atmosphere was one in which infant observation, the work of John Bowlby, and child analysis underwent an amazing development. Rycroft, quoting Susanne Langer, says that "human behaviour is not only a food-getting strategy, but is also a language". How is it—asks Rycroft—that our knowledge of interpersonal relationships is not integrated into metapsychology? Why is it—he continues—that in psychoanalysis the affects and their inter-relations are disregarded? And he recalls the communicative value of a baby's crying in the context of its relationship with the mother. Not that non-verbal communication aspects are not present in analysis: on the contrary, they are numerous—first and foremost among them, the analytic setting—but they are ignored. The analyst should realize that the patient, when speaking about himself, is trying to set up a relationship with the analyst. And the analyst's interpretations, together with the descriptions of the fantasies and defences of the patient, convey an idea of the quality of their being together. The relationship between analyst and patient does not only take place through symbols, but also through signs. Rycroft (1956) appears as a significant forerunner of the modern view of psychoanalysis as a relationship between two people.

Our overview of psychoanalytic literature on primary relationships and their mechanisms leads us to the contributions of Winnicott and Bion. I am referring here to the concepts of "holding" and "transitional area", of "reverie" and "container-contained".

Winnicott is a psychoanalyst who is familiar with children, and with their mothers and fathers, their brothers and sisters; he observes them with a paediatrician's eye. He has been able to see far beyond the peaceful family picture better known to Freud: a child's illness is an event that affects small patients, and above all their relationships with their parents, too keenly not to bring to light earlier and deeper yet observable mental occurrences.

In a brief and delightful compendium Winnicott explains what he means by psychoanalysis and points out that the analyst aims at "keeping alive–keeping well–keeping awake", while trying to behave with "stark simplicity" and underlining the fact that "the analyst displaces environmental influences that are pathological" (Winnicott, 1962, pp. 162–168). These are the sources of concepts like "primary maternal preoccupation" (1956), "good-enough mothering" (1963), and "holding" (1960). The latter stands half-way between biology and psychology: it concerns how to hold babies in one's arms and how to "hold" them in one's mind.

Bion was, I believe, the psychoanalyst who made the greatest effort to make contact, in psychoanalysis and with the tools provided by psychoanalysis, with the most primitive sheer animal aspects of man. He tried to smell out his patients and to gather affective oscillations through vasodilatation and vasoconstriction: he tried to meet up anew with what had been obscured over millennia of focusing on technical ability, of "doing" rather than "thinking" and that in the end through all this "doing" has produced a man proud of his ability at imitation.

The concept with which Bion tried to explain the basic function of the analytic mind is "reverie". The mother's and the analyst's reverie receive the baby's or the patient's pre-verbal or verbal mental communications; all those emotional messages that are resolutely directed towards finding "the Other". In the analyst's mind this receptivity must bring about an attendant transformative elaboration of emotions. The analyst must therefore be prepared to keep in close contact with these emotions, neither running away from them nor minimizing them or giving in to them, and must eventually sort them out in a way that is neither manic nor depressive. A response of this type will encourage the patient to go on seeking successive responses from without, while it will endow him with experiences of thinking objects, which, if he is capable of mourning them, will acquire the status of stable internal objects. I consider "reverie" a complex function of the analytic couple and the pivot of the basic functions of psychoanalysis. The time for symbolic exchanges will come later, and only later.

This outlook enhances the relevance of the relationship enormously. We are no longer in the rather simple context of the reel-game. For a particular experience to occur within an individual, it is not so important that the external object—parent, analyst—goes away. What is important is the way two people have been together when they were both present.

Let us go back to the reel-game. The baby has been with its mother. The mother goes away. The baby devises a game that symbolically represents the presence and absence of the mother. The events we should look at from a post-Freudian viewpoint are those that precede the mother's going away, those that occur when the baby and its mother are together.

So what about the attitude of the psychoanalyst who is with his patient at these levels?

In order to clarify this point, I shall refer to the paper by Riolo (1983) entitled "Sogno e teoria della conoscenza in psicoanalisi" [Dream and Theory of Knowledge in Psychoanalysis]. Within the broader frame of the re-definition of dream function, to bring the Freudian lesson up to date, the author defines the dream as a process of building up meaning, and not only as that of masking and concealing. Therefore the dream becomes the instrument of a mental function which aims both at creating mental reality and at acquiring knowledge. From this angle the emotional experience of the analytic couple is enhanced. A crucial question arises from this. What happens to the analytic relationship once the analyst has accepted into his own mind an emotion evoked by the patient without feeling invaded by it but, instead, being able to hold it (a microprocess implied in empathy)? Riolo believes that the further development of the session depends on the fate of this "object" in the analyst's mind. The analyst can decide to submit it to a "resolution" by the attribution of a meaning through focalized thought, or he can choose to activate his own reverie and temporarily increase contamination. Riolo reminds us that for reverie to occur two conditions must be fulfilled: the first is that the analyst keep an open mind so as to receive *all* the objects (projective identifications) coming from the patient; the second condition is that the patient should be loved by the analyst. Riolo goes on to say that *reverie* is a function of the mother's thought: *it implies the fading of distinction between subject and object.* He holds that this alarming experience of depersonalization is the fundamental reason for the preference accorded to the former procedure, that of resolving by the attribution of a meaning, even if the latter would be far more fruitful. More often there is a combination of the two procedures, with prevalence of the cognitive over the emotional one.

In complete accordance with this point of view I have indicated in the experience of "awe" the basic element of communication between minds (Di Chiara, 1990). Reverie, of course, means making oneself available, making a space for the "Other" and for what belongs to him. Reverie is defective when there is insufficient mental space for an emotional experience of "objects". In fact Riolo reminds us that the analyst who follows a semiotic procedure does not behave like a mother, but like a diagnostician or an investigator.

It is within this "dreaming–receptive" attitude (Riolo) that empathy occurs and promotes the encounter. The analyst must make himself available for this experience and not only at the beginning of analysis: meeting is a permanent characteristic of any psychoanalytic experience, and to a greater or a lesser degree must always be present if psychoanalytic work is not to be in vain. When the experience of meeting is particularly intense, the emotional states evoked have a special quality. They are similar to those evoked by the perception of beauty in the Arts, or to the feelings of serenity and completeness aroused by contemplative experiences. This is what Bion calls being in "O" (Bion, 1970).

Freud's dislike of too-intense affective tones is well known, particularly those related to contemplative or mystic states—as we can see in his letters to Romain Rolland and in the first paragraphs of *Civilization and its Discontents* (Freud, 1930a). His concern about making room for "irrationality" led him to stand back with suspicion from primary relational exchanges, particularly in the formulation of his theoretical models. Yet in his writings aspects of Jewish mysticism are detectable (Bakan, 1958) while, as Nissim Momigliano (1987) has pointed out, intuition and affective messages were of great relevance in his way of working in the sessions. This, coupled with his pathogenetic theory of fixation–regression, led in the end to an account of normal primary psychic experience which bears the non-relational and pathological characteristics of narcissism, omnipotent thinking, manic grandiosity, and denial.

But I wonder what kind of relationship there is between the world of primitive man, that of children, and the delusional phantasies of psychotics. Are they all simply the same thing, or do they correspond, for some reason, to completely different structures and developments? Can innocence be superimposed on omnipotence? Stern says that the mother "is involved in a natural process with her baby, a process that unfolds with a fascinating intricacy and complexity for which both she and the baby are well prepared by millennia of evolution". Now, is such a relationship between mother and child comparable to autistic withdrawal or to that indeterminate state of fusion from which the child still has to emerge? Under "normal-enough" conditions, what kind of events occur at the beginning of life? According to the same author they are "the fairly ordinary and common interpersonal exchanges occurring between a primary care-giver and an infant during the first half year of life" (Stern, 1977, p. 2).

I hold with the thesis that a relational exchange that is both natural and physiological exists right from the beginning of extrauterine life (according to some researchers even before that—see Mancia, 1981). Such an exchange is based on primitive mental functions, which are inborn in their premises. Their development depends on the responses of others—first of the mother, and then of the whole environment. This exchange takes place between functions of similar quality, and it is not so much the case that those of adults are better developed as that they are associated to other supporting functions that have developed in the course of time. For various reasons, which have to do either with the child or with the environment, this exchange can, so to speak, fall ill and produce deficiencies of various natures and gravities.

I believe that one of the basic elements of psychoanalytic technique is to offer the patient the analyst's primitive tendency towards relational exchange. The analytic setting is such that other functions are, as far as possible, suspended so as to put patient and analyst in the position to meet. The aim is to restore the patient's natural primitive tendency towards the encounter, which has been variously damaged by previous relationships. This physiological encounter is the premise for the expression in analysis of the patient's pathological relational patterns. The analyst, in turn, must prevent these difficulties from disrupting the analysis and see to it that they are finally overcome.

A study by Bordi on primitive mother–child interactions, holds that the child is in search of an object from the very beginning of his life (Bordi, 1985). Fachinelli, in his book, *Claustrofilia* (1983), describes those states that patients try to establish in their relationships with the analyst of intimate familiarity, affinity, sharing. Lastly, I wish to recall the book *Fusionalità*, written by a group of colleagues from Rome (Neri, Pallier, Petacchi, Soavi, & Tagliacozzo, 1990).

A characteristic of these approaches is that two different experiences are placed alongside one another: primitive fusionality on the one hand coexists with the capacity to live and relate as separate individuals on the other. The authors of *Fusionalità*, for example, maintain that very small children do not recognize the other person as different from themselves—a view peculiar to Freud and Mahler's thought; on the other hand, they point out the intense involvement of both partners in the relationship. They term the experience of fusional unity "circumscribed psychosis" but consider it as an indispensable element of every good relationship and stress the importance of "knowing how to experience it while preserving the idea of a positive and constructive identity". Tagliacozzo, in particular, examines the dual prospective inherent to fusionality and defines a pathological fusionality, which harbours the concrete need to use the other person, and a physiological fusionality, which, on the contrary, expresses "the communicative and reciprocally creative harmony of the two internal worlds". In differing ways and degrees the other authors also describe two different experiences of being together. For Pallier projective identification with the idealized object, which is the basic feature of pathological fusion, produces feelings of "grandiosity, self-idealization, falsification, persecution, and seductive attitudes", in opposition to the expression of physiological fusionality: "calm, absence of persecution, absence of manipulation, joy, possibly ecstasy, the lack of falsification and even clarity of mind".

The area of the encounter I am dealing with is that of basic trust, but at the same time it is the one in which the "basic fault" described by Balint (1968) can occur. Tagliacozzo (1984) himself considers trust as a pre-condition of every experience of physiological fusionality. The reconstructive aspects of analysis are involved to the utmost in encounter. The fact that Balint was so keenly interested in the doctor–patient relationship—and not only in analysis—is not a mere coincidence. The involvement of the two partners, at this level, is total and visceral. As Nissim Momigliano (1990) points out in her introduction to *Fusionalità*, the area of fusionality involves, above all, the body and extra-verbal and para-verbal communications.

We know that meeting is not such an easy matter. It starts off—or, instead, is inhibited—from the very beginning when the so-called indications for analysis, which must take into account both the patient and the analyst's readiness, are established. Freud stated that "not all men are worthy of love" (1930a, p. 102), and he kept to this principle even with his patients, not taking them into analysis if he felt he could not love them enough. But a purely scientific attitude, guided by loving curiosity, may help enlarge the spectrum of our receptivity.

I shall now refer briefly to a couple of difficult situations. In the first the patient's deepest emotions are impaired in their expression, their very existence is threatened, and they are constantly and successfully repressed. This can come about for various reasons; the effect of an anti-affective superego, or of the pain evoked by manifestation of emotions, or the possible numerous combinations of these and other motives. If we keep these not infrequent situations in mind, we will understand the different courses of action that the analyst may choose to follow in order to meet with his patient. But we can also see the various difficulties that he will come across. The patient's superego, for example, may attempt to frighten both analyst and patient, and it may also try to obtain the connivance of the analyst's superego—and we all know how difficult it is to resist fear and seduction.

In the second situation we are dealing with patients who from the beginning display the intense and explosive strength of a deep emotional core. In this case the analyst's task is to give an adequate response, proportional to the communication received, without recourse to defensive reactions, such as rejection, detachment, or similar defensive mechanisms.

Parting and separateness

Parting is an experience the analyst is prepared for, right from his first encounter with any patient, since the patient is another person, the analyst's "Other" *par excellence* in the analytic relationship. This is why the analyst also knows that the patient he is receiving in his dreaming–receptive state of mind will one day go away, when analysis with him comes to an end. So the analyst will set up a rhythm of presences and absences both for the patient and for himself. Within this setting the experience of separateness that patient and analyst need (and that in some difficult cases has to be built up anew) will develop and strengthen. Therefore parting and separateness are not factors that evolve only after a certain length of time. They are present right from the beginning, and the two minds involved in psychoanalytic work are prepared for this experience right from the start (Di Chiara et al., 1985). Parting is a psychoanalytic element that has to do with acknowledgement and development of the separate mental and somatic identities of human beings. It involves mourning processes and the ability to learn through introjective identification. Briefly, it concerns the very development of any normal human being. Nowadays we believe that the psychoanalytic setting, with its few but fundamental

rules and with the corresponding mental attitude of the analyst, is qualified to promote an experience of parting.

Earlier I attempted to differentiate normal symbiosis (or
physiological fusionality) from pathological confusion. My in-
tent was to point out that meeting and parting are not so far
removed from one another: they may be considered as essential
aspects of the same experience, the basic features of any normal human relationship, which the analytic relationship acquires for itself, channels, and helps to grow.

However, there is a peculiar aspect of separateness that
justifies separate treatment. While the "native" parts of the personality bring about the encounter, other structures are also
present and active, bringing their influence to bear on the process. The analyst's projective identification towards the patient
is the dangerous and pathogenic facet of such an influence.
This has been explored, together with the analyst's ability to
protect his patient from such a risk, in some recent papers
(Barale & Ferro, 1987; Di Chiara, chapter four, this volume;
Ferro, 1985).

Whereas in the encounter primary somatic and mental
structures close to affectivity are involved, in the experience of
parting and separation, I believe, other personality structures,
shaped in the course of development, are involved. The capability and the tendency to separate are predisposed right from the
beginning of life, but their development is largely dependent on
the relationships that accompany growth. We must resign ourselves to accept that personal and environmental factors are
always interwoven, even if this complicates matters. Psycho-
biological research and our experience as psychoanalysts repeatedly confirm an overlapping and interlacing of nature and
culture that render any attempt to formulate a precise discrimination between them a vain endeavour.

Nevertheless, despite all these difficulties, an effort must be
made to preserve, within the self, a cleavage between the primitive nuclei of the ego and the structures that develop later. This
sort of internal physiological fault is very important. The child's
need for care is obviously a basic condition, and excessive
dependency may render initial identifications more difficult. In

Inhibitions, Symptoms and Anxiety Freud (1926d [1925]) recalls a case of inadequate separateness and its consequences.
He writes: "The undesirable result of 'spoiling' a small child is
to magnify the importance of the danger of losing the object (the
object being a protection against every situation of helplessness) . . ." (p. 167). Is there a greater danger? Well, I believe
there is a risk, which is not necessarily greater but at least
equally serious: the loss of the original nucleus of the self.
From this point of view numerous narcissistic syndromes are
not so much the manifestation of the infantile, as the manifestation of the interior tyranny of superegoic objects from which
separation is impossible.

Kluzer mentions the contributions of Aulagnier (1975,
1979) who holds that the mother actively sets off her child's
wish to build up his own store of knowledge through a "primary
violence". This provocative term hints at the need for a cultural
"shove", so to speak, in order to build up through interpersonal
exchange an internal world, which, together with the original
ego, will form the personal substance of every individual. But
why "primary violence"? The term seems still to be obeying the
axiom of an original state of calm withdrawal, of primary narcissism, that only an intervention making a clear break—and,
in this sense, a violence—can disturb and remove from narcissistic withdrawal and direct towards object relations. As we
have already seen, the observation of the first mother–child
relationships tells another story: what is on occasions a violence, is, in other instances, simply the response of a mother
who starts off a dialogue and a relationship for which both
mother and child are programmed. True, pathological kinds of
responses that are violent and at the same time weak also exist.
Here, too, as I have said before, the original ego, with its innate
responsive ability, works together with everything that has
been learnt, and the balance between the two is difficult to
keep. Kluzer (1988):

> . . . It's a delicate equilibrium because of its exposure to the
> risk of an excessive and intruding presence of the knowl-
> edge and the wish of the parent–analyst, as well as to that
> of his abdication and absence. [p. 336]

At this point the element of separateness, proper to the analyst's mental make-up becomes crucial. For, however relevant and even vital the contribution on the part of internal objects and of what has been learnt may be, it must be felt as separate from the original nucleus of the self. An experience of interior poverty is indispensable in order to maintain "separateness". However beautiful and attractive the gifts of learning may be, they should be considered as available gifts, and not as personal property. Therefore a weak identity will be healthier and more separate, readier to part from its visitors, to doubt its knowledge, and to hold different opinions. But to what extent is separateness possible? This is really difficult to estimate. Perhaps only in a few cases, in transient experiences, such as those of the creative artist or of the mystic, is it possible to come close to an original primal essence that is maximally apart from its cultural concretions. There is no doubt, however, that intrusive and non-separating cultural stimuli are the most frequent, at least in our work and in our culture (perhaps because of some ancient social pathology). This is what leads Bordi (1978), in a paper significantly entitled "Le basi intenzionali della coscienza morale" [The Intentional Bases of Moral Conscience] to state that psychoanalysts have to follow Freud's principal indications, "that the dehumanising qualities of science can be tempered by the expansion of knowledge, by awareness of damage caused and of responsibility for it". This theme was taken up and developed by Meltzer in his studies on autistic states (Meltzer et al., 1975).

The theory of thinking developed by modern psychoanalysts is founded on these premises: that thinking is made up not of strong and fulfilling symbols, but, on the contrary, of moments of detachment, solitude, silence (Bion, 1962b; Hautmann, 1987a, 1987b; Leonardi, 1987; Tagliacozzo, 1982). And it is from these pauses of silence that "telling", the third fundamental element of psychoanalysis, develops.

Telling and communication in psychoanalysis

The analytic tale is a particular form of narration. Its importance was stressed in psychoanalysis right from its beginnings: "talking cure", chatting around the fire, and so on. An analysis is always an interweaving of narrative episodes, concerning present life or childhood, of dreams, of fairy tales and myths. The instruments for this narrative are those of all story-telling: linguistic symbols, figures of speech, syntactic constructions. But the psychoanalytic tale—which, for the analyst in the session is called psychoanalytic interpretation—is such in as much as it derives from the experience of meeting and of parting and when it expresses the emotional source of these experiences. Were this not so, psychoanalysis would be a cultural genre, like any other. Psychoanalytic interpretation, the psychoanalytic tale, connects the sphere of basic emotional experience to consciousness and to the patient's history. In this sense it proves to be an element close to our cultural heritage, from which it draws its means of expression; on the other hand, it is also an element far from the emotional sources of our experience. Its functioning is delicate and complex and not free from drawbacks. Words can be misleading. The speechless animal that inhabits us needs to find adequate expression: and even then it may be misunderstood. The psychoanalytic tale unfolds—almost spontaneously—when the other two moments, meeting and parting, have come about, and if the available language is both sufficiently simple and flexible enough. I would not hesitate to call this language "poetic", in as much as it is far removed from ideology and able to express authenticity. This is the language of achievement (Bion, 1970). The relationship between artistic creation and psychoanalysis was and still is a fascinating issue for many authors.

Russo (1990) has carried out a detailed research on two narrative levels that exist in Freud's work: one level links the affects with repressed representations, the other builds up a new story through the analytic relationship. These two levels interact dynamically, and the exclusion of either is impossible. In fact, this is implicit in "Constructions in Analysis" (Freud, 1937d), the paper in which the analytic tale is best sketched

out by Freud, though with some ambiguity between the reconstruction of past events and the construction of a story between
patient and analyst in analysis.

Ricci Bitti and Caterina, in an interesting note on emotions
(1990), take into account the discovery of the unconscious, as
well as the correspondence that exists between the unconscious and the intimate nature of emotions (using Matte
Blanco's logical–mathematical and psychoanalytic approach),
and underline the need for a linguistic labelling so as to name
and convey emotional states. Accordingly, they remind us of
the particular significance of the work of those analysts who
have placed more emphasis on the patient–analyst relationship.

Psychoanalytic literature on narration in analysis has become too exhaustive to be mentioned here. Among the many
Italian contributions, I would like to recall the meeting on psychoanalytic culture, held in Trieste in 1985 (Accerboni, 1985),
and in particular the section on "Psychoanalysis, Narration,
and Aesthetics", including papers by Gaburri, Fossi, Morpurgo,
and Di Benedetto, and the volume *Psicoanalisi e Narrazione*
[Psychoanalysis and Narration] edited by Morpurgo and Egidi
(1987). One factor should be emphasized: psychoanalytic narration, as a basic element of the psychoanalytic experience,
together with meeting and parting, is not only the "narration" of
facts and events. Therefore it does not apply to a clinical case-
presentation or to the description of a psychoanalytic theory; it
is never a text, but always a context, a plot, a relationship,
a telling-somebody-who-is-listening. It originates and develops
in a communicative web of affects and emotions that constitute
its essential and pre-verbal premise (as Di Benedetto, 1991,
has so well described). The semiology of a text is far removed
from psychoanalysis, which calls for a semiology of the relationship (Riolo, 1987).

By reason of its origin and its development, analytic narration gathers and expresses the shared emotional and relational
vicissitudes of the two chief characters. For this reason it does
not inform us but allows us to participate. For the same reason
it cannot be a substitute for psychoanalytic theory, which, on
the other hand, must show us, if possible, how to attain in our

context the narratives that are most appropriate to the need to convey the emotions that we share with our patients.

CONCLUDING REMARKS

The first and most important conclusion is of a technical nature. Psychoanalysis should provide us—as in fact it already does—with a technical instrument that fulfils three basic conditions. (1) The establishment of a relationship in which patient and analyst are emotionally involved (meeting or psychoanalytic encounter). (2) A situation in which both analyst and patient can recognize themselves as separate individuals (parting and separation). (3) A situation that makes both participants aware of the experience they are living through, rendering it explicit in the conversation between them (telling or psychoanalytic narration).

My approach leads to a second major point: a reflection on the complex relationships between psychoanalysis and the culture in which it was born, grew up, and developed in the course of its history. The idea that a natural separateness is closely linked to the unavoidable dependence of the archaic ego on developmental experiences leads us to explore the boundaries of nature and culture, a problem that will always confront us, never to be solved once and for all. After all, psychoanalysis is, at least partly, a cultural phenomenon, and in turn, it attempts to bring its influence to bear on culture so as positively to modify the nature–culture interweave. And since psychoanalysis is conditioned by the cultural system in which it operates, our approach to the mysterious nature of the object of our knowledge and of our experience should be of respect and of awe towards what is unknown (Bion, 1973; Di Chiara, 1990; Meltzer, 1975). I assume that such an attitude is peculiar to science, even if I know perfectly well that this is not the most common one among scientists. The idea that evolution follows a continuous path towards progress can no longer be upheld. This myth has lost its significance. Psychobiologists, for example, have had to recognize that certain animal species have, in the course of their evolution, adopted unsuitable behaviour patterns and cultural tendencies unable to guarantee their future survival (Oliverio, 1984). Freud formed and constructed the first psychoanalytic models in a scientific and technical environment which considered that nature should be dominated and overcome. He writes in *Civilization and its Discontents* (Freud, 1930a):

> There is, indeed, another and better path, that of becoming a member of the human community, and, with the help of a technique guided by science, going over to the attack against nature and subjecting her to the human will. [p. 77]

Horkheimer offers an alternative standpoint when he describes the stratification of western society as a "skyscraper". He casts a glance at what happens in the basement of this human construction, where, he writes, animals suffer in an indescribable hell of sweat, blood, and desperation, and the "coolies of earth" die by their millions (Horkheimer, 1934).

The differences in evaluation of artistic phenomena may be equally interesting and instructive. For Freud—or according to his theory?—art puts us in a state of "mild narcosis", and beauty gives a "mildly intoxicating quality of feeling" (Freud, 1930a, pp. 81, 82). Such a view is very different from Bion's or Meltzer's approach to the arts. Certainly it is not that of the poet who, closer as he is to man's most archaic core, discovers that

> With full gaze the animal sees the open.
> Only our eyes, as if reversed, are like snares
> set around it, block the freedom of its going.
>
> [R. M. Rilke, *The Eighth Elegy*, 1923]

Another area of interest if that of the cultural models operating in the field of economic productivity and social organization; related to them is the question of femininity. Among Freud's works, *Civilization and its Discontents* (1930a) is that in which the influence of the cultural tendencies of his time is most evident, whilst it indicates a painful conflict.

It is worth mentioning that there is a passage in which Freud clearly disassociated himself from the cultural thinking of his time. In "Memorandum on the Electrical Treatment of War Neurotics" (Freud, 1955c [1920]), he states that soldiers wished to escape from war for affective reasons—to be more precise, for fear of losing their lives, as opposition to orders to kill, and as a rebellion against superiors, who indiscriminately repressed their personalities. Well, concludes Freud, "A soldier in whom these affective motives were very powerful and clearly conscious would, if he was a healthy man, have been obliged to desert or pretend to be ill" (p. 213).

Work on the pathogenic effects of cultures, as we encounter them in our clinical work, remains a fascinating task, which is still largely ignored and which cannot be tackled by psycho-analysis alone. Freud's expectations may encourage us to do so: "But in spite of all these difficulties, we may expect that one day someone will venture to embark upon a pathology of cultural communities" (Freud, 1930a, p. 144).

I would like to make two brief clinical and technical suggestions before I end. The first regards evidence that I have gathered of the deep need patients have for an analyst free of cultural clichés (Sacerdoti, 1977), an analyst capable of being natural, uncomplicated, who knows how to create an atmosphere in which, as the poet once again describes,

> . . . a beast, a dumb one
> lifts his eyes and looks us calmly through and through.
>
> [R. M. Rilke, *The Eighth Elegy*, 1928]

The other situation, opposite to the first, is that in which the patient despairs about losing his clothes, his falsifications; he despairs because he thinks—the suggestion comes from within—that he has no core of being. This is the as-if personality, an extremely difficult one. In these circumstances, the patient is like Peer Gynt, who depicts himself as an onion, made of innumerable layers, covering nothing; layers that have grown around a void. No progress can come about if the analyst cannot uncover and activate a core of primitive experience. Can we do this with our present tools? Perhaps in part, and certainly not always. To Peer Gynt's desperate plea: "Tell me, then!

Where was myself, my whole self, my true self? . . ." Ibsen makes Solveig reply: "In my faith, in my hope and in my love."

Thus the poet.

How we can transform these elements into proper tools for therapeutic activity is what contemporary psychoanalysis is trying to discover.

CHAPTER THREE

From a play between "parts" to transformations in the couple: psychoanalysis in a bipersonal field

Michele Bezoari and Antonino Ferro

> To docket living things past any doubt
> You cancel first the living spirit out:
> The parts lie in the hollow of your hand,
> You only lack the living link you banned.

Goethe: *Faust*, part one, p. 95

Bion and the revolution of perspectives

Our clinical–theoretical itinerary takes as its starting point Bion's revolution of perspective concerning the way the analyst's mind functions in the session and his attitude in the analytic scenario.

With Bion the analyst's place is no longer outside the patient's mental functioning and personal history. Analysis becomes an authentic adventure—a new meeting between two strangers, and the possibility herein of writing a new story out of the many possible ones, according to the reciprocal interaction of the two minds involved in the session and to the extent they are prepared to be open to new thoughts.

Thus the analytic situation can be seen, on the one hand, as *symmetrical* to the utmost, since in the consulting room there are two frightened people, two fierce, dangerous animals, and the analyst himself is seen as a "mess" while the patient is considered "his best colleague". On the other hand, the relationship is *asymmetrical* to the utmost, since the analyst is wholly responsible for the way the analysis proceeds: he is like an officer who is entrusted with command but shares risks and fears with his men, being himself exposed to the Ps ↔ D oscillations (Bion, 1973, 1978, 1980, 1983).

According to this model, the analyst is no longer the guardian of a predetermined process, which he observes with benevolent neutrality, modulating anxieties and presiding over a reliable setting. Nor is he a decoder–interpreter of phantasies (including very primitive ones), which do not concern what he actually is but only what the patient believes him to be.

The analyst at work as conveyed by Bion, especially in the *Discussions* and *Seminars*, is someone who is not only a participant but also the driving force of the new story that is developing, inasmuch as he helps to point out the itinerary and proceeds along it with the patient.

In this perspective, for example, the primal scene is not only a phantasy, which is more or less related to childhood experiences; instead, it becomes a "realization" brought about by the coupling of minds in the session. It is thus possible to observe the development of the analytic dialogue from an angle that considers it as an expression of the actual vicissitudes taking place in the consulting room, with the knowledge that, as concerns mental exchanges, what one *does* far exceeds what one *says* (Bion, 1987).

This way of looking at things also implies recognition of the patient's capability to indicate almost constantly his unconscious perception of the mental functioning both of the analytic couple and of the analyst. The latter is called upon to join his patient and dare to act in unison with him.

There is a very significant passage in *Bion in Rome* (1983) in which Bion says that it is tantamount to a revolution to state that on the one hand we can become mentally absent when we don't like what the patient is saying, and on the other hand the patient (particularly the borderline patient) always knows when the analyst has become mentally absent. This poses the problem of the quantity of truth about the patient and about himself that the analyst can bear. Gaburri and Ferro (1988) say that in these cases the patient thus functions as a mirror of the analyst's distancing. He allows him to mend the relationship and gives him also the opportunity to observe those emotions that he has been unable to tolerate (his hidden dark zones or too painful scars). Thus the patient functions like an analyst's countertransference dream. Furthermore the patient reveals when the analyst is getting too close to the truth that this is not tolerable to him (p. 317, note 33).

In this sense the patient is someone who can constantly tell us how we appear to him from angles we are unfamiliar with.

The Barangers and the model of the field

The convergence between the work of Bion and that of M. and W. Baranger constitutes an important cross-roads on our theoretical itinerary.

These two French authors—who work in Argentina and write mainly in Spanish—have in the course of the last thirty years published a number of works of considerable originality in which they have developed a point of view that considers the analytic situation as a *dynamic field* structured by a *bipersonal relationship*.

The Barangers never quote Bion (at least in the works we are familiar with), although they seem to have worked along parallel lines, and in the same period too (their paper manifesto was published in 1961–62). It is, however, significant that they quote John Rickman (Bion's first analyst) and regard his work as fundamental to the specificity of psychoanalysis as a "bicorporal psychology" (Baranger & Baranger, 1969).

Their argument starts out from the observation that although the psychoanalytic experience was founded and technically defined by Freud in relational and dialogical terms, the majority of the concepts that make up the theoretical corpus of psychoanalysis are formulated in terms of a one-person psychology. The prototype of such metapsychological constructions is in Freud's conception of the psychic apparatus as a system that can be studied *in itself.*

As Petrella (1988) points out, this Freudian perspective bears the stamp of an original self-analytic quality. But today, we can echo Nissim Momigliano's (1987) affectionate critical notes and accept without too much difficulty that Freud—for good or ill—was not rigorously "Freudian".

This discontinuity between theory and technique was less obvious as long as the analytic situation was conceived of as a place in which the patient—more or less regressed—externalizes his psychic processes to an impartial listening–observing analyst who can perceive and describe them objectively.

But this simplistic schema has become more and more incompatible with the clinical experience and has been contradicted on the theoretical level by observations that the Barangers group around two central concepts: countertransference and projective identification. The Barangers theorization stems from the Kleinian model, but this is supplemented by the original contributions provided, in the 1950s, by a group of South-American authors (Racker, Liberman, Pichon-Rivière, Bleger, Grinberg, etc.).

On these grounds these authors conceive of the analyst's position in a new way and acknowledge his inevitable and complete involvement as an equal partner in the analytic process. But since analyst and patient make up an inextricably linked and complementary couple and are involved in the same dynamic process, it follows that no party of the couple can be understood without the other (Baranger & Baranger, 1961–62). From this programmatic stance stems, for the Barangers, the usefulness of adopting the model of the field, which appears better suited—above all descriptively—to the characteristics of the analytic situation.

The use of the concept of the *field* in the study of psychic phenomena has fairly well-known precedents in *Gestalt* psychology and in the work of Kurt Lewin, in which it acquires greater epistemological autonomy by freeing itself from any physicalist implications. Less well known is the elaboration of the concept as carried out by Merleau-Ponty (an important author in the Barangers' philosophical background). He takes the notion of the *field* in Koffa and Lewin's sense as being useful in founding a *situational* human psychology in which psychical events can be observed and understood for the meaning they acquire in the context of intersubjective relationships. In this way the historic choice between naturalistic objectivization and solipsistic introspection would be overcome.

An exemplification of this is a passage in which Merleau-Ponty (1964), following Husserl, states that getting to know the other is "a phenomenon of coupling" and stresses that this expression is not only a metaphor, because "We perceive the body of the other and we sense in him the same intentions that motivate our body, and the other does the same with us".

Beyond these extra-psychoanalytic references the Barangers trace the notion of the field in the works of Freud, in particular in the metaphors of the battlefield and of the chessboard.

In this perspective the analytic situation is endowed with a temporal and spatial structure of its own, oriented according to certain lines of force and animated by particular dynamics: this field is "the immediate and specific object" in the psychoanalyst's observation (Baranger & Baranger, 1961–62).

The analytic contract and the fundamental technical rules determine a first organization of the field, the setting, the field's potentially stable background. Against this background the predominantly verbal manifest material of the communication between analyst and patient gives rise to a second level of organization. But what is specific about the analytic experience is its possibility to arrive, starting out from these two levels, at the unconscious phantasy that constitutes the latent structure of the field.

In keeping with the above premises, the Barangers hypothesize that the unconscious phantasy actually active in the session does not belong to the analysand alone—it is, rather, a phantasy of the couple (similar to what happens in the case of group phantasies). It should be understood as a new structure created by the two members of the field within the couple they constitute during the session.

The unconscious phantasy that organizes the analytic field is thus a bipersonal phantasy, which cannot be reduced to its habitual formulation—as, for example, in Isaacs—that is, as an expression of the individual's instinctual life.

For the Barangers, the unconscious bipersonal phantasy is made up of an interplay of projective identifications, which to various degrees involves both the patient and the analyst.

We wish to emphasize in passing how the authors have made projective identification a veritable key to the construction of their bipersonal metapsychology by developing the original Kleinian formulations in a direction that in many ways seems to be extraordinarily reminiscent of the works of Bion. If projective identification is not only one individual's omnipotent phantasy but a "two-way affair" (Bion, 1980), it is no surprise that it is of decisive importance in the structuring of every couple (Baranger & Baranger, 1961–62).

Today these ideas are fairly widely accepted, though ambiguously and inconsistently. As Di Chiara and Flegenheimer (1985) point out, in the light of recent definitions proposed by Ogden (1979) and, in Italy, by Manfredi Turillazzi (1985), projective identification seems today to offer a basic model for the relational phenomena in analysis.

This radically bipersonal model of projective identification also produces important changes in transference–countertransference dynamics. According to the Barangers, what is traditionally defined as a "transference neurosis" (or psychosis) should be considered, in terms of the field, as a "transference-countertransference neurosis" (or psychosis)—that is, as a function of the couple. The patient's pathology as such only enters the field in relation to the analyst, who in turn contributes actively (although hopefully to a lesser extent) to the formation of that pathology of the field which will be the object of analytic work.

In those areas of the analytic field, which the Barangers call *bastions*, an interchange of projective identifications brings about an unconscious collusion between analyst and patient, which tends to immobilize them both and to prevent the analytic process from developing.

The analyst's specific function will thus be to avoid total involvement in these phenomena and to maintain a vigilant "second glance", as the Barangers call it, over what is going on in the field (Baranger, Baranger, & Mom, 1983). By working though his own countertransference, the analyst will be able to arrive at an effective interpretation which promotes insight.

It follows that the Barangers consider analytic insight as an experience of the couple, which differs from the self-understanding that an individual can have of his own psychic reality. In the analytic situation insight is achieved when analyst and patient acquire a common understanding of the unconscious phantasies that are active in the field at that moment. This coincides with a restructuring of the field itself, since thought and communication—both affective and cognitive—spread to areas previously occupied by the bastions, which are thus mobilized and dissolved. What the couple has split and deposited in a confused and random way in the bastions can now be reintegrated, symbolized, and discriminated by the two, thus enabling both analyst and analysand to achieve a better self-awareness in relation to the other. In the analyst such awareness will be "conscious and silent", in the patient "conscious and expressed" (M. Baranger et al., 1983).

The bipersonal field of analysis is thus the theatre of a dynamic process characterized by the couple's tendency to form bastions (that is, symbiotic bonds in Bleger's sense), and by the work required to transform these experiences into authentic object relationships. This endless dialectical exchange gives the analytic process a "spiral" course, as the Barangers, following Pichon-Rivière, called it.

The heuristic value of the model of the *field* in psychoanalysis was recently underlined by Corrao, who defined the psychoanalytic field as the "optimal specialized situation for exploring . . . the affective–cognitive phenomenologies which develop intrinsically within it" and stated that the "observables" are not to be placed in the static categories of "objects" and "subjects", but, rather, "in the mobile transactions of reversible exchanges and coupling among themselves" (Corrao, 1989, p. 530).

In a previous paper, Corrao (1986a) had dealt with the same topic, applying to psychoanalysis some peculiar aspects of modern physics' model of the field. One of those aspects is, for example, the fact that the existence of a clear distinction between the observer and the facts observed is no longer plausible. In quantum physics, as Heisenberg demonstrated, it is impossible to state, except in an arbitrary way, which object should be considered as part of the observed system and which one as part of the observing apparatus. It may be worth recalling that Heisenberg's well-known principle of indetermination is founded on the acknowledgement of a mutual interaction between the observer and the observed object, an interaction that can no longer be considered negligible, or at least sufficiently controllable to eliminate its influence by means of calculus, as the classical theories suggested. It is fairly significant that these same words might be used for what has happened in psychoanalysis as regards countertransference.

We shall try, now, to show how these theoretical reflections have influenced our way of conceiving analytic work and the technical problems related to it.

The parts and the functional aggregates

Since we are accustomed to thinking in terms of split parts, we have perhaps made excessive use of those clumsy interpretations that start "it's a part of you that . . ." (as if it were really possible for the analyst to be nothing more than a mirror), with all the problems involved in deciding how to consider the characters that come into play in the session: whether they are figures from external reality, projected aspects of the patient's self, representations of internal objects, and so on. We have become increasingly dissatisfied with interpretations of this type, as regards both their therapeutic efficacy and their theoretical validity. (We need only mention the risk that the analytic dialogue runs of degenerating into a stereotyped jargon, when the patient himself furnishes the simultaneous translation of his feelings in terms of parts of his self, of which he speaks in the third person.)

Recently Gaburri and Ferro (1988) pointed out that while Klein used toys in child analysis as personifications of internal objects cathected with love and hate, Bion shifts this model to what we might call the split parts of the personality. Just as Klein used play analytically, Bion *uses split parts analytically* rather than merely interpreting them.

If it is true that the exchange between analyst and patient goes beyond the verbal level, and that words convey far more than their linguistic meanings—if, that is, the reciprocal projective identifications form a bipersonal field, as the Barangers hold—it follows that, when their effects become apparent in the session, it will not always nor immediately be possible to allot the split parts to one or other member of the couple. It is worth recalling here that the patient may dream split parts of the analyst's mind—as Rosenfeld (1987a) emphasized.

Meltzer, following Bion, considers dreaming as a continuous process, which takes place both in sleep and in the waking state—a process lending shape and meaning to experience, making it thinkable. Thus, during the session, too, an oneiric function is at work in the two minds, which dream of each other in a reciprocal flow of stimuli and projective identifications. We can understand the derivatives of these "waking dreams" as they emerge in conscious fantasies, in free associations, and, by extension, in all the material; they are perhaps more clearly apparent in those particular phenomena that Meltzer (1986a) describes as oneiric flashes in the waking state.

In this perspective the characters, the narratives, and the memories evoked in the session—in addition, that is, to genuine dreams—can be reinterpreted as representations of the type of relationship the couple is unconsciously experiencing in a given moment.

Basically, the bipersonal field requires that we develop a perspective that has an important and often-forgotten forerunner in Fairbairn (1952), who holds that, fundamentally, dreams are not wish fulfilments, but the dramatization—or a "short", in the cinematographic sense—of situations that exist in the dreamer's inner reality. The situations portrayed by dreams—and daydreams—represent relationships that exist between endopsychic structures.

To underline the specific meaning this concept has when placed in its new context, we have introduced into our technical vocabulary the term *functional aggregates*, as an alternative to the classical term *personified parts*. In this way we wish to indicate that we avoid deciding whether characters appearing on the analytic scene belong to one of the authors or actors rather than to the other. Instead, we think of these characters— and of every other significant element of the scene as well—in a transitional dimension that respects their composite quality.

We speak of *aggregates* since the images of the manifest speech and in general the *Gestalten* of the analytic field are a synthesis of heterogeneous elements (verbal, emotional, corporeal), stemming from both analyst and analysand.

We call them *functional* because the forms of this variable combinatorial geometry are linked to the mental functioning of the analytic couple and to the communicative needs of the moment.

We shall try, now, to illustrate these ideas through some clinical vignettes.

> Marta, a language teacher married to an Englishman,
> talks about her jealousy for Pat, a foreign friend of her
> husband's. The subject crops up fairly often. . . .
> Obviously it is tempting to interpret this jealousy in
> various ways, but the analyst manages to wait. One day
> Marta tells the analyst how her husband goes "pat–pat" to
> women friends as a way of greeting them or reassuring
> them if they have problems, thus managing to have
> physical contact with them: and this is what she really
> can't stand!

Thus at last the analyst notices that his patient is indicating how sensitive she is to all the possible betrayals of the analytic function that he might indulge in (reassurances, pat–pat, eroticization of emotional contact), even if these are perhaps attitudes that the patient herself activates in him through projective

identifications. At this point the perspective of a possible interpretation changes, or there can even be a "silent interpretation"
(Spotnitz, 1969), a settling phase in countertransference work.

Moreover, it seems that quite frequently a session begins
with the account of the previous one from a perspective that is
unknown to the analyst (and also unknown at a conscious level
to the patient himself). Successively, indications concerning
the current functioning of the couple and reciprocal "signalling
one's own position" (Gaburri, 1986) are given. The various
characters—i.e. *functional aggregates* that come into play—are
thus the expression of a conscious process whereby the members of the couple tend to dream and to communicate to one
another what is going on between them, almost moment by
moment.

Thus, for example, Carla is unable to choose between two
boyfriends, Luca and Luigi; in this way she describes two ways
in which the couple functions in the session. The former is
discreet, affectionate, and makes it clear that he is interested in
a long-term relationship. . . . The other, with his urgent and
impatient way of courting and his passionate declarations,
makes her feel highly desired, but, as soon as she shows she is
willing, a sort of "Turkish chromosome", Carla says, starts to
work in him, and he pesters her "like a drill". Of course these
characters represent two possible ways in which two minds
can meet in the session, with the projective identifications of
incontinent aspects of the patient . . . which activate the interpretative incontinence of the analyst . . . who then tries to understand what has happened by using the patient's unconscious indications in his own working through. Each of these
characters, who, from time to time, enter the session, can undergo further metamorphoses. "Luca" can become "Lucio", who
tends to make fun of people and makes derisory remarks in
response to everything that is said to him . . . and so on.

From this technical viewpoint we can thus reflect over our
initial perplexities about those interpretations that go ". . . it's a
part of you that . . .".

The split parts of the field cannot be attributed *tout court* to
the patient rather than to the analyst, because basically they
are confused, symbiotically agglutinated parts, to use Bleger's

(1967) terminology. It is thus no surprise that an interpretation that induces a forced introjection of these "parts" arouses persecutory anxieties in the patient and legitimates negative therapeutic reactions.

Rather, it seems to us that the analyst's priority should be to foster the progressive interaction of these areas into the couple's communicative work, so as to arrive, through successive transformations of what we have called *functional aggregates*, at a shared vision and an experience of emotional syntony relative to what occurs in the field. Only then is it possible to discern and redistribute what had been confused by the overlapping of projective identifications. Each member of the couple can thus better identify those aspects of his inner self that have been activated in the relationship.

Two-part interpretations

Previously (Bezoari & Ferro, 1989) we discussed the nature of analytic interpretation and showed how profoundly the models we adopted changed our views on the matter. Through our clinical experience, we came to realize that difficult patients are somewhat reluctant to accept transference interpretations, formulated according to Strachey's "strong" model. This led us to give more value to those verbal interventions of the analyst that do not convey a clearly defined meaning and are not intended to explain "truth", but contain instead a highly unsaturated semantic projectuality, which needs the patient's active contribution to become more precise and actual. To give an idea of what we mean, we have called these formulations "weak interpretations", for the patient's contribution is essential to the establishment of meaning, and not merely to confirm or add something to it. In such a perspective, it is the very image of the analyst that is weakened, for he is no longer regarded as the sole depository of power and hermeneutic competence. The term "weakness", however—employed in order to evoke the philosophical themes of "weak thought" (Vattimo & Rovatti, 1983)—is in fact intended to indicate the radically intersubjective and dialogical nature of interpretation. Indeed, Meltzer spoke of the analytic couple as a two-person working group; and it is again Meltzer who recently indicated as one of the most important changes in his technique the reduced importance of accuracy in interpretations. The same author states that attention should be shifted towards the interaction and the relationship in which the interpretative ideas originate. The container–contained model, too, turns out to be inadequate if understood in terms of the analyst being the container; it is, rather, the mutual adaptation between the analyst's attention and attitude, and the patient's tendency to co-operate, that form and seal the container (Meltzer, 1986b).

Corrao (1986b) speaks of a "hermeneutic field" produced by the analytic situation, whose "functors"—that is, the mental operations constructing meaning—are representation, symbolization, dramatization, and narration. Each of these functions can be performed both by the analyst and by the patient in a relationship of "hermeneutic reciprocity and complementarity".

We are thus entitled to believe that all the analyst's verbal observations which produce transformations—including transference interpretations *apertis verbis*—carry out their specific function and become authentic mutative interpretations of the analytic field only when they manage to make contact with the patient's mental processes, thus encouraging their development (and not blocking it, for example, through badly timed saturation of meaning). A couple of short clinical examples will illustrate these statements, showing, so to say, their negative side.

> A patient dreams he is in a hut looking out happily at two white mountains, when suddenly he sees an avalanche start to come crashing down from them. This fills him with terror . . . a chick he is holding in his hand is at risk of being suffocated.

It would seem easy to interpret the dream in terms of unconscious body-phantasies about the patient's internal objects, and possibly about the vicissitudes of his relationships with his mother's breast (the original experience of ecstatic admiration of the breast, which is spoiled by envy; then the good milk becomes threatening and oppressive, etc.). But we find it more useful to think of the dream as a precious indication of what had occurred in the previous session or of what the patient fears might happen in the next one; it is as if the patient were saying to the analyst: "What you say overwhelms me, even though you speak the truth. . . . If you go on like this, you'll risk suffocating my new-born thoughts . . . slow things down a little".

Another patient reported a dream after a session in which the analyst had concluded a long preliminary dialogue with a rather "strong" transference interpretation prompted in him by a sense of respect for his theoretical beliefs. In her dream the patient goes to see Prof. X, who is helping her to prepare her thesis. They normally have a profitable and amicable relationship. But on this particular day Prof. X looks different, quite unlike his usual self: he harshly criticizes the way she has written her thesis, he even goes so far as to tear it up before her very eyes and says: "Read my book instead, and learn from it . . .".

It should not be forgotten that an interpretation conveys far more to the patient than its mere cognitive content. Together with meanings, our words tell the patient what sort of emotional attitude we have towards him (Rycroft, 1968b). They tell about how the analyst's mind has managed to approach that of the patient, thus creating an experience of intimacy in separateness (Di Chiara, chapter two, this volume).

The balance between the semantic function—that is, the identification of meaning—and the affective involvement is thus one of the fundamental criteria for gauging our interventions in the analytic dialogue.

Sometimes the analyst is too actively in search of meanings—not those belonging to the patient's past, nor those pertaining to his internal phantasy world, but meanings connected to the present analytic relationship. The patient can prove incapable of accepting this, even for a long time, and develops intense persecutory anxieties. Such patients often appear to be extremely receptive towards the methods, the feel, and the quality of the relationship, and the fact that the analyst finds a meaning, or, rather, expounds it directly, is perceived by them to be a form of defence on his part. They feel that the analyst is

refusing their affection or is defending himself from that temporary disorganization of the mind that should allow him to be in
tune with them. They emphasize, often through their dreams,
that excessively assertive ways of interpreting are perceived as
mechanical, non-relational, or even autistic.

A typical situation is one in which the analyst notices that a
mistake on his own part has provoked the patient's pain or
anxiety. In such an event the analyst has two choices: either he
silently readjusts his mental attitude and tries to be more cautious in his interpretations, or he makes explicit pronounce-
ments. A technical measure—proposed by Langs (1975, 1986)
in particular—is to go back and show the patient what happened, where the misunderstanding, the impasse in communication, or whatever else set off the sense of persecution took
place. It is possible to do this only with certain patients, and in
certain phases of analysis. But other patients cannot tolerate
this—they find such an operation even more persecutory. In
this case the analyst should work the situation through within
himself, avoiding interpretations. It thus becomes necessary
to absorb and metabolize the anxieties of the moment, even
those of the current session, which are perhaps caused by
something that happened the day before, without displacing
them onto the past—even a very recent past—thus producing a
distance.

Such patients seem to have a particularly strong need
(which is, in any case, felt by all patients): the need to experience a genuinely intimate relationship with the analyst, in contrast to which a "strong" interpretation represents a too-abrupt
break, a tear.

When we speak of intimacy, we do not mean something akin
to fusionality, but, rather, a condition in which the interpretation of what is going on in the field remains a *fil rouge* in the
analyst's mind—a real Ariadne's thread that helps him not to
lose his way—but also a condition in which meaning is allowed
to develop freely during the session, using the elements that
the patient is providing as if they were Lego or Duplo bricks.
The analyst and the patient can play with these, as it were,
without taking them apart "to see what they are like", but trying to form new creative combinations.

To play with the patient during the session without unmasking him constantly (and . . . unmasking ourselves) recalls Alvarez's (1988) description of anticipatory identification, in which "masks" are not used as disguises or distortions, but as ways of experiencing and trying out a new identity in advance.

In such an atmosphere, interpretations will not lay out or uncover supposedly known meanings, but they will be transactions of affects rather than of meanings, to construct a truth that both members of the couple first experience, and then share.

Here is how some of our patients responded to interpretations that leant too heavily on the intellectual–explicative side, at the expense of sharing and understanding.

After an interpretation of this kind, a patient talked about a film in which an angel seized the disembodied essence of what a girl held in her hands, leaving her—the patient remarked—the sad and hard task of carrying something devoid of meaning.

Another patient dreamt she was wandering about her house in a worried state, switching off the lights that someone had left on for no reason and looking for *Gente* (People), the magazine her mother used to read when she was a child.

A third patient dreamt that a famous surgeon was carrying out a heart transplant on him and on another person, even though they did not need one. He stuck a tube down their throats . . . it was a most painful operation . . . And who knows whether the stitches would hold after the operation . . . Then the scene changed: the patient was on a boat with a friend who was fishing, and had caught a big fish . . . But he noticed that it was a little man, a doll . . . it couldn't survive, so that he had to kill it. With his interpretation the analyst had transplanted into the patient the feelings of a sick child in need of much care and attention. The first meeting between this patient and his analyst had occurred in a hospital, and this sick child had been evoked several times in the course of analysis. Now, however, the patient felt such an interpretation to be an unnecessary operation, and a very painful and risky one; he thought the same about the analyst's having suddenly brought to light his infantile self, which, if taken out of the aqueous matrix of what cannot as yet be spoken, gasps and must be killed—that is, denied.

And, finally, here is a dream that seems to show—positively, for once—how the analytic situation can act as an incubator for affects and thoughts that are not yet fully developed, and how the analyst's principal task is to safeguard the delicate and decisive transitional area between the spoken and the unspoken, the experienced and the thought, the self and the nonself.

> In a little bay, within several piers and berths joined by small bridges, there are lots of tiny "foetuses and newborn babies" swimming in the sea. They are tied to the piers, which support them and keep their noses out of the water, thus allowing them to breathe. Close by there is a lifeguard who watches over them, and as soon as any of them seems to be in danger of sinking below the surface, he gives them a little prod with a stick, and so they stay afloat.

Relationship ↔ transference

The mental encounter of the analytic couple seems to proceed according to two different basic ways of functioning, which alternate. One can be defined as *relationship* in the specific sense of a new intersubjective experience fully respectful of the partner's otherness, which can be continually symbolized. The other is that of *transference* (including its necessary counter-transference complement), in which actuality is experienced in a stereotyped and repetitive way, where one member of the couple tends to force the other into fixed roles, predetermined by unconscious phantasies and induced by projective identifications.

The analyst's basic task is to guarantee a microclimate that facilitates the development of transference phenomena in a relational sense. So as to effect this, temperature, timing, distance (Meltzer, 1976), and other specific qualities of his mental array must be adequately dosed by the analyst. This process, which proceeds from *transference* towards *relationship*, is not only arduous and laborious, but also hardly as linear and unidirectional as certain ideal patterns of treatment would make it out to be, not even in successful analyses. Common experience—which is also our own—indicates an oscillation between the two ways of functioning of the analytic couple. This oscillation is analogous to the one between Ps and D described by Bion—and we could likewise represent it with the symbols $R \leftrightarrow T$.

The convergence between Bion's and the Barangers' approach explains this oscillation without ascribing it to the patient's resistances, envious attacks, or negative therapeutic reactions, nor to the analyst's technical errors or personal defects, with the various degrees of apportioning of guilt to one or the other that this implies.

Indeed, the specific potential of the analytic situation lies precisely in the opportunity it offers the patient to structure the relational field with his projective identifications, by means of which he can express anew his unsatisfied needs for mental growth and the unresolved conflicts of his affective life. The fact that the analyst also takes part in the structuring of the analytic field through the limited use of projective identification, neurotic elements, and other unanalysed residues of his own, thus experiencing a "countertransference microneurosis", is not an undesirable though inevitable inconvenience. As M. and W. Baranger state (1961–62), "it is part of the analyst function to let himself become involved in these configurations". The formation of a transference–countertransference neurosis (or psychosis) in the analytic situation will make an evolutionary transformation possible.

In other words, so as to be genuinely receptive towards the patient's projective identifications, the analyst must be willing to live under his own skin the corresponding experiences that they evoke in him, and to activate obscure and unfamiliar zones of *his* personality (since, as Manfredi Turillazzi says, there are no "foreign guests" in the mind). In short, Freud's (1912b) classical definition of transference is applicable to projective identification as a relational phenomenon: one cannot expect to work it through *in effigy*, that is, by treating it as if it were merely someone else's phantasy.

It is thus inevitable, but also necessary, that the analytic situation should involve powerful feelings that cannot become immediately conscious.

There is a myth that the analyst can always discover what is going on in the session by "using" his own countertransference as a pointer. Bion exploded this myth in a few simple words when he stated that one of the founding characteristics of countertransference is that it is *unconscious*, and thus the analyst cannot make any use of it, since he does not know what it is (Bion, 1980).

This has also put paid to the illusion that it is always possible to identify and interpret the moment where the anxiety emerges; one must accept that the couple needs time in order to make the exchange of certain experiences possible and thinkable.

Thus the $R \leftrightarrow T$ oscillation must be considered physiological. For the analyst this implies, among other things, that he is subject to various sorts of countertransference micro-actings, even interpretative ones, during the long and difficult journey towards a thinkability of nameless emotions. In this perspective the interruption of R permits the emergence of T, which can be metabolized and transformed by working through. It thus becomes possible to reach a mental and interpretative attitude suitable to the re-founding of R.

Risks and benefits for the analyst's mind

In conclusion we would like to propose some reflections on the implications that work on the analytic field, as outlined above, can have for the analyst's mental health.

If we accept that it is an essential aspect of our therapeutic function to allow ourselves, within limits, to be receptive towards the patient's projective identifications, then contact with mental pain, whose intensity and quality cannot be estimated at the outset, is inevitable. A crucial question thus arises: what risks are we willing to run in order to accept and metabolize the still unknown experiences that the relationship with the patient might activate in us?

As the planned end of his analysis draws near (after seven years), Nico, a serious case, is, for perhaps the first time, going through the painful and, for him, heart-rending experience of separation, which he perceives and imagines as his last hour, a death foretold. During a session in which it is causing him a great pain to talk about these feelings (which he had never experienced before, even though he had been submitted to traumatic separations from his mother in the past), this patient says he is smoking a lot at the moment, more than forty cigarettes a day, although he knows it can damage his health. Suddenly, he asks the analyst to smoke at least one cigarette with him. Somewhat perplexed, the analyst interprets, thinking that if he hits the mark the problem will be solved, and he will get out of this tight spot. So he says something about the patient's wish to overcome his hate and anger towards the analyst (which had emerged previously), who, he feels, is about to abandon him, by smoking the calumet of peace with him (metaphors derived from cowboy Westerns are a common way of communicating within the couple). Nico nods in agreement, but insists on offering the analyst a cigarette he himself has lit. The analyst has no choice but to accept it. Then, when the patient's attention seems momentarily diverted, he takes advantage of this and drops a bit of ash into the ashtray. At once Nico remarks, "Doctors want to remain healthy, so they don't smoke . . . Only I have to smoke so much". Unable to understand, and worried about the possibility of an acting-out of his own, the analyst feels that at this point he must run the risk anyway, and is about to bring the cigarette to his lips, when he is panic-stricken: he could become infected . . . the spectre of AIDS flashes into his mind.

Only then, when he has got over this moment of terror, does the analyst feel he has really been "in O" with the patient and with what he was being asked. Whether, that is, he was observing the patient's suffering from a safe position, from behind a glass screen, or whether, on the other hand, he was willing and brave enough to share this terrible and painful experience and to run, albeit to a lesser extent (one drag of a cigarette as opposed to the patient's forty a day), the risk of becoming infected. The analyst tells the patient about these thoughts. The patient replies: "That's what I've been asking myself for years".

Of course, the safety net represented by the setting is fundamental, but in this perspective it cannot be considered either all embracing or always equally efficient, as countertransference dreams—a form of patching-up "after hours"—show (Barale & Ferro, 1987).

We must also allow for our understandable and very human tendency not to stray too far from the safety of trodden paths. Recourse to models and theories during the session—and at times after hours, too—can cater to this need. This area includes many problems concerning the limits of analysability (it would be more accurate to say, the limits of a certain patient *with us*) and perhaps also certain cultural phenomena of entrenchment in theoretical positions, which, however innovative they may have been originally, thus become obstacles to the development of thought.

When during the session we make excessive use of our theories, normally our patients are quick to remind us of this, for example through dreams in which they receive old records as presents, or come up against bureaucrats who are reluctant to renew their expired identity cards. Indeed, records with words and music that are most familiar to us or the most familiar images of our patients—and of ourselves—represent whatever we cling to every time we are afraid of going where the patient is and from where he calls to us. Wittenberg (1988) states very explicitly that to avoid such calls we can use our theories mentally, as autistic children use their autistic objects.

As Leonardi (1987) reminds us, we should always bend down next to the patient, so that together we can take a better look and grasp the specific physiognomy of the objects and of the bonds that are at play in the relationship. It might thus be possible to avoid the phantasy of an omniscient analyst who possesses universal truths about his own psychic life and that of his patient: such a phantasy may perhaps reduce anxiety and procure analgesic effects, but it may also have a "malignant and cancerous" effect on the mental health of both members of the couple.

At this point, however, we must not overlook the other side of the coin—namely what Bion (1980) aptly calls the supplementary benefits of analytic work—those that lead to improved self-knowledge and to mental growth.

If it is true that with each patient the analyst experiences a new countertransference micropathology (Baranger & Baranger, 1961–62) a successful analysis will have transformative and liberating effects not only on the patient, but on the analyst too. As A. and F. Meotti (1988) say, every analysis that is successfully, if imperfectly, terminated is also the successful analysis of a part of ourselves as yet unknown to us.

We would like to end our consideration of this somewhat disquieting topic on the risks involved in our profession by a quotation from a text we feel expresses similar disquietudes poetically, while at the same time indicating which resources we can rely on. It is a passage (a dream?) from *The Diaries of Franz Kafka*, dated 19 January 1915.

> I had agreed to go picnicking on Sunday with two friends, but quite unexpectedly slept past the hour when we were to meet. My friends, who knew how punctual I ordinarily am, were surprised, came to the house where I lived, waited outside awhile, then came upstairs and knocked on my door. I was very startled, jumped out of bed, and thought only of getting ready as soon as I could. When I emerged fully dressed from my room, my friends fell back in manifest alarm. "What's that behind your head?" they cried. Since my awakening I had felt something preventing me from bending back my head, and I now groped for it with my hand. My friends, who had grown somewhat calmer, had just shouted "Be careful, don't hurt yourself!" when my hand closed behind my head on the hilt of a sword. My friends came closer, examined me, led me back to the

mirror in my room, and stripped me to the waist. A large, ancient knight's sword with a cross-shaped handle was buried to the hilt in my back, but the blade had been driven with such incredible precision between my skin and flesh that it had caused no injury.

Nor was there a wound at the spot on my neck where the sword had penetrated; my friends assured me that there was an opening large enough to admit the blade, but dry and showing no trace of blood. And when my friends now stood on chairs and slowly, inch by inch, drew out the sword, I did not bleed, and the opening on my neck closed until no mark was left save a scarcely discernible slit. "Here is your sword", laughed my friends, and gave it to me. I hefted it in my two hands; it was a splendid weapon, Crusaders might have used it.

Who tolerates this gadding about of ancient knights in dreams, irresponsibly brandishing their swords, stabbing innocent sleepers who are saved from serious injury only because the weapons in all likelihood glance off living bodies, and also because there are faithful friends knocking at the door, prepared to come to their assistance?

PART TWO

THE ANALYST'S MIND

Interest in the analyst's mind, which is already evident in the previous chapters, is more thoroughly developed in the two that follow. In the tale of the "green hand", listened to with pleasure by children and remembered with anxiety by some patients, Di Chiara acknowledges the representation of the projective identification of parents towards their children and of the analyst towards his patient during analysis. The cathartic value of the tale lies in the fact that the "child" cunningly has the better of the intruding, domineering "grown-up". But what is more likely to happen in reality? The anxious hypersensitivity of some patients towards the analyst's interventions is seen as a sign of fear for such an intrusion. This takes place at an unconscious level for both analyst and patient. The analyst may be unable to defend himself from the patient's projective identifications. He may develop a forced countertransference reaction and no longer be in control of himself. This is a genuine "professional risk" for the analyst and a serious threat to the patient. How can both

be protected from such a serious danger? Di Chiara
believes that the solution lies in the *analyst's mental
setting* and in the peculiar way it works in analysis. One
essential characteristic of a mind working analytically is
the capacity to relate to internal objects that are the result
of a successful separation from the original objects. This
separation creates a space (between the analyst's ego and
his objects) where the patient can be welcomed with the
assurance of respect for his own potential individuality
and separateness. A structure of this type is the mental
model of *psychoanalytic setting.*

Vallino Macciò arrives at similar concepts by somewhat
different paths. She tells us about dealing with patients
who suffer from a feeling of not existing that the analyst is
led to share through the "enigmatic, undifferentiated"
experience of anxiety. The analyst who agrees to suffer
such an experience within himself accepts communication.
This is the point at which the particular make-up of the
analyst, his specific working tool, comes to the fore. The
analyst must be able to receive anxiety and suffer it. He
must be able to run the risk of losing all certainty, at least
temporarily. This does not, however, imply loss of mental
health. His internal make-up must allow him to make
room within himself for the patient's emotional states
without losing his own identity. During the phase when
the patient can hardly survive, the analyst's mental
survival, understood as the ability to think and to imagine
emotions, is also in danger. "Excessive" projective
identification may lead a person to identify himself too
much with the feelings of another, up to the point of losing
awareness of his own. Another danger is then that the
analyst, once a working alliance has been set up, may
become an internal object imposing rules on the patient.
Separation is a basic feature of the analyst's mental make
up for Vallino Macciò too. She understands separation as
an establishment of boundaries, the creation of an
optimum distance from both emotional involvement and
one's own theoretical models. In order to create an

emotional experience with his patient, the analyst must keep an imaginative area for himself and, at the same time, respect the other's individuality. This ability of the analyst's can never become a permanent acquisition. Each patient requires us to be "new" for him, rich in experience and free from prejudice. Here psychoanalysis is presented as a continual, active struggle against uncritical acceptance of preconceived models or scientific dogma that can never be doubted. Otherwise, I believe, the latter can turn into our "Green Hand". In Vallino Macciò's mainly clinically oriented chapter we observe parallel changes in both analyst and patient. The latter is seen as a person who has something to teach us.

The authors of both chapters mention the danger of uncritical acceptance of an ideal, which for the analyst can be his theoretical model, and for the patient an analyst who is never wrong. In a true psychoanalytic relationship, however, the point of reference for analyst and patient is the *psychoanalytic method*, which is the exclusive property of neither of them. In the analyst's internal world, alongside the other objects, we also find the "object psychoanalysis", which, hopefully, is able to inspire and advise, rather than impose rules to be followed.

In this light, countertransference is no longer seen in its former aspect of a reply to transference (and a defensive reply, as suggested by the prefix "counter-"). Rather, it is conceived in the wider sense of the analyst's disposition to a relationship. The responsibility taken on by the analyst for his internal world, which requires great care on his part, is obvious. The analyst, however, while being alert against his own resistances and defences, is also open to his emotions and does not consider them as obstacles, but, rather, as a guide and source of inspiration. A developmental value is given to the capacity for feeling emotions, for both the analyst and the patient.

Andreina Robutti

CHAPTER FOUR

The tale of the green hand:
on projective identification

Giuseppe Di Chiara

I had known the tale of the green hand since my childhood. In my clinical practice, it appeared during the analysis first of one patient and then later of two others, as an association to a dream in one case, of recalled anal erotism in another, and of anxiety-ridden vicissitudes of anal sadism and masochism in the third. In two of these cases the recalling of the fairy-tale aroused anxiety, and the tale had failed in its aim of making tolerable the psychological experience to which it alludes. The patients remembered it as having been a source of anxiety, when it was told to them as children.

At the beginning I had thought that there might be a correlation between the contents of the fairy-tale and events caused by over-stimulation, as they are described and studied by Shengold (1967), but I did not continue along this train of thought. Similarly, I had abandoned the idea of linking the tale with anal masturbation and projective identification (Meltzer, 1966), even if there were a number of clearly possible connections in this sense. But it was Grinberg's work (1976, 1990) on identification that induced me to take the matter up again.

71

The tale

First of all I shall give the version of the tale that I knew and that my patients recollected, which is probably a regional variant of a text transmitted by word of mouth.

Once upon a time, on the outskirts of a densely populated village, there stood a beautiful mansion, surrounded by a magnificent park. In the mansion there lived a very rich lady, who promised an extremely rich reward to any young girl who could pass a test to which she would be submitted. The reward would make the fortunate girl a princess, endowed with rich clothes and jewels. The test consisted in the girl having to eat a green hand, made of a mixture of worms, earth, and parsley. The first girl arrived to pass the test. The rich lady left her to look after the house and gave her the green hand. She told her to take good care of everything and during her absence to eat the hand. When the lady had gone away, the unfortunate girl was left with the hand, which seemed to her to be far too disgusting to eat. In the end she decided not to eat it and swiftly threw the hand into the well. When the witch came back—because you must have realized that the rich lady was nothing but a witch—she asked the girl whether she had carried out all her tasks. The girl replied promptly that she had. The witch then called out, in a loud voice: "Green hand, green hand, where are you?" "I'm at the bottom of the well", replied the hand. "So, you didn't obey me. For this you will die!", said the witch to her victim. In this same way many a lovely girl lost her life in the mansion just outside the village, for the same thing happened again and again, differing only in the place where the victim hid the hand, which always replied at once to its mistress's call, from rooms in the attic, from the cellar, from the oven or from the barn. Then one day the heroine of this story arrived. She was a young country girl who was brighter than the others. On being left alone with the dilemma of the revolting meal, decided to crush the hand up well and apply it with a bandage like a poultice to her stomach. When the witch came back and asked the girl if she had eaten the hand and called out the usual words to the green hand, it replied: "I'm in Antonia's stomach", for Antonia was the winner's name. In this way the trick, worthy of Ulysses, was played on the wicked witch, who, once vanquished, was in her turn punished with death, while the girl came into possession of all her wealth.

Somewhat different and richer in detail is the version written down by Giuseppe Pitré, entitled "The Slave", which I shall briefly relate (Pitré, 1875).

A father goes out with one of his three daughters to gather wild cabbages. They come across one that the daughter tries to pull out of the ground. But it is well rooted. They have to labour at it. When the cabbage is finally extracted from the ground, a slave appears who—turning to the father—asks him for his daughter, saying he will make her a queen. The father asks his daughter whether she will accept and when she does, takes a bag of money from the slave and goes home.

The slave's palace is underground, and it is built of gold, silver, and jewels. The slave orders the girl always to do what he asks her and always to be faithful to him. Then he goes away after having given the girl a "hand of living flesh" and bidden her to eat it. The hidden hand answers the slave's call, and the girl is beheaded. The slave returns to the father and, with the excuse that the girl is bored and would like to have one of her sisters for company, persuades the father to give him another of his daughters, again in exchange for a bag of money. And once again the same thing happens with the third and last daughter, who gets the better of the slave with the trick of the poultice. The slave then opens the doors of secret rooms, full of riches, but also of the bodies of his victims. The slave gives all these riches to the girl who has outwitted him and brings his victims back to life. Among these there is the little king of Portugal, who marries Antonia. The slave thinks up a revenge. He makes himself tiny and has himself shut into a cabinet that is bought by the king of Portugal. However Antonia, who is still just as astute as a queen, hears the slave moving about in his Trojan horse as he tries to get out, and so the slave is captured and put to death.

Psychoanalytic observations

I do not believe that we can psychoanalyse a fairy-tale. A tale of this kind can in some respects be analysed with other tools. However, it is possible to carry out a psychoanalytic exercise on a fairy-tale since unconscious and primary psychological events and vicissitudes are represented in it—all the more so when the fairy-tale appears as an association during a session.

The patients observed by Shengold (1967) had suffered as children from overstimulation consisting in seduction and sexual violence by an adult—often one of the parents—exposure to the primal scene, and frequent and violent beatings. These patients often had psychotic parents. There was often a "cannibal" animal in their dreams, in their fantasies and in their symptoms, most often a rat. The relationship that they had with the analyst in the transference was intensely sado-masochistic. The overexcitement caused by the trauma produced a hyperactive character in the patients, and therefore they were ill at ease when having to keep to the rules of the analytic setting. The childhood trauma tended to be negated, and, when it reached the conscious level, phenomena connected with splitting of the ego occurred, with self-induced states of reduced consciousness and alterations of identity. The superego appeared to be compromised, both in the sense of an excess of severity, with requests for punishment, and in the sense of extreme perversity. Psychopathological behaviour was produced by identification with the psychotic or psychopathic parent.

As a consequence of all this, I related the narration of the fairy-tale of the green hand, a traumatic event for some of my patients and associated with sadomasochistic anal erotism, to the syndrome described by Shengold. Some elements corresponded: the fairy-tale appeared to be the expression or the screen memory of sexual seduction, of anal manipulations, and of a father's beating-up of his daughter. But all this did not seem to be tied up solely with such traumatic and blatant events. On the contrary, it seemed that many patients had passed through less severe experiences, which nevertheless had aroused a reaction similar to the one described above, even if less evident. I observed a general hypersensitivity to the analyst's interventions, or even a start when the analyst broke into a silence. There were frequent states of obnubilated consciousness during sessions. My growing interest in countertransference helped me to realize how important it was to proceed cautiously, prudently, guided by the impression that otherwise I would be excessive, intrusive, or incomprehensible. My patients were teaching me, reminding me, at the end of an analysis or when emerging from a period of more intense suffering, how important it had been for them that I had been able to wait. But they were also letting me know that although what I had given them was good, they had at times suffered because of the form in which it had been offered to them. All this seemed to indicate that we were confronted here with a more general phenomenology of the analytic relationship, determined by structures and functions that were present and active in all cases, even if in different ways and in a different measure.

Meltzer's (1966) work on projective identification and anal masturbation was presented at the Amsterdam Congress in 1965 and published one year later. The aspects relative to anal erotism that he describes should not have been missed by Shengold, who, strangely enough, makes no mention of them. From Meltzer's standpoint my clinical material appeared more transparent, as did the possible associations aroused by the fairy-tale. I could see a clear link between separation from the analyst in the transference and from parental objects in the

past and the masturbatory practice of anal erotism. The aim
was to recuperate the lost object with projective identification
by forcefully intruding into the object with the split part of
oneself. In the light of Meltzer's work, some characteristics of
particular patients and analytic relationships could be seen
with greater precision, but I still had the impression that we
were again confronted with a widespread mechanism, which
was functioning in every case, even if possibly at less manifest
levels. In fact, Meltzer's brilliant individuation of the cryptic
character of anal masturbation allowed the phenomena to be
recognized in a much wider range of events. In the fairy-tale
there is an allusion both to overstimulation and to anal masturbation. Both phenomena were also present in the mental situations of my patients. Meltzer's work was based on an analytic
concept that had been discovered by Klein and then gradually
developed—namely, projective identification. I decided to proceed along this path.

An exercise on the fairy-tale

As I have already said, I do not think that work on a fairy-tale,
or on a literary or film text, is psychoanalysis: it is an exercise.
It can be useful, as long as we keep in mind that it is just an
exercise, which can provide us with cues, with examples that
must find evidence in the real context of analytic work with
patients. Let us therefore take this fairy-tale as the background
for our research and examine it more closely for a moment. The
written version is more pedagogic. A girl, presumably of marrying age, is induced by her father to take account of her own
sexuality. But an excess of interest will cause her to turn not
only to her own genital organs, but also to fantasies and to
the exploration of cloacal meanders; masturbatory rubbing will
make the slave appear, like the one from Aladdin's lamp. Fantasy and a desire for omnipotence will cause her to give in to
the slave's seduction, and he will become the master. It is the
same for both the girl and the father, children and parents,

men and women (the little king of Portugal comes to the same end). Anal masturbation leads to the rectum, which is equated with the source of all wealth but activates the claustrophobic anxiety of being a prisoner. The unleashed masturbatory part becomes the master now and leads to mistaking the anal bolus for food available during the object's absence. A bad part is forced into the victim's ego: the victim has little choice, risking death and—by beheading—madness. The alternative of eating the hand is not taken into consideration, but in any case it would have results not dissimilar to death or service to the slave. Strictly applied to a social reality, the fairy-tale suggests a solution that rewards astuteness, makes the protagonist rich, and later, once married, will make her capable of resisting the masturbatory temptations of the slave who is stirring in the cabinet.

I must say that all this alone would not have persuaded me to take up this work again and carry on with it. But I felt that in the way my patients recalled the fairy-tale there was a particularly great apprehension and that their anxiety could cover up a deeper understanding of a hidden mechanism, which, they feared, might also be at work in their analysis. The simpler version of the tale, and the one that had been brought out in analysis by the patients' associations, contained something more evident. If read as being directly correlated to the analytic situation, it threw light on a peculiar kind of analytic relationship in which the patient, who had come to analysis in the hope of obtaining omnipotence, had found to his despair a colluding analyst who gave him this chance, through projective identification originating from the analyst and directed towards the patient. Therefore, I found myself confronted with a rather alarming but now definitely clearer view, which gave me a better understanding of the analytic situation. But now, as far as the fairy-tale was concerned, I had to come to a conclusion: the most representative element was projective identification of parents towards their children. In psychoanalysis this appears on the scene under the name of projective counteridentification, and was individuated in 1957 by Grinberg (1976, 1990).

Projective counteridentification
or the dangers of psychoanalysis

Projective identification represents the dangerous side of analytic work for the analyst, exposing him to a professional risk
(the real and effective possibility of a professional illness), when,
having become the object of an experience of intense projective
identification by the patient, he may develop a compulsory
countertransference reaction. In Grinberg's (1962) words: "The
analyst may have the feeling of being no longer his own self and
unavoidably becoming transformed into the object that the
patient, unconsciously, wanted him to be" (p. 437). This reaction has been called projective counteridentification. A reaction
of this sort is so intense and above all so specific as to obtain the
same type of result with different analysts, as can easily be
observed in groups (Nissim Momigliano, 1980; Speziale Bagliacca, 1982c). So-called paranormal-type experiences are very
probably based on these same mechanisms (the intensity and
dramatic effect of such phenomena are described by Micati
Zecca, 1982). However, while there exists a risk for the analyst,
there exists a threat to the patient too, above all in cases where
the analyst is not able to face up to the powerful stimulus
that comes from the patient and replies with his own negative
countertransference; that is to say, he colludes with the patient.
This happens most often when the analyst is bombarded by the
patient's actings, especially his acting-in, and responds in turn
with his own actings (Grinberg, 1976, 1990). This can also
happen as a consequence of a countertransference identification with the patient's superego, which is incapable of reverie.
Grinberg (1976, 1990) indicates authors who have dealt with
such phenomena, among whom we find Fenichel (1926), Greenacre (1950), and Gitelson (1962). These authors do not use the
concepts of projective identification and counteridentification,
but their descriptions are quite precise, and sometimes the
terms they use approach those that we use now. Grinberg de-
votes particular attention to such phenomena and gives some
excellent examples observed by himself and by analysts in
supervision. He also points out their quite frequent association
with acting out.

If the projective identification of the analyst towards the patient was always and only determined by particularly serious situations, the analyst could more easily be warned to pay attention to it. But the point is that there is evidence, already to be found in literature, that points to a different reality—that the protection of the patient by the analyst's projective identification is a constant task of the analyst himself. This point may not have been sufficiently well identified and studied. Of course the personal analysis of the analyst also has the purpose of preventing the analyst from doing so. This would confirm, once and for all, the importance of the analyst's personal analysis and the need to carry out analysis in a proper relational context—that is, in the analytic setting, which naturally includes the "analyst's psychoanalytic mind". I should like to mention here a paper by Tagliacozzo (1980) on analysis as a drug, and also Balint's concept of the "unobtrusive analyst" (1968), and Speziale Bagliacca's "comitial interpretation"—i.e. interpretation as electioneering speech—(1982b), but first of all I should mention Langs (1980), an author who is most attentive to this subject and who describes the relationship between projective identification and "technical errors". He states—perhaps a bit too categorically—that "every technical error, since it's an incorrect intervention for the patient, constitutes a projective identification of the analyst or therapist, a placing into the patient some aspect of his pathology" (Langs & Stone, 1980, p. 109). Given the consequences it may have, this seems to be too important a subject not to merit further study. But in order to do this, a short digression on projective identification may be useful.

Projective identification, the structural model, and the internal objects model

It is difficult to find a clear definition of projective identification—a definition that takes into account all the phenomena that can be gathered under this heading. If we read the description and definition initially supplied by Klein (1946, 1955b), we find them convincing and consistent with the area explored and the clinical material used. The same can be said about all the contributions made to this subject by various authors over the years. Grinberg (1976, 1990) tries to gather all the situations that have been labelled as projective identification in the course of time. He proposes a classification of projective identifications based on their qualities, orientations, purposes, contents, and effects, both on the subject and on the object. This is an attempt at putting some order into such a complicated matter, keeping the same label for phenomena that are different from each other but have a basic issue in common: a mental function originating in one part of an individual's mind ends up in the mind of another—or in another part of the same mind from which it originated—producing an alteration both in the projector and in the recipient. All this corresponds to a widespread tendency to think of projective identification as a more general phenomenon, which includes both the most normal and the most pathological form of communication in a relationship. There is a note on this subject by Speziale Bagliacca (1982c) in the margin of the text by Grinberg that I have quoted above. I think that difficulties arise when we consider the concept of projective identification as being valid both in the structural theory and in the internal objects theory. In the first concepts of projection and identification are used. Projective identification, on the other hand, had its origins in a model of the mind in which the ego relates with its internal objects. Rosenfeld (1969, 1987d) refers to both models when he defines projective identification as a narcissistic object relation and, at the same time, describes it as being correlated " . . . first of all to a splitting process of the early ego, where either good or bad parts of the self are split off from the ego and are as a further step projected in love or hatred into external objects . . ." (Rosenfeld, 1987d, p. 157).

I do not intend here to go into the merits of making a comparison or a more thorough study of the two models. I do, however, wish to point out that it is not the clinical content, the observed phenomenology, that is in crisis, but the ability of the theory to represent the facts. For this reason it is not surprising to hear people speaking about narcissism of object relations.

We can imagine that they are referring to facts that we observe time after time—such as the fact that a person can treat somebody or something with strictness and control, outside or inside himself and in the transference, while at the same time having or trying to have power over him or it. Nevertheless, if it seems to me that the "mature object relation" should be quite free from "narcissism", it is hard for me to be satisfied with an expression like "narcissistic object relation". Laplanche and Pontalis (1967) underline how the concept of object relation is foreign to Freud's thought and that it rarely appears in his work. Significantly, it appears in "Mourning and Melancholia" (1917e [1915]) and, as we know, with regard to the formation of the superego and the description of what was to become the point of departure for the formulation of structural theory—that is, narcissistic neurosis. The superego, in fact, is placed within the very sphere of the ego, and is built up in the memory and as a reward for the loss of the object. The difference between normality and pathology, mourning and melancholia, is not determined, in this context, by the presence or absence of narcissism, but by the presence or absence of affective ambivalence.

Meltzer (1973) dealt particularly with these issues in his study on the clinical phenomenology of narcissism and the formation of the concept of the superego-ideal. But, clearly with a few exceptions, there is generally a tendency to superimpose the superego of structural theory on the internal objects of the object relations theory. I personally wonder whether this is worth doing and, above all, whether, to understand the facts, it is useful to hold that: (1) the superego is always in the narcissistic sphere, and (2) the internal objects with their qualities express different stages of the same superego, from its forerunners to its mature form. If we adhere to this model, then we must attribute the same amount of narcissism to the internal objects.

A volume edited by Mancia (1979) gathers together a number of papers dealing with superego, and ego-ideal, their structure, functions and so on. Among these, an article by Manfredi Turillazzi (1978a) is pertinent to our subject; the author establishes a connection between internal objects, superego, and ego-ideal, in the sense that the latter two are not to be considered "structures", but "functions" of the internal objects. This same author had previously initiated her research on this theme in an article on interpretation and its relation with internal objects (Manfredi Turillazzi, 1974). The introduction of the concept of introjective identification (Klein, 1946), and its functioning together with projective identification supplied an explicative model of the relations that the ego has with its objects, from their most archaic, confused, and partial forms to the most developed, complete and clearly individuated ones. Grinberg (1990) gave us a very eloquent description of introjective identification. In it the object is given

> . . . space within the mental apparatus . . . the object is felt as coming and going out freely, doing what he likes. It functions . . . like a foreign guest who has full liberty to move within the country that shelters him. [p. 36]

Together with Flegenheimer, I have tried to summarize psychoanalytic thought on projective identification in a note published in 1985.

The Green Hand, projective identification, psychoanalytic practice

Let us return to our fairy-tale for a moment. We can see above all that what is ordered to be taken inside is a cut-off part of the human body. This gives us the idea of something that comes from a whole body that has been mutilated. Such a cut-off part has the power to subjugate the victim by entering into her, requiring blind faith and obedience. The victim agrees to play the game because of her avidity. As is common in fairy-tales, the story is about an astute victory over evil. Nevertheless, the atmosphere is one of mania and of a clear-cut splitting between good and bad.

I think that projective identification of this kind deserves a particular place among our models, and perhaps a specific title. The ego mutilates a part of itself and sends it into the other or may produce a resonance in him, thus inducing him to slavery. The vicissitudes, among others, that Leonardi (1976) speaks about, concerning perverse relationships between internal objects, or those that Speziale Bagliacca (1977, 1982a) remind us of regarding dictatorial techniques and phallic ideology, are based on a similar mechanism. Tagliacozzo (1980) makes it clear to us that we must be capable of resisting demands to supply psychoanalysis as a drug, to transform ourselves into the wealthy witch who lives in the beautiful mansion just beyond the boundaries of human society, or into the tyrant slave in his underground realm. Neither should we ignore the "anal" aspect of the operation: the search for wealth, the gaining of a great treasure, which is the background of the story; the disgusting characteristics of the hand, the underground places and the astuteness; and, finally, the masturbation in that pulling-out from the ground. Meltzer (1966) pointed out how important it is to analyse projective identifications correlated with anal masturbation, which can easily escape our notice because of their cryptic character and which produce pregenital false selves. This may also happen on the analyst's side, so that he warns us all to be on the look-out not to be analysts just in order to analyse ourselves.

We must therefore ask ourselves how the psychoanalyst can protect his patient and himself from projective identifications with such characteristics, which are not necessarily particularly violent or massive, since they are serious, even if they are of a modest consistency. Ways and means to protect the analysis from such an intrusive projective identification do exist: these are the mental organization of the analyst and the way he works in analysis. In other words, the best instrument is the identity of the analyst and the analytic technique that best suits that identity. I should like to recall, at this point, the contributions of Carloni (1979) and Carloni et al. (1981) on the professional and personal identity of the psychoanalyst, at the Fourth Congress of the Italian Psychoanalytical Society. On re-reading my own intervention at that meeting, I realize that I owe much of my present work to their contribution. But now I would like to approach the analyst at work in the particular situation that arises when transference and countertransference merge, as proposed by Usuelli Kluzer (1980). I make use of this interesting paper because it comes very close to the problem with which I am dealing here, and it is useful for individuating a standpoint that I intend to confront critically. The author asks herself what the function of the analyst is in analysis and what specific adaptations it requires of him. She wonders how the analyst can carry out his function of being a container, a mirror, an elaborator of another's desire. What about his own? Does it condense and hide itself in the interpretation in order to parasitize the "disciple"? How close we are to the Green Hand! But above all I want to point out what this work says about the ego-ideal, that part of the ego that is indicated as "the third personage on the analytic stage", the one to whom the ego of the analyst directs his discourse, his demand (p. 111). The analyst would be protected and would protect his patient precisely through the relationship that he has with his own ego-ideal. The author then underlines how the ego-ideal has archaic and omnipotent roots filtered and redimensioned by the Oedipus conflict, and how, above all, since pleasure in our work comes from the ego, from the approbation given by the ego-ideal, such pleasure has a narcissistic character. In substance, the analyst is protected in his work by his own narcissism. This is in line with the structural theory, as can be seen. The context in which Usuelli Kluzer's research is carried out is especially pertinent to my work, given that she studies the possible perversions of the analytic relationship due to countertransference reactions.

At the Fourth Italian Psychoanalytical Society Congress in Taormina, a panel of Milanese analysts dealt with this subject, and their work was later published (Di Chiara et al., 1981). In a previously published paper E. Gaburri and G. DeSimone Gaburri (1976) spoke about the "third interlocutor" on the analytic stage. They say that the analyst does not seem to be the patient's only interlocutor. The patient also communicates with *his own representation* of psychoanalysis (italics in original, p. 195). The patient is not the analyst's only interlocutor, and the analyst always has to keep in contact with *psychoanalysis as an object in his own internal world* (italics added, p. 195). The Gaburris' work, which is dedicated to the psychoanalytic setting, gives me the opportunity to make two comments: (1) that their formula is consistent with the internal objects theory, and (2) that the psychoanalytic setting is the principal means of safeguarding the analytic situation from the intrusion of the analyst's projective identification. This is particularly true if we consider the analytic setting as a function of the analysed mind of the analyst in which the presence of a third party protects him from plagiarizing the patient. As we can see, up to this point to a certain degree the two lines of thought go together; the "third interlocutor" is the ego-ideal (Usuelli Kluzer, 1980), the "third" is psychoanalysis as an internal object (Gaburri & Gaburri, 1976). I should, however, like to point out one difficulty: if the analytic mental operator is the ego/ego-ideal couple, since they come from the same matrix and have the same basis, we could imagine that the ego-ideal ceases to be the third and overlaps the ego (the first), as effectively happens in mania.

If, on the other hand, we give the third element a special statute that frees it as far as possible from the ego, underlining its characteristic of being something else and delivering it from narcissism, then we have a better guarantee that the third remains the third and a better explanation of the phenomenon of protection that both lines of research study. This is not just a play on words, even if it may seem so; put in another way, the internal objects model has a heuristic advantage over the structural theory model, inasmuch as "the internal object", in the fullness of its functions, is over and beyond the mature superego or the ego-ideal. If we think over what Freud says in "Mourning and Melancholia", we have to consider that the ego, having lost its object, agrees to take it in, as something different from the ego itself, in a state of separation. It would, of course, be interesting to reformulate all this according to self psychology theory (Kohut, 1971).

In one of her papers, Nissim Momigliano (1979) relates a dream in which she, the analyst, protects her parents against persecution. This dream, I believe, is an eloquent and very fine example illustrating the real meaning and value of the formulation I proposed above. Starting off from these premises, together with a group of colleagues, I have developed the view according to which man's mind is organized from the very beginning in an oedipal sense, and not in a primary narcissistic sense (Di Chiara et al., 1985). This is why I think that meeting with the Other and making a place for him inside ourselves is a physiological and fundamental step in development (Di Chiara, 1985).

CONCLUDING REMARKS

I think that the analyst, in order to protect himself and his patient from the intrusive and parasitic operations alluded to in the fairy-tale of the Green Hand, must establish and know how to maintain sufficiently stable relationships with "internal objects", taking these to be the product of a successful separation from original objects (Di Chiara, 1978), through the analytic vicissitudes of the relationship with the analyst in analysis. If the analyst comes to the encounter with the patient equipped in this way, he will have an analytic relationship with him in which the danger of intrusion is minimal, and he will be able to establish a correct analytic setting. In this case it will be easier for the analyst to refuse to supply a "drug-analysis" (Tagliacozzo, 1980), by analysing idealization. His interpretation will not be peremptory, but "provisional hypotheses on the nature of the unconscious processes of the analysand" (Meotti, 1981); the interpretations are not forced into the patient's ego, but placed where they can be taken up. The patient's ego and the analyst's ego, so to speak, must not overlap. The interpretation that originates from the relationship of the analyst's ego and his good parental objects (Nissim Momigliano, 1974, 1979; Meltzer, 1973) must end up in the space provided by the separation between the patient's ego and his internal objects. If this happens, the analyst will be protected from being a "brander" (Fachinelli, 1982, personal communication). We must admit that a real interpretation is such only because the patient has allowed us to formulate it: we owe it to him and to our personal and professional internal objects. From this point of view we can say that an interpretation originates from an object relation, and does not have a narcissistic source! It is produced by separation, and it produces further "separation", both in the analyst and in the patient. The analytic setting remains the crucial instrument for establishing—and for spoiling if it does not work properly—a relationship that can protect the patient. Langs and Stone (1980) quite rightly confirm this, the former with great rigour, realizing, above all, that the reserved behaviour of the analyst is "involved not only with the principle of confidentiality but with the transference . . ." (p. 117). Behind failures in our setting, whatever they may be, we will find a change in the relationship between the ego and its object, and a displacement towards narcissism. Such failures often have their origin in countertransference residues, in more or less evident expressions of our narcissism. The patient who has taken them in will find separation from the analyst even more difficult.

CHAPTER FIVE

Surviving, existing, living: reflections on the analyst's anxiety

Dina Vallino Macciò

April is the cruellest month, breeding
Lilacs out of the dead land, mixing
Memory and desire, stirring
Dull roots with spring rain.

T. S. Eliot, *The Waste-Land*

There is a "cruel" quality to the difficulties of analytic work, to which psychoanalysts more and more frequently give voice, overcoming their reserve and the pride they have in their knowledge. The point in question is the following: to what extent is the analyst, while engaged in his process of understanding, exposed to disrupting anxieties? Facing these anxieties within himself is unavoidable, if the analyst wants to understand and intervene in patients' mental difficulties. Even though personal analysis and training are sources of inspiration, knowledge, comfort, and encouragement to persevere, analysts can only partially take advantage of their "psychoanalytic" equipment. The analyst at work cannot be protected from the anxieties transmitted by patients by means of either his technique or his scientific knowledge; the quality of understanding is personally endured. Bion's (1967b) well-known advice to the analyst that he should work without memory and desire indicates how much *emotional discipline* the analyst must exercise over himself so as to be able to face the unknown transmitted by patients' experiences. The more the analyst neglects this particular capacity for the assimilation of the confusion and the despair in others' minds, the more such a defensive stance will render him incapable of understanding and powerless during analysis. The rich store of the psychoanalytic conceptual apparatus will be used rigidly, and an authentic, vital emotional growth relationship with patients will be missing.

Clarifications regarding countertransference

Conceptualization regarding "countertransference" (Alvarez, 1983; Brenman Pick, 1985; Heimann, 1950; Little, 1951) only achieves partial understanding of the problem, since, although the inevitability of anxiety in the analyst's mental set-up is emphasized, its consequences are not fully faced up to. A number of Italian studies (Di Chiara, 1985; Di Chiara et al., 1985; Ferro, 1987; Nissim Momigliano, 1974, and chapter one, this volume) have highlighted the relationship between transference and countertransference, making clear where they overlap and establishing their respective boundaries. The result has been further development in countertransference conceptualization. These studies deal with the impact the patient's anxiety has on the analyst, concentrating on what takes place in the latter's mind. The analyst's phantasies and interpretations can be influenced by experiencing the patient's anxiety (Nissim Momigliano, 1974), and the result can be projective identification towards the patient on the analyst's part (Di Chiara, chapter four, this volume; Ferro, 1987). However, the analyst's working mind is also considered to possess special equipment, a set-up that, when it functions satisfactorily, can work through what the patient communicates and return a method of work to him, together with the interpretation (Di Chiara et al., 1985).

Understanding and aiding the analyst's mind has been the cause of a step forward: the analyst is committed to subjecting himself to constant revision of his tools of investigation and relationship modalities with patients, accepting them, listening to them, modulating transference interpretations, attributing meaning to acting, answering requests, accepting non-verbal communication, etc. For the analyst it is a question of not side-stepping any new individual features, which, during analysis, a person should, with his own tempo, mode, and rhythm, be able to contemplate, not suffocate.

The analyst's anxieties

Reflecting on the analyst's mental set-up, with special reference to terminated analyses, I realized that, both at the beginning and at the end of particularly demanding ones, an almost always latent particular death anxiety context could be singled out. I had to take this into consideration from a certain stage onwards. This death context is present in every analysis (Bonasia, 1988), whether it appears openly or passes unnoticed. The relationship between analyst and patient can be thought of as being on the way to becoming vital if it survives the anxieties and emotions that *also* impede the analyst's thought. No analyst will deny that some analyses come out better than others. Perhaps what is meant by this is that what happens in an analysis, just as in everyday life, can coincide with what two people experience together and communicate to each other. However, what two people try out on the emotional level may be excluded from communication for most if not all of the time.

The analyst may talk about this with his supervisors or colleagues and the patient with his friends, but the question is not dealt with during analysis. It is thus necessary, in such cases, to be clear about what obstacles and deviations analyst and patient encounter in understanding each other, talking to each other, and making their *relationship* as a couple a vital one. Thinking of the analytic couple relationship under the sign of its "vitality" allows me to go one step further in outlining the types of risks encountered with non-psychotic patients suffering basically from a feeling of not existing. They feel their real life as if it were a dream and show a special difficulty in realizing an authentic self-representation, buried deep inside them. It is as if the analyst finds himself for some time at the bedside of someone who is seriously ill, and his affective mental activity, which is full of hope, is the only resource left to the patient to overcome a deathly condition. If the analyst finds it difficult to endure his own emotions, his capacity for understanding may be undermined by serious worry about the patient's life being at constant risk. Under such circumstances the vitality of his thought is the loser. An analyst can *survive his role, exist* in his role, but not live to the full his function of thinking for the patient and with the patient.

Use of the term "experience of death" by the analyst may seem exaggerated. However, I am unable to find an alternative way of highlighting what takes place in the analytic relationship with patients suffering from a lack of revelation of their self. It is not so much the question of the self not being very substantial—rather, it is one of an exact, strong, and cumbersome perception of self, which, no matter what it is like, is totally rejected, so that the best solution is to hide it until not even the "owner" can find it and recognize it.

In such cases the patient suffers from an internal situation that we can imagine as *excessive adherence to one's own internal objects*, which prevents him from distinguishing his own emotions from those of others. He suffers from this lack of revelation of himself, which is necessary to be able to recognize, understand, and express what he feels. His suffering is expressed in the enigmatic, undifferentiated way, which Freud appropriately called "anxiety". If the analyst wishes to understand, he must accept different kinds of anxiety reaching him from patients, precisely in order to make giving meaning to the patient's feeling a possibility. This will allow a vital relationship to blossom and, in the case of successful analyses, shared thinking to emerge.

Surviving

During what I call the "survival phase" in the phenomenology of the analytic relationship, patients show a strange aptitude for ignoring and encouraging us to forget the problem that is the reason for their asking for an analysis. This resembles what happens in child analysis.

These patients are not at all clear about what they are suffering from and why, neither do they openly ask themselves what they are expecting from the analysis (Joseph, 1978). Their communication is often fragmented, and references to specific mental suffering are rare, outside emotional contact. In fact, they are so confused about themselves that they entirely depend on the intentionality developed by the analyst towards them. As they have always done throughout their lives, they adapt to the "task" of analysis with apparent docility. Only after some time will they be able to re-establish contact with the great strength of the repressed "anger" they direct towards themselves. The problem is that their specific symptomatology and inability to live derives from marked obedience to the commands of some Other who is not oneself. Thus they request analysis because of the discomfort, the lack of a will to live, and the loneliness originating in a mental structure and behaviour that they highlight as soon as they begin analysis. Their suffering is so closely linked to non-expression of self and at times has such marked undifferentiation from an internal object with whose humiliating and scornful dictate they must comply (Rosenfeld, 1971), that the analysis requires considerable time to bring about a meeting of experiences on the analytic ground. The internal experiences are so strong that they are neither accepted nor communicated, until they end up by revealing themselves as new-born emotions and thoughts during analysis (Vallino Macciò, 1992). Such very intense emotions will allow an authentic mental love relationship to be experienced. Since I believe that a successful analysis cannot fail to inspire willingness to love in a person, I also hold that the time of the psychoanalytic meeting does not differ from the time of the patient's life (De Simone Gaburri, 1982a), in the sense that the analyst finds himself experiencing with the patient what the latter is experiencing in his own existence. It is not only the transference process that is brought to life during a session, but also a countertransference process of the same intensity.

In these analyses the first obstacle is secrecy and an enigmatic aspect of these persons, who have no personal sense of identity. Winnicott's (1965) model of the false self brings us close to the problems I am trying to describe, but it leaves out the indications coming from the analyst's own feelings, which can, in fact, guide him towards the solution of the enigmas proposed by the patient. In what I call the "survival" phase, the analyst is inspired by not yielding too much to abstract, intricate thought but by use, with due caution, of *observation of evident facts*. They are facts of the immediacy of the analytic field, to be observed, understood, acquired. They are connected with the patient's sufferings and the analyst's difficulty in attributing meaning to them. Talking about survival at this stage means not ignoring the fact that, while the patient's life may be at risk (in cases of serious depression, perversions with dangerous acting out, mental anorexia, childhood autism), the analyst's mental existence in his disciplined, imaginative role of thinking the emotions of the relationship is in serious danger.

Cecilia

The analysis of an eighteen-year-old girl, which lasted eleven years, and the changes in the way I worked and, as a result, in the relationship with my other patients, became clearer in my mind over a long period of time, during which I was on occasion worried about losing my patient. By this I mean the patient's possible death, at first because of her serious anorexia and, following that, because of difficulties in getting her out of the blind alley of depression. When I asked myself why her analysis was accompanied for so many years by this chilly feeling of death, I came to the conclusion that the very fear that she was incapable of thinking about was initially the patient's and subsequently mine. [Many of the features of Cecilia's story were suggested by her and accepted by me, after her careful reading of this report of an aspect of our psychoanalytic experience that was very useful (for me). Cecilia is the pseudonym suggested by the patient herself for the narration of her analysis: so that eyes may see the mind must have a frame of reference and a language for understanding. It was essential for Cecilia to understand in order to recover the will to live.]

Cecilia suffered from anorexia. The extreme frailty of this pale, emaciated girl (she weighed only 33 kilos) when I first set eyes on her is still vivid in my memory. I was struck by the fact that, despite her obviously painful physical condition, she greeted me with a kind smile, evidently thankful for the interest I was showing in her. She had fallen ill at the age of thirteen, when her mother was away and she had been asked to look after a younger female cousin. She also had considerable responsibilities for her grandmother. Her clearly worsening condition, which was now marked by frequent stays in hospital for feeding by intravenous drip, had convinced her that she needed analysis, her motivation being in particular her parents' concern for her condition.

Aspects of confusion and secrecy in her way of speaking made it difficult to work out where she was. She claimed that physical aspects should not exist; her mother and father would remind her to eat and would look after her and take her to hospital when she was in danger, but she denied feeling hunger, pain, etc.:

> "I don't know what I feel. I don't know whether I feel heat
> or cold, hunger, or anything else. In winter other people
> put on warm clothes; I only wear light ones. When I come
> here, I realize that perhaps I'm all head, only thoughts.
> But when I leave, I feel as if I'm on the edge of a precipice I
> could fall down into. So then I know I have to do
> something, anything."

She was clearly afraid that there were too many needs and desires, but her self-defence from feeling them led her to a dead end, which later on, during analysis, was expressed by a recurrent dream in which she followed somebody's car and ended up in a cul-de-sac.

Her language was rarefied and lacked concrete form, consisting of sensations tailing off, with no descriptions connected to her own daily life, and I did not know then to what extent it was the expression of non-existent self-revelation. What had made her insubstantial or extremely weak in her capacity for self-expression was a development that had taken place in an opposite direction: identification with her mother, to make the mother's world, with her experience, feelings, and discontent, her own.

The Kleinian model of a psychoanalytic process allowed me at that time to make some hypotheses and enable the patient to go back over her earliest developmental stages, to outline the grammar and syntax of the language of her passions. She was terrified of being invaded by something that differed from her sensations and ideas. It was as though there should always be "such a good little girl" in place of the real Cecilia. She had built, in defence of her insubstantial identity, a barrier of silences, secrecy, and, eventually, rejection of food and of any mental nourishment outside her own rumination.

Cecilia's interest in her analysis and in communicating her mental states was very intense. However, the deep sensitivity and high intelligence of the initial situation could not come out owing to her basic despair. This did not allow her to concede vital space to her sensations and emotions. Cecilia was fading away in silence, like her words, since, although she was searching for a reason to live, what did not belong to her was especially important in her mind, where it occupied a great deal of space.

She most frequently dreamed about boxes, wrappings, windowless rooms in which she found herself. Here are two examples:

Dreams about closed containers

Cecilia saw a room completely lined with pretty little flowers. The wallpaper covered the room in such a way that it was impossible to make out the difference between the floor, walls, ceiling, furniture. . . .

She was shut up in a red velvet bag, which held her
mother's jewellery. When she woke up, she went to see
whether the bag was still on the desk, but it had
disappeared.

She connected the dream to the sudden "disappearance" of
beneficial results experienced during analysis, at the end of
each session: as soon as the sessions ended, she was unable to
remember that the analyst had helped her. The patient was
right. What was going on during analysis was connected to
my being a *voice*, wrapping up her feelings and emotions. The
transference relation was impregnated with such a lack of differentiation between me and her that she was unable either to
remember it or understand its meaning. This agreed with what
happened to her with her mother, to whom she was tied by a
primary identification totally devoid of distances:

"When I was a child, Mummy asked me what kind of
snacks I wanted. I expected her to guess, and so I didn't
answer. If Mummy didn't guess, I would get angry, as
though she had done it on purpose, because Mummy
should have known."

Getting angry with me because she wanted the right snack
without asking for it, wanting to be understood without feeling
the need to explain and inform me was connected to not putting
up with any diversity between me and herself. However, all this
was not verbally expressed. The information she gave me was
so brief and vague that there were not sufficient elements to
understand what she was talking about. She never spoke about
her nutrition, but her frailty was enough to remind me constantly that this was definitely a problem.

One of the lines of work that helped her was attention to the
concrete, which was achieved by encouraging her gradually to
talk to me about her daily habits. I asked her questions, made
brief comments, paid attention to her observations, in order to
communicate my desire to listen to her and give her a place in
my mind (Di Chiara, 1985).

She was very hungry, but she could not accept food from others. She only ate if she was alone. In order to encourage her to eat, seeing that she denied that this was necessary, someone had to feel as she felt when forced to accept things that did not belong to her, things that were unpleasant. I tried out something that as an analyst I had no experience of: cooking "meanings" at the patient's level. Later I found out how putting oneself on the patient's level means giving up elaborate interpretations and imaginative conjectures hinging on complex constructions, but limiting oneself to elementary exchange processes. For patients it is a question of finding someone who manages to realize what being what they are means to them (Nissim Momigliano, chapter one, this volume). The required listening level is that which allows floating attention: to perceive and follow the music of the patients' words, their harmonies and dissonances, their pauses (Bion Talamo, 1989) rather than their content.

Cecilia expected me, without asking, to pay careful attention to the most insignificant aspects: small, simple things in her life she wanted to talk about, without knowing how to. For example, she did certain things during a session that made me think that my intervention was urgent and, at the same time, mistaken. While she was talking, she suddenly stopped and showed that she was waiting for me to take my turn. It was an inexplicable, highly urgent silence. At the same time I was losing her mentally, and I had difficulty in answering her and in finding out the meaning of that strange interruption in the discourse. Often there was no reason why I should or could answer her, and I pointed this out to her. I asked her what she was expecting of me. She seemed to be happy about the fact that all I could do was point out this strange silence of hers. Eventually I realized that she was afraid that her ideas could contaminate and invade others. Thus she selected the things that came into her head, until, on certain occasions, she had nothing left to say; or else she preferred to leave thoughts unworked-out so as not to run the risk of being misunderstood. Verbal expression thus meant loss of the little "self" that she managed to hold onto. She therefore stopped talking. Her reserve had the scope of protecting herself from possible misunderstanding on my part and from my impulsive reactions, which she partly studied on the basis of my tone of voice.

I realized the patient was asking me to feel what she was feeling; to be aware of the area of isolation that was building up between us, just as it was between herself and all the *others* she could not approach. The reason for this was that human relations were soon emptied of emotional meaning to her, since she was prevented by an invisible internal obstacle from accepting her own emotions.

This invisible internal obstacle is nothing other than the by-product of an inflated use of projective identification, which leads a person to excessive interest in what the Other feels, to the point of losing awareness of his own primal feelings.

To my selective attention both to her need to survive even physically and to her silences, she began to reply with significant communication about what she was feeling in her dialogue with me. She told me she was very lonely. She spent whole days in silence and was intimidated by contact with people outside her family. At home she expected to be understood without speaking. But this was an illusion. Nevertheless, she was painstaking about her studies and co-operated with housework. This appeared to me to be a sign of a desire for life and existence. She often spoke about feelings such as *worry, terror,* and *fright,* and it was her monotonous, weak tone of voice, rather than her actual words, that allowed me to enter into contact with unmentionable terrors of being invisible and disappearing even from me, like her utterances, which trailed off into unexpected silence, even though she made great efforts to cooperate in the task of analysis.

The setting-up of intense transference of a maternal type was parallel to the possibility of containment that the analysis allowed her. With me she could begin to give a name to unmentionable and unthinkable experiences that prevented her from living; she could not speak, could not approach her fellow students at university, could not eat. She could only feel the torture of being unable to do anything.

What I expressed in Kleinian language about her small-child relationship with her mother (Generali Clements, 1982; Generali

Clements & Mori Ferrara, 1980; Lussana, 1984) allowed me to use nursery language, which diminishes shyness and fear of the outsider, adult analyst. In this language, borrowed from the small-child family relationship, everything takes place in the present, with no evolution; the protagonists being child phantasies and passions (Vallino Macciò, 1981). The advantage for the patient was in not noticing further requests from the analyst. However, it is well known that consideration of the extreme expression of the violent, fierce quality of child passions is implicit in the Kleinian model. I was faced with a dilemma: how was I to lead this delicate, fragile, silent little girl to the problem of aggression? In her internal world there was no room for a dyadic relation, and, in the absence of the Other, she could not help turning what disturbed her destructively against herself, by not eating.

How could I bring a slow, progressive revelation of these aspects into being? The possibility presented itself again from the modalities of her way of relating to me. This again took on concrete form in the structure of her language and behaviour, including her silences. I again had to take into account what I could not speak about, but was worrying me. Dressed like a little boy, always in the same way, as if she were in uniform, she would smile at me pleasantly and also listen to me in a particularly gentle way. She was always ready to find an excuse for saying that I was right and for showing me that the situation I was describing had in fact happened when she was . . . years old, etc. She made frequent references to her childhood. I remember that I was able to take a cue from one of her admissions:

> "I can't think of anything to say, and I'm afraid this
> analysis will end up as a monologue . . . I'm contradictory.
> If my parents show interest in me, I get angry. If they
> don't, I feel bad just the same . . . Part of me is
> irresponsible. Other people don't know about it, but I have
> to put up with the harm it causes me and with being made
> fun of."

The impression of having to proceed delicately so as not to hurt her and make her disappear could lead us to a block and a monologue, just as the patient observed. A way needed to be found of working through her annihilation anxieties and my fear of hurting her. Thinking it over, my fear of damaging her may even seem "mad", except that accepting my anxiety means both accepting *her* fear that I should invade her, and being able to talk about it together up to the point of enabling her to notice that the danger of my influencing her was of secondary importance, compared with the danger she was putting herself into. I had, thus, to accept that her frailty was real, that she really was in danger and that, as her analyst, I had to help her, first of all, to want to eat.

It was of fundamental importance for me to admit to both my fear and my preconceptions; only later could I show her how her terror related to her not eating. She was thus really ill and was afraid of dissolving like a bubble, since she ate hardly anything. We could not treat this question lightly and go on as though it did not exist, because she would suffer harm as a consequence, and I would make a fool of myself by, through my silence, joining up with these dangerous aspects.

I noticed the aggressive valences of our relationship expressed in hostile silences, answering back, repetitions, but I could only deal with them by telling her that she felt that I was the cause. She often said that she felt confused or that I had made her mind untidy, or that she could not feel what I was telling her because it had happened to her the day before and was now distant. Sometimes she asked me for "proof" that she had said or thought something close to my interpretations. She also complained that she was unable to have more spontaneous relationships with the people she worked with. She said:

> "It's certainly not analysis that makes me feel better. I'd say that my way of seeing things is changing. I'm the cause of my depression. It's something inside me . . . as heavy as a rock, where nobody outside can do anything about it."

Cecilia was really better now, but there were still too many dangers for her to be sure she had been helped and to feel gratitude. It was more important for her, at this stage, to notice how much potentiality she had left and how much we could both count on the existence of a strong will to live and love, expressed through the appearance of children in open and closed places in dreams. Room for burning, vaguely structured child passion, after two years of analysis, seemed to have at least removed the danger of her self-destruction by fasting. More normal rhythms started up again, both in analytic communication and in daily life. For example, she began to get irritated with me and criticize me.

Existing

After the obstacles of secrecy in communication and of risk for the patient's life had been overcome, another equally difficult one came to the fore. If a satisfactory relationship of containing and friendship has been set up between analyst and patient, there is an equally serious risk of the patient's passively adapting to the analyst, who imperceptibly becomes his *internal object*, imposing rules to be followed. Thus Cecilia, after becoming competent in showing her rebellion, was very susceptible to me at the same time.

There is a dream from the second year of analysis that illustrates this theme of complex interlacing between inside and outside, both in the patient's mind and in that of the analyst.

Dream about the little girl inside and outside

"I was holding a pretty little red-and-white baby girl in my arms. Perhaps she changed colour because I kept her in a bag, and I was always putting her in and taking her out of it. I don't know why I did it, but it was as if I were showing her all over the place and felt awkward."

Connected to the dream was her remark that she realized her chances of getting better depended on her to a great extent, and this thought relieved her, since she felt that she could achieve something. She certainly felt less depressed, but outside things like eating and her pain might go on as before.

In the dream the child patient begins to come out of the bag. I pointed out to her that she desired to come out, and this was connected to her desire to get better, which was in conflict with fear of having to face the experience of birth, of being small, of having to put up with waiting, asking, letting me cure her. She was conscious of the risk of not feeling she was anywhere, a risk of cancelling herself, getting lost, when she perceived she was outside, that she was not alone, but there were things that did not depend on her. It was also a picture of her relationship with me: going in and out of the bag, like her coming out during a session, allowing herself to be approached, only to go back inside immediately afterwards to hide and escape from me. Here is an example of this eccentric movement: at the end of the session, in order to keep me close to her, she tried to reconstruct word by word what I had said to her, or she complained about the great confusion that entered her mind after listening to me. Both experiences mentioned regarded a suffocating wrapping-up in the analyst's mind, which had become an intrusive internal object. At that time I was not fully aware of the danger of such a situation. The patient's adhesiveness and her "going inside" could be cured only following my being able to avoid being adhesive and intrusive as an analyst.

I propose the hypothesis that, as in child development, it may be easy for the patient at the outset to install himself partially in the analyst's mind or easily make use of the things learnt. The phantasy of installing oneself in the analyst's mind (Rosenfeld, 1971) is not, however, a position that is willingly kept up. On the contrary, patients pass from "coming out to going back in". This allows one to glimpse both their vitality and incentive to exist as differentiated persons, and the risk of being suffocated again by the analyst himself in his position, which is so fundamental, of ideal object. To avoid this danger, it is also important for the analyst to know how contagious a quality adhesiveness is.

Child analysis, that terrain of unusual explorations and discoveries for psychoanalysts, has taught us how the tie between a small child and its mother can be of such an adhesive quality (Bick, 1968) as not to permit the formation of a feeling either of bodily separation or of individual identity (Tustin, 1986). However, it is impossible to believe that what is so difficult for a child patient to bring about does not end up by being difficult for us as well. For the analyst, adhesiveness is connected with repetitive submission to his scientific beliefs (Nissim Momigliano, 1991), the renewal of which requires a profound, painful revision of his prejudices.

Alice

It was precisely the analysis of a four-year-old girl that made me think again that the "reverie" function, which, as Bion (1983) has shown us especially in his seminars, is so indispensable, is also so difficult to fulfil. Alice's parents asked for an analysis because of feeding and sleeping problems and a very evident withdrawal into a delusional world, where there was only her monologue, without verbal replies to her parents, despite a richly developed linguistic competence. She was unapproachable through a common parental relationship that was due to rather extensive autistic areas.

Alice was a graceful little girl: light in her movements and very delicate in all her manifestations, including her use of clothing and underclothes, which were always too coarse for her. Analysis of her way of playing was useful for me in approaching her wild child passions, which began to be represented by Alice in the game of a mother looking after her little girl. The whole of her infantile self was revealed in play: her relationship with her mother, the need to be restrained in rage, to show it, a need for tenderness, presenting herself as the balancing element between her parents as a couple—she who restores the equilibrium between the two. I talked to her about this. However, Alice was unable to answer me, even though she listened to me.

Interpretation of play meant nothing to her, since she was unaware of the distinction between herself as a child and her mother. Even the I/you differentiation had no emotional overtones. Alice, due to reasons connected with her primary experience as a newly born baby, was terrified of being a tiny baby; she would have to wait, obey her mother and have to do without her. She had built up the delusional idea of being with her mother in a vague amalgamation by means of which she protected herself from an anxiety of being abandoned, which was one of death. However, this came out later in analysis only when differentiation began again.

During the four weekly sessions, for more than a year, she would be Mummy and I had to be an onlooker. She was very happy to come to me. She was allowed to play in a way that expressed her lively internal world. But she found no meaning in her pleasure, since she was unable to understand anything in her play that could be useful for living a better life with Mummy and Daddy. It is important to realize that analysis must help patients to have better relationships and not represent our theories.

During sessions Alice led me to understand that she did *not exist* as a child. In her play she was acting the part of a mother, pleading and in despair, trying to look after an unresponsive daughter. The game realistically reflected what happened with her mother and with me. Alice did not seem to hear what she was asked or told at all. Shut up in her monologue, when asking, she said, "you want, you don't want", instead of "I want etc.". I was certain that this was a case of paroxysmal expression of projective identification in which the child's ego dissolved in the "you" object. At this level she gave her mother no respite, but she bullied her. Controlling her mother resulted in her being able to put the maternal functions of taking care, thinking, and reverie out of kilter, but she also dismantled her own functions (Meltzer et al., 1975). This could be clearly seen in analysis: she must not listen to me, and she raised her voice if I spoke to her. She must not look at me; she had a curious posture, she gave me sidelong glances or glanced at me while keeping her head facing the other way from me. She dismantled her sensoriality, but something reached her. Thus I was able to notice that some of my words got stuck onto her speech, or else she paused when she wanted to know what I was saying. My anxiety was that I might not be able, as an analyst, to break this delusional, megalomanic shell and to lose the child, this time in the sense of a mental development that could get worse and worse and not allow her an affective, learning relationship. My understanding of her disrupting separation anxieties was unable to find a suitable means of communication for the patient. I had to give up a way of working that up to that point had had good results with other children in analysis. The method was descriptive, which was correct from the adult point of view but mistaken from Alice's. In short, a capacity really to listen to patients and ourselves, beyond our beloved theoretical frames of reference (Nissim Momigliano, 1991), was impeded by the desire to reach certainty by means of my faithful adherence to a theoretical system of reference that had proved satisfactory with other patients.

I needed to learn what being a tiny baby meant for Alice from the experience of not receiving replies from her. However, identification with the child was certainly not enough to enable me to transmit trust in me as an adult. Her first games involved cooking, where she played the mother. There was an air of good things in the session. I could feel and understand Alice's pleasure in her relationship with food from the way she spoke about dishes of ravioli, about mozzarella cheese with olive oil, about cakes. But there was no way of setting off a single spark of emotional contact. She fluttered around like a butterfly without listening to me. I started drawing butterflies for her, to show her how she fluttered around. She started drawing filled-in and empty circles, full and empty plates of baby food. I talked to her about the good things going from her to her mother and from her to me.

My interpretation made use of the images in her drawing, to show the emotional experience of something good, which was allowed to exist. It had been drawn by Alice and, therefore, belonged to her. One of the first emotions of which she was aware was the feeling that there was no need to fight me to obtain recognition. Her desire to draw was an expression of her need to communicate with me. Beginning to trust me as an analyst was of fundamental importance for her feeling that she existed, with all her needs and difficulties as a child. Her getting closer to me went on for the whole second year of analysis, until we discovered a mutually acceptable language. This was achieved through drawings, which became our most frequent means of communication. If I talked to her about herself, she answered in despair, "I don't want to become Alice; I can't get tiny". But by using drawings, I was able to put questions to her, viz.: "Is Alice at the children's party?" She answered: "No, she's invisible." "She's too tiny, you can't see her." After that, she would say: "She's hidden away"; and, further on in analysis: "She's wearing a wedding dress, she's dressed like a Mummy."

I had had two problems: one was not being able to use a descriptive interpretative style I knew well and which had proved useful with other patients, the other was setting up, in sessions, that separation and differentiation function (Di Chiara et al., 1985), while such primary levels of communication were under way, in which my way of talking to her was not emotionally assimilated. Melanie Klein began by playing with her little patients and by describing personification in child play (Klein, 1929); only later, working through the use of interpretation, did she give them an account of their internal conflicts (Klein, 1955a). With his concept of maternal *reverie*, Bion indicated a fundamental function of the adult mind. This is being able to make use of several means of symbolic communication to give meaning to mental pain and thus help to ease it (Bion, 1962a).

With Alice, it was a question of putting symbolic experiences at her level back into circulation. If I could not reach her by talking, I had to take an active role in her play-acting. I had to draw when and how she asked me to. I had to make room for and highlight all the experience of her being a little child, which she was unable to express in words, but only by playing and drawing (Milner, 1952, 1969; Artoni Schlesinger, 1989).

Living

Alice's analysis was profoundly instructive for me concerning attention to and respect for patients' concrete, daily, "external" lives. I became aware of something I had always known but not profoundly respected. This is relevant to the concept of integration of internal and external experiences. For Alice, *existing* as a child also meant accepting the existence of a parent couple living outside her control. Its literal meaning was that her parents, like her analyst, had an existence that was independent of hers. Once this had been recognized, she was able to relax her omnipotent control.

I believe that attraction to patients' internal worlds and the passionate happenings within them can occasionally tempt the analyst into a megalomanic design involving the idea of being able to help a patient to change his life by changing his feelings. This is partly true as far as analysis is concerned, on condition that the analyst acquire detailed, intimate knowledge of his patients' external lives, so that the analytic relationship manages to inspire changes in this area, which allow patients to feel people and things in a different manner, to love them more and not suffocate their emotions in ill-feeling and inhibitions. It thus seems necessary to me that one should learn from what patients tell us how and where they live, what they eat, how they sleep, who they associate with, and what their intimate and superficial relationships are like, so that all this can supplement their dreams, which can illuminate their external lives and be illuminated by the latter in turn.

Living an analysis as a phase of thought experience where integration between internal and external worlds is real is a crucial stage, which is usually preparatory to its termination. For the patient, transference is an experience of awareness whose interpretation enriches rather than irritates him. The analyst as an internal object is accepted, but the quality of character and honesty of the analyst is also explored, as are his limitations, together with his good points, his coherence, and above all his affective competence. The patient can excuse many of the analyst's mistakes, if the latter gives up the role of ideal, infallible internal object. "Living" as a stage of analysis is a unique experience, even for the analyst. It is the point at which one has the marvellous impression that a patient is able to bear his difficulties with the support of the beauty of the psychoanalytic method and of the intense human relationships that it helps him to face. However, all this cannot only be valid for the patient. It is also a deep, almost "sacred" feeling, which accompanies the analyst in his meeting with the patient. I am rather reluctant to provide a conceptual shape for this experience, which was, for me, inspiration both in my personal analysis and with patients towards whom I have less guilty feelings and to whom I feel close. What follows is the story of one of them.

Francesco

Francesco began his analysis at the age of twenty-one. It lasted only for one year, ending ten days before he died of cancer, which was already at a very advanced stage. He had asked me for analysis six months previously. At that time there had been a problem about his name—the officially registered one and the one by which he was normally called. For me, he was Francesco.

[The narration of a psychoanalytic "route", even if based on biographical elements, cannot expect to reach the level of a historical reconstruction. It can only shed light on "one possible account that has been built up through a selection, on emotional grounds . . ., of certain aspects of an experience rather than others . . ., and that experience is unfailingly more complex and goes beyond both that account and any other account that can be given" (Barale, 1990, p. 916). On that premise, I should like to recall what Francesco's sister wanted to say about him. She was anxious to point out that during that year of illness Francesco "was able to live very enthusiastically", so much so that he found the time for a good holiday and had the chance of "delighting" in the happiness he was allowed. Francesco's sister's recollections remind us all of the special character of the mystery of people like him. Although he had to face the sudden and relentless outbreak of his illness, he was able to say things like (as far as I remember):

> "I am able to be happy, but how is this possible? There are emotions of such intense happiness that are not suited to my pains and worries. I'm so different from before. . . . I would never have imagined I could feel like this. How can one get used to precariousness? And yet there's something strange that puzzles me. . . ."]

Right from the start, an experience of Francesco's was present in his mind. It was unthinkable for both of us, like something mysterious that was conjugated in his personality with intense curiosity and particular reserve. I remember that he mentioned his fear that no analyst would accept him, because there were not sufficient signs of suffering apart from his desire to get to know himself. On the occasion of our meeting in September, when we were going to decide on the beginning of analysis, he told me that there had been some serious family problems and that economic difficulties prevented him from planning an analysis. He spent a long time talking about things he had to do and which worried him, showing responsibility and a capacity for organization unusual in someone of his age. I again noticed something mysterious in him, and so I asked him to think over his decision not to start analysis. He appeared to be a person with an intense capacity for thought, and thus the motivation he provided for giving up something he had been thinking about for some years seemed all the more incredible. I was frankly unable to find a reason for this change of heart, but guessed that the only way of understanding the meaning of what was going on was taking some time over it. I was aware of the fact that he was not providing me with sufficient means to understand him, and I suggested that we meet for a specific number of sessions to think over his change of plan. He immediately accepted this new plan, and we left each other after fixing a definite appointment. The day before the first session he sent me a letter from hospital, where he had been forced to go in the meantime due to a return of his cancer,

which had started two years previously. After telling me about
his illness, he went on:

> "That's why I won't be able to come to our appointment
> tomorrow, and I'm sorry about it. Everything happened so
> quickly that I couldn't arrange things better. I'll contact
> you as soon as I leave here. For the moment I haven't the
> faintest idea if, how, or when it will happen, but I haven't
> given up hope, and, what's most important, I really do
> want to start the analysis in January, if I am physically
> able to."

A month later he answered a message I had sent him, telling
him that I was willing to begin his analysis when he was ready:

> "I'm going to start chemotherapy this week . . . then I'll
> have to go back every three weeks, but nothing has been
> definitely arranged yet. I should really like to have a talk
> with you by November, but I'm afraid that we'll both be too
> busy."

With the expressions "if I am physically able to" and "I'm
afraid that we'll both be too busy" (for a talk in November), he
began to be able to attribute the uncertainty of his illness ("I
haven't the faintest idea if, how or when I'll be leaving here") not
only to his condition, but also to my availability for him ("we'll
both be too busy"). The whole meaning of that beginning of
analysis was already there in outline: to accept his death anxiety and not to leave him alone. I realized how emotionally demanding his analysis was going to be. Would it be too much for
me? Certainly no time had to be wasted; we would have to
reach a level of truth in our work, and I did not really feel
adequate—I mean truth in words corresponding to thoughts
and emotions, whose degree of painfulness was unknown. In
any case, I could see no reason, at the time, why someone
suffering from a secondary tumour should stop himself from
having an analysis, and, after all we were going to look into the
question together. He really wanted analysis, and he began the
following January.

I thought that he wanted analysis so as to gain recognition from somebody else in something that was fundamental but unknown, and also in order to be able to accept going on living at such a tragic time. Although he wanted analysis, he had thought that he would not be able to have it, and he expected me to confirm his decision. At the outset he had not even asked; he would be the first to give up, so as not to endure a verdict from me that might be: "psychoanalysis has nothing to offer someone in your condition." The experience he had expressed to me at the surface level had been this fear of being abandoned. I realized this retrospectively, even though I had immediately noticed how intense his capacity for not despairing was. Lack of time was the most immediate factor in my uneasiness about being up to the task of analysing him. He had great difficulty in keeping up a rhythm of four weekly sessions, which he had asked for. His chemotherapy had serious toxic effects, and he had to stay in hospital for some time, both for the therapy and because of its after-effects. I noticed that the analysis would have to take these needs into account and suggested a minimum of two sessions per week. We would make arrangements to make up for this reduction, taking into account both his and my availability. This allowed us to keep a regular analytic set-up, even though it was flexible, but not to the extent of making him feel he was a "special case" or that he should idealize a "special" though theoretical analysis. The first dream he presented at the outset was about the hope brought by being able to talk about death, when death was approaching:

The dream about the leap in the dark

"In hospital I was really afraid of dying, but I was lovingly cared for and realized that if you can love and be loved even at times like that, fear vanishes. Then I dreamt that a green man leading a gang of aggressors was attacking me. I was running quickly and I jumped out of the window into emptiness to escape from him, but I was prevented from hitting the ground and being smashed up by some

washing-lines. These washing-lines were my analysis . . .
the hope I have that you will understand. But you must
help me to succeed. And if I feel lack of understanding,
then there's the terror of disappointment. . . ."

In that year of analysis a dilemma kept coming back—the dilemma of not giving recognition to his fear of death, violent and
persecutory, but present in his mind in the nightmare of the
leap in the dark and the hope that the homely washing lines,
his analysis, could hold him in an intimacy with himself that
would not throw him into a state of panic. However, Francesco
was ready to forget the fear of death as soon as he felt better,
since he immediately felt alive and was very happy about it.
This happiness was so intense that, after leaving inside the
idea of dying, room was left for an unchanged passion for life in
all its manifestations.

Both of us were aware from the very beginning of his analysis that we were constantly subject to its being interrupted by
his visits to hospital for chemo- or cobalt therapy treatment,
with the added complication of long, unpredictable periods of
discomfort, which prevented him from leaving hospital. Inter-
rupting sessions for chemotherapy was something that deeply
affected him. He said:

"There's this feeling ill, which uses up the time I've got,
and these thoughts keep me prisoner: I can't do my
chemotherapy because I've got a temperature, and with
this pain I'm afraid of not being able to do it. If I do it, then
I'll feel ill again. . . ."

"I always dream I'm late, and I've got to come to analysis,
and there isn't much time."

His pain was not only physical, but mental. It was the pain of
not succeeding. I could be near him, accepting the idea that his
thought was not static for him while his physical pain often
was, and his mental pain caught him in a trap. Sometimes the
mental pain appeared as a kind of keeping-at-a-distance, a
coldness, a hesitant way of speaking, which gave off an air of

prevention, rage, and despair. We later gave these phenomena the name of "The Triad of Hell": pain, protest caused by pain, and a guilty feeling caused by the rage he felt. I must admit that it was this experience that I felt less able to face. He was facing a task that was still beyond my reach. I had to accept the idea that I had nothing to teach him but everything to learn. How can one die, when one still wishes to live? All I did was listen to him. Or else I listened to him and tried to recognize how much life there was in his feelings.

He passionately loved all the significant members of his family and wanted to save them the trouble of looking after him. In analysis he asked to reveal fully all his passions through fear of being envious of life, which continued to flow easily beside him. He was afraid of asking too much and of being overbearing, destructive and fussy. This was precisely because his relatives and friends were helping him, lovingly and efficiently. The real difficulty was dealing with a mental pain that took on the cruel connotations of a feeling of guilt, just when he felt most fragile. All this came down to the problem of the time we had available. I learnt that the sense of time could be extended in our relationship, but I would have to accept both its interruptions and its silences. Francesco frequently asked me whether interruptions for his chemotherapy would disturb his analysis; if they were intolerable for me, then he would interrupt the sessions. I was embarrassed by the way the question was put: if I, as an analyst, were troubled by the interruptions, then he would give up the analysis. I was embarrassed by this question not only because death is an embarrassing subject, but also because feeling affection for a patient is embarrassing. We have always been advised to be neutral, thus protecting our patients from our projections. I must admit that I did not immediately understand the question. He was metaphorically asking me whether I would tolerate dealing with a problem of death, or whether the only thing I had in my mind was that he was dying, and whether I was certain that he would not survive. In short, there were several complex reasons and only later on did I realize that he had become free to express himself—freer than I was.

*The dream about setting off in fourth gear
and about flowers*

> He got very angry with a girl, who was a friend of his, for
> using the fourth gear, and then cried with rage if people
> around him offered him flowers, which are good for
> cemeteries—an unacceptable gift. His father would
> certainly have been able to think of something good for him.

The dream clearly showed two things he did not tolerate: that
I should impetuously offer him four sessions (setting off in
fourth gear) and that in interpreting I should be careful not to
give him gifts of death. Only he would speak about such feelings, when the time was ripe. First of all I had to come out into
the open myself, to face how much the uncertainty of his illness
and suffering was reflected in our relationship, as in the other
relationships in his life. There was nothing I could control with
my knowledge. All I could do was admit that his presence was
important for me, as mine was for him. This had a consequence
for the setting of our sessions, which I learnt to modulate on
the basis of my or his availability. We made up for missed
sessions whenever we could. The meaning of setting as a modulation of the relationship that is useful to the patient to make
himself known and to live with his emotions became clearer to
me and we reached a very intense stage in our work that was
not damaged by interruptions due to illness, although they did
highlight all the difficulties.

Francesco had a very strong desire to be capable, to be able
to face particular situations, to behave maturely with the members of his family. He was capable of affection and through
analysis realized that he had grown up too quickly, "when", he
said, "I was obviously not ready to take on things that made me
feel bad, but I behaved as though I were". For him loving was
very important. In that year before his death it became vital for
him to be understood for what he was and what he slid into in
dreams: the little koala, the dormouse, the bear, the little bird,
his dog, which in his mind were like an unthinkable experience
of being small, fragile, wild, passionate; all unknown aspects of
his personality. They were parts of his wild, withdrawn, solitary

existence, that felt elementary, agonizing desires; pre-emotions in his words, of which he was ashamed and which did not fit his lucid, logical rationality with its incisive questioning, or his desire to love, even when he was unsuccessful.

As soon as he felt better he returned to analysis, taking up again his plans for living, which had become extremely realistic. There was a change in his university studies. He decided to follow a more individual study programme presenting this change to me as his giving up his former curriculum to enable him to think. Accepting, I think, in making this choice, that he would not live long enough to graduate. Right from the start, I was aware that he was looking for such deep understanding of himself that I would be unable to avoid disappointing him. I think I spoke to him about this, asking him to let me know when the "lines" of what I was saying were not holding him, since he was the only person who could know. I have already mentioned that I was unsure whether I was up to the task of analysing him, since he was grappling with a task that overhangs us as human beings. We both knew that our analytic relationship was dominated by something we both depended on: a natural but impenetrable transcendence. I detected a message for me in his decision to "change faculty": I should be closer to him in a simpler way without infringing on the modes and rhythms of his existence. I was aided by the thought that Francesco would help me understand what I was not yet able to experience, but what would sooner or later happen for me too. With this feeling that we were sharing an experience that sooner or later would involve me personally, I found it less difficult to be close to him, and I achieved a cautious but constant confidence when facing being anxious and continually afraid. There is a dream that Francesco left me from the ninth month of his analysis, just before chemotherapy treatment:

The dream about the bear and the naturalist

"There was a naturalist feeding a bear, and I had to go and watch them. I was at the top of a mountain and could see an apocalyptic sight: rivers overflowing their banks, avalanches sweeping everything before them, thunder and lightning. In the dream I said to myself that it was a pity I had not been able to study Nature."

The patient's associations were of a light tone. The bear was him, who was hiding in his lair instead of going out with his friends. He made a brief remark about his chemotherapy, which would keep him away from analysis for two days. I was dismayed by this dream of an ecological disaster, a premonition of death, and thought that the patient's neutral stance might reflect an indifferent attitude on my part. I thought that he would have found things easier if we had talked about his dismay every time he had to go to hospital and about the self control he was capable of, so as not to provoke anxious feelings about him. He certainly appreciated the naturalist's approaching the bear, without expecting too much.

Then he came to his last session . . .

An analyst gets closer and closer to his patient, almost without being noticed. Then one must stop. There are moments that everyone would like to keep to himself:

I shall know why—when Time is over—
And I have ceased to wonder why. . . .

[Emily Dickinson]

CONCLUSIONS

There are phases in analysis where the patient's suffering is so all-embracing that for a long time there appears to be no way out. In such conditions a person thinks that he can do nothing by himself, and thus asks the analyst for guidance about what to do in life. The appointment with the analyst is already one step; it is something to do tomorrow, the day after, etc. In such situations a patient can express himself in acting, gifts, photographs, or bringing personal belongings. Children bring drawings and toys from home. The analyst must supply the patient with convincing answers. I remember a patient, who was about to graduate, drawing a plan for her dissertation in architecture but without being able to stay at her drawing board. For months we dealt with what was happening to her in her work room. She was hoping for instructions that would help her in an external situation.

Apart from despair, these people have an unquenchable thirst for *being understood* in something to which nobody pays attention, and which is inseparable from the feeling of being themselves. The will to live is so intense and so complete that they can externalize it only if they feel understood in something fundamental even if it is something small and hidden. One could use the term overwhelming will to exist even though paradoxically they avoid expressing themselves and noticing what they feel. In the context of child analysis it is very clear that *being understood* is as essential as nutrition for the life of a small child (Harris, 1975). It is also clear that if experience of mental existence is missing the effect is complete suffering that on occasions has depressive traits, but is closer to an annihilation anxiety and to those primary feelings of disintegration, dizziness, and losing oneself in the void that are very close to psychosomatic states.

What I wanted to emphasize in connection with Cecilia, Alice, and Francesco is how, during analysis, our relationship, for very different reasons in each case, risked becoming colourless. When the patient begins to notice his own existence as a person, he often reproaches the analyst and is not happy with the results achieved. The analyst has allowed him to exist but he has also thrown him into the outside world, where the patient feels deeply unhappy. Death wishes return. This time they are conscious, since there is a refusal to be born completely as persons until, much later and together with the analyst, the patient is able to understand that one can exist mentally insofar as one works through the profound unhappiness and pessimism towards oneself. These are long years of analysis during which a basic, chronic, despairingly recurrent depression is faced. For Cecilia there appeared to be nothing that justified her being "sentenced to live". As for Alice, it was rather difficult to be able to speak to her realistically about her unhappiness over her parents' separation and the conflicts in her phantasies of abandoning her mother to be with her father, and abandoning her father to be with her mother. To abandon, to her, was the same as "dying or causing death".

What should be emphasized here is how much "energy" I needed each time to work through the anxiety–impotency impasse when faced with the patient's pain, which risks being perceived with irritation. It is very difficult indeed to pass from understanding to experiencing a relationship.

"Life is violent" said a patient when speaking about her conflictual wish to have children. By quoting the lines by T. S. Eliot at the beginning I wanted to evoke how much of my experience as an analyst has seen the periodic alternation between harshness, pain, and hope in those that I consider my most successful analyses. This has led me to the conclusion that no vital analysis can be completely successful unless it centres on an experience of death worked through by the analyst.

If we adopt the analyst's viewpoint, it is a question of psychoanalyses implying such an intense emotional condition that, at the beginning, it is difficult to separate what originated in the analyst's difficulties in assisting a traumatic birth of the Self and what originated substantially from patients' catastrophic anxieties of how to survive, of not existing, or of dying. Vital exchanges with patients come into analysis relatively late, and perhaps this is connected with the analyst's being closed up in other worlds. I believe that how the analyst works through his own countertransference with the help of colleagues is fundamental at these stages in analysis. A friendly atmosphere in Psychoanalytic Centres is a necessity for the analyst's mind in order to accomplish the working through and to understand the meaning of patients' pain. The analyses I have described in outline would not have given me such food for thought if they had not been periodically dwelt on during meetings with colleagues in small groups or under individual supervision. Regarding this precious help provided by friends and colleagues among analysts, I should like to add that contact with different models of psychoanalytic conceptualization is only one of the sources of inspiration for integration between the analyst's internal world and that of the patients. But there is more to it than that.

The work of the analyst is far too disquieting and demanding for it to be reduced very generally to conceptual models. The analyst's mental activity, including that *outside* the sessions with patients, is boosted by sympathy and firmness towards oneself and towards others. It is a matter of enduring personally that change that will be explained to the patient when he has been shown what to do and how to do it. The analysts' peaceful and interested attitude, listening and replying to each other, is one of the qualities that brings nourishment to the emotional experience in our consulting rooms.

Another type of help comes from the trusting opening up of our patients towards their inner world. As the analyst gradually becomes able to penetrate deeply into the patient's internal world he can show the latter the appearance of the first manifestations of rage and aggressiveness that were once feared so much that the patient turned them against himself. The analyst must know that this is the first occasion the patient has to express himself concerning the analyst as a new internal object. Only after this will a less idealized relationship with the external analyst begin to appear. This is the phase that I call that of "mental existence", and it involves especially the development of the patient's self in relationship to his object–analyst. It is very important to highlight, both in the transference and in the countertransference, what the patient is able to perceive in the analyst—namely, the defects, mistakes, and character he begins to notice. This helps us to become aware of our own vulnerability to criticism, as well as of our incoherence, indifference, and mental closure.

PART THREE

THE CLINICAL FIELD

In this section the general approach to the analytic relationship presented in the first two parts can be traced in the description of some specific clinical situations.

The theme of *interruption of analysis*, dealt with by Gagliardi Guidi, is of such a painful nature for analysts that it is generally avoided, despite its occurring rather frequently. The author approaches the problem from the standpoint of the analyst's difficulties, recognizing an unconscious collusion between both the analyst's and patient's narcissistic–omnipotent aspects as a possible cause of interruptions. Collusion occurs in "blind spots" of both minds. The analyst's mind at work is thus examined here at the difficult stages of failure. When an analysis is interrupted, the analyst finds himself alone, facing a process of reparation that concerns only him. There is the danger that the problem may be dismissed through reliance on the idea of the patient's non-*analysability*. However, if analysability is not seen as being linked merely to the patient's characteristics but rather to those of the analytic couple, observation inevitably shifts towards the analyst. The author suggests constructively that interruptions of analysis should be faced without discouragement or condemnation. At the initial stage of our professional experience or when we have to deal with very difficult patients, our internal equipment may not succeed in the task of accepting and sharing the patient's anxieties. Personal analysis provides the analyst with new objects on which he can rely, but no analysis can defend us from the reappearance of long-standing problems. On the other hand, a scientific approach that regards countertransference not so much as a disorder but as a useful working tool is the operational basis for trying to avoid interruptions, or for newly working through our failures when an interruption has taken place. Careful study of our interpretative style can highlight moments when unconscious collusion occurs and help us overcome difficulties. When an interruption has taken place, the problem is to deal with a disparaging superego, which may provoke persecutory guilt, splitting, and denial. At this point the theme of the *narcissism of the analyst* comes to the fore. Its constructive transformation to the benefit of the patient can be the result of a process of reparation, starting off from the analysis of our failures.

There is a close link between these themes and *negative therapeutic reaction* (NTR). The latter is briefly dealt with by Gagliardi Guidi and covered in greater detail by Barale and Ferro, who consider this phenomenon from a relational point of view. They warn us against seeing analysis as a mere re-establishing of a "natural" balance following a disturbance caused by some "external" accident, and they remind us of the complexity, unpredictability, and contradictoriness of human mental development. However, they also state that to pay careful attention to the transference–countertransference dynamics, to what takes place in the here and now of the session, is all we can do. The theme of a possible collusion between patient and analyst is taken up again here, and the analyst's possible errors are also considered. But the authors go further. When NTR bursts into the analytic field, it is no use trying to find out "who started it", who initiated the attack, who took the first wrong step. It is more profitable to consider the phenomenon from a *communication* standpoint. NTR can be the way in which a communicative failure in the analytic relationship is expressed. In this case it is important to recognize the "microfractures" in analytic communication. Close attention to what the patient is going on to say, and to the analytic dialogue, will help recognize the possible precursors of NTR. Here the characters appearing in the analytic narrative become essential. They are considered (as in chapter three, this volume, by Bezoari and Ferro) as a product of the encounter of aspects belonging to both patient and analyst and are used to monitor the developing relationship and to deal with difficult moments. However, NTR can also represent the emergence during analysis of aspects of the patient's internal world that had not yet had access to thinkability. In any case NTR is not considered to be so negative, and the analyst's self-analytic vigilance is seen as the fundamental tool for overcoming impasses.

The *transference psychosis* that intruded into the analysis of a borderline patient is a theme closely connected with those previously discussed. De Masi shows how the risk of rupture is overcome by the analyst's effort to discover whether a communicative failure has taken place. In the case described the analyst had temporarily failed to reach the patient where he actually was. He had thus aggravated the distortion and confusion of the patient's internal world dominated by the presence of a seriously damaged object, which may lead to madness. The analytic work permitted, in this case, the recognition of this object and the reconstruction of a past reality that had not yet had access to thinkability. At the moment of transference psychosis it is the actual story of the analytic couple that is experienced dramatically and worked through. The analyst who accepts the patient's version turns delusion into shared knowledge and offers himself as a new object, capable of admitting his own errors and defects without letting himself be destroyed by guilt and persecution.

In the final chapter, the myth of Cassandra (the prophetess who tells the truth but is never believed) is seen as an emblematic model of communicative fracture. The drama of the hypochondriacal patient who complains of physical illnesses that cannot be demonstrated and are thus "unbelievable" is seen in this light. Robutti suggests that the *hypochondriacal symptom* be accepted as a warning that communication has been interrupted and that relational meanings, which can no longer be shared, are lost in the concreteness of the body. In the case of hypochondria, she advances the hypothesis of a defect at the level of *introjection* stage. When the hypochondriacal symptom appears during analysis in a concrete expressive form, the analyst must set off a reverie to save both his and the patient's imaginative area. The myth and its poetic expressions help the analyst, outside the session, to reflect. The myth of Cassandra, which puts forward an unending series of irreversible misunderstandings, is illuminating in the search for those moments in the relationship when fractures have occurred, when the analyst's and patient's discourse have begun to diverge, and when the meaning they should build up together is lost.

Andreina Robutti

CHAPTER SIX

Premature termination of analysis

Rosanna Gagliardi Guidi

The problem of premature termination of analysis falls within the wider area of acting-out and is intimately connected to issues that the psychoanalytic literature has thoroughly discussed: analysability, transference, counter-transference, negative therapeutic reaction. The development of these issues plays an important role in the history of psychoanalysis.

It is not my intention to retrace the history of these milestones of our science, but simply to examine their connections to the specific subject of my interest. First of all, I would like to highlight something that struck me when I started investigating the problem of premature termination: the attitude taken by analysts towards it. Then I shall make a few considerations of my own and try to sort them out.

The very first thing that attracted my attention was that, as far as I know, premature termination is an event every analyst, sooner or later, has to face; not only do the essays written by many a "master" mention it, but all the colleagues—both Italian and foreign—to whom I put the question as to whether they had any experience of premature termination answered in the affirmative. On the other hand, no one seems to have written anything specific on this well-known subject: the bibliography on the topic is scarce and often only apparently pertinent.

As to the Italian literature, I have come across two contributions. One is a peculiarly written booklet, by Cesare Viviani, a *neo–avant-garde* poet, the other is a paper written by a group of colleagues from Rome. Viviani's book is a collection of interviews made in Milan with people who had begun an analysis with analysts belonging to different schools ("Freudians" and "Kleinians" are also represented) and interrupted it. These short interviews are often contentious even though they frequently betray some grief and perturbation. This work is of no utility for a psychoanalytic understanding of the problem; still the author claims an unquestionable element of novelty: "it is the first essay, as limited as it may be, on interruption of analysis in Italy" (Viviani, 1975, p. 13). Another interesting point is the vast number of interruptions the author has uncovered, and this is rather surprising especially if we consider that in that period (and to this day) no psychoanalytic paper on the subject was published by analysts in Milan.

The other contribution (Calvesi et al., 1981) is a paper that was read at the Fourth Congress of the Italian Psychoanalytical Society in a panel on the formation of the analytic couple and on the identity of the psychoanalyst, co-ordinated by Bellanova (Amati Mehler et al., 1981). This work presents some cases of premature termination in relation to problems that arise right from the "first encounter" between analyst and patient. The authors wonder whether each interruption of analysis is motivated by resistances and defences present both in the patient and in the analyst towards a basic unconscious instance (separation) that seems to determine the outcome of the treatment (Calvesi et al., 1981). All things considered, they wonder whether the specific element of premature termination lies in the incapability of the analytic couple to confront the question of separation adequately. They believe that the conclusive unconscious vicissitudes that seem to be basically debated within the couple, from the first encounter, hinge on the possible fate of separation (p. 120).

Except for two very recent papers dealing specifically with this issue (Tyszblat, 1990; Zanin, 1990) I came across a whole series of promising titles that seemed connected to the problem but actually concerned those interruptions of the treatment that could be traced to holiday or other absences either of the analyst or of the patient. Other papers discuss the problem of interruptions of child psychotherapies, and some statistical researches deal with interruptions due to external factors: parental decisions, change of town, of school, and so on.

I would, instead, like to focus on those situations in which termination derives from a particular dynamic that develops within an analytic couple that has established itself without apparent difficulties. I am not referring to extreme cases, to patients who suffer from particularly serious pathology or who are insufficiently motivated. I am, rather, interested in those patients an analyst decides to treat in the conviction that he will be able to make the analytic journey with them and who, at a certain point, say good-bye and walk away. To quote Di Chiara (1975), these patients have been given credit for the capability to grow and achieve a certain insight, and their narcissistic infantile wound has been considered by the analyst to be strong but not in so overpowering a way as to irremediably prevent the process of development from being resumed.

The lack of researches on this particular way an analysis may end is of considerable importance, since in contrast bibliography about the numerous problems that may emerge during an analysis and the ways it may come to an end is superabundant. We have many items regarding termination problems, interminable analysis, relationships occurring between patient and analyst after the end of an analysis, and so on, but very few contributions dealing specifically with premature terminations.

Still, many an author punctually refers to interruption. Meltzer (1967), for instance, hints at what he calls "the unhappy problem so frequently encountered, interruption of analysis" (p. 46), and further on he states that the impasse interruption is "the most frequent outcome in our work with adults, especially with the preponderant group of borderline cases . . ." (p. 51); but he does not hesitate to drop the question by simply saying that "it is a huge technical area" (p. 52). Although I subscribe to this opinion, I do believe that such a difficulty is not the only reason accounting for the reluctance shown by analysts: *there is something more personal that may be difficult for us to face* and the undeniable technical difficulties support our wish to withdraw.

My experience as a supervisor and the interest shown towards this particular subject by my younger colleagues have stimulated my interest in this topic, on which I have held a series of lectures at the Institute of Psychoanalysis of Milan. I do believe that, as regards both the psychoanalytic movement and the analysis proper, it is always profitable "not just to be prepared for 'the good analytic hour', but rather for the difficult hour, the hour that may lead to a possible failure of analysis" (Di Chiara, 1975, p. 173). Analytic failures are a thorn in the side for every analyst, since "whatever defects we find in our patient's co-operation, we must accept the burden that these are all analytic failures, due to limitations of the science itself and our individual practice of it" (Meltzer, 1967, p. 52). To quote Winnicott (1956, p. 388) ". . . every failed analysis is a failure not of the patient but of the analyst", who must search for his own errors whenever resistances turn up.

Premature terminations may occur at any point of an analyst's career even though it has been ascertained that it is more frequent at the beginning, when our analytic function is as yet unrefined and we are subject to drawbacks and difficulties, before we reach a greater stability (Rosenfeld, 1978b). This means that interruptions occur at a time when we need, more than ever, some reassurance about both our analytic capabilities and psychoanalysis itself. Working through the experience is far more difficult in these formative years.

I think however that another element, though not so obvious, also interferes: when an analysis breaks down, we can repair or clarify something to our sole advantage, since the other person is no longer there, and there is nothing more we can do in order to help him. *The reparation—when it is possible—is just an issue between ourselves and our internal world.* This is very difficult to bear.

As we know, phenomena that used to be considered mere incidents or disturbances, such as transference, countertransference, or acting-out, have been understood and better employed in our daily work, once they have been considered as physiological. I wonder whether a change of attitude towards premature termination might not improve our self-knowledge, and not only in our function as analysts. I believe that such mishaps highlight, more than other relational impasses, the areas of difficulty for the analysts.

Although it seems that premature terminations can occur at any phase of analysis, the risk is magnified in specific moments of the analytic process: I am referring to that situation known in the Kleinian context as the "threshold of the depressive position". At these moments the main problem of analysis becomes "the concerted attack on the strength of the good object that is mounted by the most split-off destructive parts of the infantile personality" (Meltzer, 1967, p. 83), and the capability of the analyst to make the distinction—concerning himself and his patient—between responsibility and omnipotence turns out to be vital. At this very moment—as we have learnt from Bion (1962a, 1967b, 1970)—the analyst must be prepared to accept his patient's projective identifications, to endure the painful feelings the latter evokes, and to "contain" them.

In this situation, which is difficult for both, the analyst's task consists mainly in the analysis of countertransference as the only solution for his patient and for himself. This is far from easy and the analyst is not always prepared to follow it through. As Nissim Momigliano (1982) reminds us, when his anxieties are symmetrical to his patient's, "the psychoanalyst may be hindered from being favourably disposed and responsive towards him."

Nowadays we are accustomed to thinking that there are no general termination criteria for analysis and that the attempt to formulate them may be unnecessary (De Simone Gaburri, 1982b, 1985). Similarly there are no general criteria concerning interminability and interruption. The problem is why, how, and when, within a specific analytic dyad, a project on the fate of the relationship takes a malevolent turn, bringing the analysis to a premature ending.

An investigation of the problems connected to such failures inevitably leads to an oft-debated issue: *analysability.* Was there an indication for analysis in the case accepted for treatment? To this day opinions differ greatly: either—according to certain schools—psychoanalysis can treat any pathology, or—from a different viewpoint—there are no neuroses, even the most classical ones, that can be reached at their core (Nissim Momigliano, 1975). Still, it is undeniable that clinical experience has modified our outlook on indications for analysis. For many categories of patients who were thought to be unanalysable in the early days of our science (psychotics, narcissistic personalities, etc.) the psychoanalytic treatment is now considered the treatment of election. Analysability is less and less associated with diagnostic criteria, but some reserves still exist towards certain categories: for instance, patients involved in a *folie à deux* (Meltzer, 1967), or severely narcissistic patients with acting-out tendencies, or serious forms of sadism and masochism (Rosenfeld, 1978a).

Aside from these extreme cases, however, if it is true that—as I previously stated—nearly every analyst can count some cases of premature termination in his professional career, we can conclude that *unanalysable patients* do exist: they are *those patients that a particular analyst is unable to analyse.* In this context the problem of analysability can no longer be tackled by determining whether or not a category of patients is analysable. The context in which the problem needs to be examined is that of the patient–analyst relationship. "The only reliable criterion of indication or contraindication for an analysis is to be found within the couple, in the mutual possibility for that specific couple to establish a relationship" (Amati Mehler et al., 1981, p. 105). And we are aware of the fact that some patients, who are unable to continue in analysis, would not necessarily encounter the same difficulties with another analyst, and not necessarily because this latter analyst is more skilful. All things considered, premature terminations sound like failures of the relationship between an analyst and a particular patient even though we now tend to place more stress on the analyst's responsibility than on the patient's (Meltzer, 1967; Winnicott, 1955).

A quite peculiar aspect of our profession is the relevance of the analyst's personality for his work. To quote Freud: "Among the factors that influence the prospects of analytic treatment and add to its difficulties in the same manner as the resistances, must be reckoned not only the nature of the patient's ego but the individuality of the analyst" (Freud, 1937c, p. 247). That is why personal analysis is the fundamental element of our training. It should enable us to acquire the self-awareness and self-experience that are vital to our task (Rosenfeld, 1978b). In spite of personal analysis, however, the constant contact with the repressed past of our patients may be—as Freud (1937a) reminds us when discussing the "dangers of analysis"—a noxious factor, as well as a risk for the analyst. Nowadays we are all more aware of the fact that if on the one hand the daily practice of psychoanalysis is unquestionably enriching, on the other hand it may elicit several problems, mainly linked to the profound narcissistic challenges inherent in this profession.

This is a particularly relevant point, since we know that the most fragile elements of the personality, which are also the most difficult to keep under control, are to be found in the narcissistic structure. This structure, as far as we are concerned, plays a fundamental role in the choice of analysis as a profession. Grunberger and Chasseguet-Smirgel focus on the subject in a paper on the psychoanalyst's narcissism; they observe that those who choose to be analysts take special pleasure in dealing with the unconscious. To have access to the dimension of timelessness, infinity, and omnipotence of the mind affords profound narcissistic satisfaction (Grunberger & Chasseguet-Smirgel, 1978). Tagliacozzo (1976) highlights the fact that the decision to become an analyst entails a phantasy "not to modify that much something inside oneself, but rather to acquire the capability to modify others", and he adds that "we can presume the existence of mechanisms of omnipotence and negation" (p. 41).

At this point, I would like to put aside the issue of the analyst's narcissism and of its drawbacks and examine the difficulties our daily activity entails. To contain our feelings, anxieties, and fears and to subordinate them to analytic work is unquestionably a difficult task. Despite our personal analysis, there are still areas, deep inside ourselves, over which we do not have total control. Each of us is burdened by unresolved conflicts; through self-analysis we struggle to acquire increased awareness of their existence, though this too will never be totally liberating. We shall always have to cope with our touchiness, the narcissistic needs that may collude with those of our patient and lead us to burden him with what is ours alone (or, at least, ours as well). Although we may become more skilful in coping with transference and countertransference, we can never fully eliminate these psychotic, primitive, or narcissistic residues. There will always be some moments or areas in which an analyst does not function properly.

In 1912, Freud—quoting Stekel—said that what is repressed determines blind spots in the analyst's perception. Still, it is true that nowadays our improved knowledge of transference and countertransference and our heightened familiarity with these phenomena often help us to realize when our personal difficulties collude with those of our patients, either actually or as a risk.

The changes that have occurred in our conception of countertransference and of the analytic process have been reciprocally influential. The analytic process has evolved from being a situation in which one individual "observes" another into a relational exchange, "a relationship, albeit of unique kind, between two persons" (Rycroft, 1958, p. 414), between two co-actors. Countertransference, in its turn, from its status as trouble or "source of trouble", has become a precious and indispensable tool both in clinical practice and in psychoanalytic research (Heimann, 1950). This process has been aided, notably by the Kleinians, with the introduction of the concept of projective identification (Klein, 1946, 1955b) particularly since Bion indicated the existence of its communicative nature alongside the defensive use. In this context, countertransference has come to signify not only "a reaction of the analyst to the patient, but, rather, the way an analyst experiences deep inside himself certain aspects of his patient's personality and deals with them" (Albarella & Donadio, 1986, pp. 19–20). Thus, countertransference becomes a privileged area where the analyst can recuperate and decipher messages, for which a more suitable language is not yet available (Grinberg, 1976, 1990).

There is, however, a facet of patient–analyst reciprocity—already remarked by Freud (1910d, 1937c)—that prevents the analyst from understanding in his patient what he has not yet understood within himself, or what he is unable to understand at that moment. "No psycho-analyst goes further than his own complexes and internal resistances permit" (Freud, 1910d, p. 145). To quote Money-Kyrle (1956, p. 361), "in particular, his understanding fails whenever the patient corresponds too closely with some aspect of himself that he has not yet learnt to understand". The inevitable consequence is that in every analysis, and notably with a certain kind of patient, there will be periods in which the analyst is simply unable to understand what is going on.

I have not forgotten that countertransference has "its causes and effects" in the patient as well (Money-Kyrle, 1956). I am perfectly aware of the fact that the patient's personality influences the analytic process, quite apart from the quality and the gravity of the pathology involved. There are patients who are able to communicate with the analyst and to accept his difficulties in understanding, and who are genuinely interested in exploring their own mental processes. But on the other hand—as we all know—there are patients who appear too frightened or simply not able to cope with their deepest anxieties, and consequently try to avoid them or only pretend to know about them. If the analyst is in a similar condition, having to deal with unconscious malfunctioning areas of his own, then he will be caught in the trap of unconscious collusion, which blocks the interaction and thus the analytic process. In this context the analyst is no longer able to understand what the patient is telling him, because he, too, is engaged in the effort of not thinking and of getting rid of feelings he can neither recognize nor contain, by giving interpretations that sound superegoic and accusatory.

This interpretative style, even if only occasionally, nonetheless affects the patient and may lead to *negative therapeutic reaction* (NTR) as the greatest possible hindrance in the analytic process (Grinberg et al., 1968). I shall not go into detail on this topic, which is unquestionably linked to premature termination. Most of the authors who have dealt with it (Abraham, 1919; Horney, 1936; Klein, 1957; Riviere, 1936; Rosenfeld, 1968, 1987a) cover topics already linked by Freud to NTR (guilt, superego, omnipotence) (Freud 1923b, 1924c). Since Abraham, the link between NTR and narcissistic structure and envy has been particularly stressed. I believe that a detailed analysis of the technical norms for dealing with NTR or avoiding it can prove profitable in understanding premature terminations as well.

Riviere (1936) suggests careful attention, particularly with narcissistic patients, towards phantasied relations with internal objects in order to get in touch with the latent depression underlying the narcissistic structure. Excessive and insistent interpretation of aggressive impulses should be avoided. More recently, Olinick (1964, 1970) recommended tolerance towards the need some patients have to revive in analysis painful experiences of the past by inverting the roles and handing the analyst the incapable role. In this context the development of a NTR and the analyst's ability to put up with it are considered vital for success. Barale and Ferro (chapter seven, this volume) seem in tune with such a view.

When the analytic work makes a break in the defensive structure, a dependent part that is prepared to receive some help appears. However, as soon as a relationship with this dependent part has been established, a NTR may occur; the omnipotent narcissistic part feels ousted from its supremacy and counter-attacks, trying to regain control over the ego (Rosenfeld 1968, 1987a). If the analyst does not understand and cannot put up with this situation, the chances that the analytic process will proceed are diminished. I have attempted to clarify this issue, for it is tempting to interpret the patient's desertion as a NTR on the part of someone who is too narcissistic and omnipotent to carry an analysis through. I confess to having resorted to this kind of self-reassurance in two cases of interruption that occurred at the beginning of my career.

I believe, in spite of NTR, an analysis can be resumed and profitably carried, on even with this kind of patient. This becomes possible if we succeed in reaching the overwhelmed, unavailable dependent part and support it against the narcis-sistic–omnipotent one. As I said above, this becomes possible only if the analyst *is not trapped into a collusive countertrans-ference*. Otherwise, there would not only be a NTR but also acting-out of increasing severity and finally interruption. As Rosenfeld (1968, 1987a) says, the attacks to the dependent self are vital for the narcissistic structure, which in this way denies both need and envy. But these attacks would, at the very most, make our work harder, producing further NTR, further acting-out, more splitting mechanisms, and so on. If the analyst's characteristics and difficulties were not implicated, there would be no interruption. Undoubtedly, when a therapeutic impasse occurs, it is advisable to discuss the whole situation with a colleague who, being an impartial observer, is more likely to spot where the clash is occurring. This is often revealed by those interpretations that tend to sound accusatory or superegoic to the patient (Rosenfeld, 1987a).

This kind of interpretation has the quality of an acting-out on the part of the analyst, a way of ridding himself of tensions his ego cannot contain. According to Bion, acting-out is linked to difficulties in thinking, when elements of sensuous or emotional experiences that have not been metabolized through alpha function are evacuated. Thus, it happens that in analysis, something coming from the patient at that moment is disturbing to the analyst, whose interpretations—although words—take on the nature of acting-outs. And, in fact, Bion (1973) described a language that does not communicate and is not different from acting. Pertinent to this topic is Manfredi Turillazzi's note that our language "may easily hide our interpretative acting, which is probably impossible to avoid, but always worth recognizing" (Manfredi Turillazzi, 1978b, p. 238).

I shall now briefly summarize my theses with a view to making some conclusive remarks. All analysts find it difficult to cope with interruptions, which are more likely to occur at the beginning of one's career. Such incidents should be considered as natural events, particularly when they occur before our experience and awareness of our analytic function have acquired stable characteristics. Interruptions can be seen as the possible consequence of a persisting collusion between patient and analyst, where the latter tends to act out through his interpretative activity. Such an event tends to be particularly frequent with narcissistic patients and is linked to the analyst's narcissistic response.

There is probably nothing new in considering interruptions as the consequence of a collusive relationship between analyst and patient, when the analyst—either under the patient's pressure or on his own grounds—cannot work out what is going on until the patient has left and, often, not even then. As I said earlier, I believe that premature terminations should be considered part and parcel of our work. Were we prepared to discuss and share such experiences with our colleagues, we might become better acquainted with them and be enabled to make use of them for our personal and professional growth. These considerations, which may sound obvious, nonetheless lead to further reflections.

Freud wonders which are the legitimate demands that may be made on the analytic therapy and whether "it is possible by means of analytic therapy to dispose of a conflict between an instinct and the Ego, or of a pathogenic instinctual demand upon the Ego, permanently and definitely" (Freud 1937c, p. 224). Basically, he believes that not even a successful treatment can preserve the individual from the risk of a sequel to his neurosis, which is bound to have the very same instinctual roots as the previous one. He accepts for psychoanalysis the statement of an Austrian satiric writer: "Every step forward is only half as big as it looks at first" (p. 228). As to development and the psychoanalytic treatment, Freud says, "there are nearly always residual phenomena, a partial hanging-back". And further on he declares: "The transformation is never complete and residues of earlier libidinal fixations may still be retained in the final configuration." He reminds us that "what has once come to life clings tenaciously to its existence" (p. 229).

Many an analyst would subscribe to this point of view: analysis cannot solve all pre-analytic problems; nor does it claim to modify the internal situation of a human being once and for all. Brenman (1980) states that all through our lives we are dealing with basically the same internal objects. To these original objects analytic work adds others that are more mature, better integrated, and sounder; but the original object is always there, and we tend to return there at the critical points in our lives. It would be an omnipotent claim to believe we can analyse it away. What has come to life clings tenaciously to its existence. When things go well, analysis furnishes the individual with a good internal object, something that was previously inadequate or lacking. As Klein says in *Envy and Gratitude*: ". . . the introjection of the analyst as a good object, if not based on idealization has, to some extent, the effect of providing an internal good object where it has been largely lacking" (Klein, 1957, p. 90). It would be dangerous to believe that the new object built up in the course of analysis becomes a permanent reference point. The analyst should accept for himself as well as for his patients the persistence of the original object and be prepared to come across it again even after a long period of work, without dismay and without the feeling that his mission has failed. If he knows and accepts this, he will be prepared to tolerate his own regression and that of his patient; he will also be able to think over the situation, discuss it with others, and start over again. It is tragically different when the analyst believes this stage has been overcome once and for all, both for himself and for the patient; this is impossible. It is vital to remember that Klein described "positions" and not developmental "stages", which means that more primitive ways of functioning can always be re-experienced by analysts and patients, at any stage of our lives.

In this view, reparation stands on the chance that the two objects—the old and the new one—coexist, not on a radical change that should have occurred. The possibility of moving from these primitive relationships to more mature ones set up during analysis is enhanced if we are prepared to accept, for ourselves as well as for our patients, without condemnation and discouragement, the fact that we may back-track, as it were, to the inevitable accompaniment of pain. In my opinion, this conception of analysis is not merely convincing, but also agreeable, since it protects us from those experiences of discouragement and idealization that every now and then peep through our phyles and those of our patients.

All through the history of our science, the therapeutic model has undergone an undeniable change, becoming more radically grounded on the patient–analyst interaction than on the patient's problems; and the analyst's interest has shifted in part from the therapeutic factors to problems arising within the relationship (Bordi, 1985). Brenman (1978) has discussed the effects of the analyst's narcissism in analytic practice. Starting from the Kleinian conception of the cannibalistic narcissistic processes as incorporation of the object's good and desirable elements, with simultaneous projection of the bad ones, he wonders to what an extent this might not be acted out by the analyst as well. He firmly believes that such a process, which is similar in his opinion to the destructive narcissism described by Rosenfeld, "can lend itself to the negation of the worthwhileness of the patient with the analyst behaving as if he were the ideal breast rather than a person who may have something useful to say" (Brenman 1978, p. 2)

The analyst's narcissism has been the topic of the second EPF Congress. In her report, Berry (1978) highlights the fact that, aside from the analyst's libidinal cathexis on the patient, there is also a narcissistic cathexis, both positive and negative, which, being neither recognized nor theorized as such, the analyst controls with greater difficulty than the libidinal countertransference.

Nowadays we know that the most stubborn resistances to psychoanalytic treatments are connected to narcissistic states. We are growing progressively more convinced of the fact that a correct understanding of destructive narcissistic structures—particularly concerning the attacks made on the libidinal relationship and on dependency need (Rosenfeld, 1971)—is essential for all sorts of pathology: psychosis, neurosis, or perversion. *But this is true for the analyst as well.* I believe that such malevolent collusions, leading to that particular kind of death that is the destruction of the patient–analyst relationship, also have something to do with the destructive aspects of the analyst's narcissism. Having to cope with the loss of a patient, the analyst's ego experiences a sense of depletion, which leads to very primitive defences: splitting, projection, denial.

When our personal analysis comes to an end, we try, with the aid of self-analysis, to take more and more control over those primitive structures that concern narcissism. Still—as Zaccaria Gairinger (1970) say—on the one hand, self-analysis is a process that lasts for a life-time (an interminable analysis, assuring neither stable nor definitive acquisitions), on the other hand it allows—at the very most—the integration of all those problems that fall within the context of depressive situations. "Self-analysis at this (more primitive) level simply does not exist", and "the psychotic residue, which is concealed in everyone, always remains inaccessible" (Zaccaria Gairinger, 1970, p. 85). Along the same lines Tower (1956), stated that self-analysis is in part an illusion, since it implies conscious control over one's own unconscious.

If analysis leaves certain areas unexplored and self-analysis is unable to reach primitive levels (and interruptions have to do with those very levels), who or what can help us?

It is true that analysts, as their experience increases, run less risk of losing their patients. This is normal, we think, because they are far more expert. But expert in what? In everything that goes on deep inside the patient, of course, but mainly they are more aware of what happens within themselves as regards their analytic function. Young analysts can be amazingly skilful in reaching the contents of their patients' communications and interpreting them, but their interpretations tend to be used as a defence. This has to do not so much with the acquisition of knowledge about the patient's mental state as with the awareness of how our own mind reacts to what is forthcoming from the patients. To quote Carloni (1984), what might make our interventions more personal and humane—and I would add more effective—"is not so much their cognitive but the affective content that reflects the profound responsiveness of the analyst, his capability to feel rather than to understand" (Carloni, 1984, p. 203). However, if we are to feel and be in tune, we need to overcome our defences and to be less afraid as to the "place" of our rendezvous, a place that is always chosen by the patient, who asks us to reach him where he is (Nissim Momigliano, chapter one, this volume).

Nowadays, we are accustomed to considering the analytic relationship as a process of profound interaction leading to some change not simply in the patient, but in the analyst as well. We are inclined to see it as a process of growth, a therapy that is not just meant for the patient, but also for the analyst. In this context, our work with patients becomes—together with personal and self-analysis—the element that allows us to acquire an improved ability to explore the universe of our unconscious.

Is it possible to believe that those levels that are—partially—accessible to analysis and not to self-analysis, may be reached anew when the analyst allows his patient to treat him? In this case, the patient would turn into the analyst's best ally twice over. I do not know whether this is possible; moreover, I do not think that our improved analytic skill always coincides with a benefit for our internal health. We may be aided merely in our analytic function, for as to our difficulties in other relationships, both internal and external, personal analysis remains the only reliable point of reference.

As we have seen, psychoanalysis owes a good deal of its clinical progress to the elaboration of situations that were considered to be negative. This should encourage us to continue our research in the same area, to which premature terminations unquestionably belong. Nevertheless, analysts seem to be unwilling to explore in that very direction. What I have called the analyst's "reluctance" is to be seen as an indication of their feelings of responsibility for such drawbacks. Their refusal may conceal a sense of guilt, which, as we know, often follows an attack, but also persecutory anxieties due to the pressure of a contemptuous and disparaging superego, which is always particularly difficult to bear and inevitably leads to splitting and denial.

In this context we can therefore suppose that a patient who interrupts his analysis may be a patient whom the analyst, deep inside a split part of his self, wants to send away, envisaging him as too harmful a person. Thus, the analyst's unwillingness to face his own failures seems to be linked to his difficulty in getting rid of those residues I have defined as narcissistic and omnipotent. Nowadays we are inclined to believe, however that narcissism and omnipotence, are the manifest aspect of some hidden, intensely suffering parts, which have not yet found a space in more tolerant and benevolent areas of our consciousness, in which to be treated, comforted, and soothed. That is why I believe that we should accept sharing and discussing our painful experiences of interruption, recognizing them as something we can have in common with more renowned colleagues. This may not provide us with new technical discoveries but will certainly help us to cope with those alienated residues that cause us so much trouble. And, eventually, we may also feel less lonely.

Italo Svevo always showed an ambivalent interest towards psychoanalysis, which was at its dawning in his day. His novel, *Confessions of Zeno* (1923), is best known as a report on a self-analysis, but, in fact, if we read it carefully, we realize that it is the story of an interrupted treatment. The novel begins with a short preface, written by a certain Doctor S, Zeno's "psychoanalyst", who tells us how it was that the report came to be written. To overcome his patient's reluctance to go on with the treatment, he had suggested to his patient that he should write his memoirs, hoping that "his autobiography would be a good preparation for the treatment". But the results "would have been better still if the patient had not suddenly thrown up his cure just at the most interesting point, thus cheating me of the fruits of my long and patient analysis of these memoirs" (p. 25).

I shall conclude here, with the intuition of the novelist who highlights how deeply an analyst is tied to his patient and how impoverished he feels by his decision to give up the cure. Still, it is important that the grief for our failures be free from secret revengeful feelings. From the painful experience of being abandoned by our patients we can gain some benefit on condition that we free ourselves of collusion in revenge and succeed in working through and mourning our human fallibility.

CHAPTER SEVEN

Negative therapeutic reactions and microfractures in analytic communication

Francesco Barale and Antonino Ferro

What is a negative therapeutic reaction?

This chapter was conceived in the conviction that a good starting point for a general reflection on clinical experience might be to propose an image of analytic work that approaches everyday difficulties as far as possible. It is precisely work on these difficulties (and an awareness of our limits and setbacks, and those of analysis) that may perhaps give birth to ideas on the still unexplored aspects of the analytic relation. At the very least we may hope to gain perspective points from which usefully also to reconsider clinical phenomena that, like those we shall discuss, have always been familiar in their overall outlines.

What is meant by a negative therapeutic reaction (NTR) is, at a basic level, well known: the NTR is part of the basic conceptual storehouse of every psychoanalyst and is probably part of his experience as well. But if one turns to the literature, the question quickly becomes more complicated: one finds, in fact, that the original descriptions in Freud (1914c, 1914g, 1923b,

1924c) and Abraham (1919) were followed both by a vast range of ways of conceptualizing and understanding the phenomenon and, consequently, by a considerable extension of its boundaries. Thus, under the heading "NTR" we find descriptions of quite diverse clinical phenomena. Indeed, as Pontalis (1981) notes, having been identified everywhere the NTR cannot be localized anywhere, and the greatest risk is surely that this extension is used to give an entirely nominalistic explanation for any situation of impasse or failure in the analytic relationship, and especially so as to blame the patient: "He dealt me a negative therapeutic reaction!"

Various publications present useful histories of the concept and bibliographic reviews. The reader may wish to consult those in Rosenfeld (1975, 1987c), Arrigoni (1987), Giannotti and Grimaldi (1987), and the chapter on NTR in Etchegoyen (1991).

Some, however, have also questioned the usefulness of maintaining this concept. Pontalis (1981), for example, entitles his article, "No, and Again No: An Attempt to Define and Dismantle NTR". Even Rosenfeld, who has worked on this problem throughout his life, stated at a seminar in Rome in 1986 that he did not feel comfortable in continuing to use the notion of NTR. Indeed, from a certain point of view, the notion may appear appropriate to the concept of transference, though requiring reformulation if considered within the framework of the analytic situation seen as a dynamic bipersonal field, which encompasses the continual interaction of transference and countertransference phenomena [Rosenfeld's position, at least as it is expressed in *Impasse and Interpretation* (1987a), is not actually so clearly defined. There coexist, in fact, both a more "classical" view of NTR, linked to the theme of destructive narcissism, and (but only in "certain cases") the suggestion that NTR may be fitted within the problem of possible dysfunctions in the analytic dialogue, due, for example, to the analyst's difficulty to make room for, welcome, and recognize certain psychological parts of the patient or other aspects of his communication.]

Whatever the case may be, discussion of the NTR issue has continued unabated throughout the history of psychoanalysis; indeed, this is true also of the works of Freud, who began to speak of "negative reactions" as early as 1909, in connection with the Rat Man (1909d), and finished in "Analysis Terminable and Interminable" (1937c). It is likely that one reason Freud left the subject is that the phenomena that surround the question of NTR are those more directly connected with mourning for our feelings of omnipotence and omniscience and for the idealization of analysis and of its power to transform. From this perspective, the lesson of Freud's "Analysis Terminable and Interminable", the great lesson on the bedrock and the death instinct, is, as Pontalis (1981) reminds us, one that still bears consideration; as is well known, it definitively situates NTR (like all forces that radically oppose growth and change) in a tragic scenario, in zones of what we are that lie beyond and precede all representational order and the knowable itself (it is only, in Freud's words, the portion of the death instinct "psychically bound by the Super-Ego" that is expressed in guilt feelings and in the need for self-punishment, thus making itself recognizable). This lesson continues to constitute a healthy antidote against those softened, psychologistic, or oversimplified interactional views that fail to perceive the complexity, unpredictability, and contradictoriness of the growth of mental life. This antidote also serves against those pre-analytic views that conceive of the process of cure as an effort to re-establish a patient's presumed harmony and "natural" balance, previously disturbed by some "external" accident. The authors' reflections on NTR, on the other hand, seek to steer a course between this "tragic" awareness and the apparently opposite position recently stated by Guillaumin (1989)—that is, that the recourse to such radical options as the death instinct may in reality have a "defensive and degenerative function that enables the expulsion in theory of what is not resolved in countertransference". While we are aware, in short, that there are certainly many more things at work in the mind than those accounted for by our models, we cannot help but centre our study on the "incessant calling up of the misalliances between transference and countertransference". This is, quite simply, our perspective, and it is this that we are able to do.

Despite the broad range of opinions on the nature of the phenomenon, then, recent thinking has tended to take NTR back to its original clinical configuration. Negative therapeutic reactions are increasingly defined as those that surface after a period of solid work, characterized by sensations of evolution in progress, integration, good contact. They correspond, that is, to a "paradoxical" progress in the clinical relationship, excluding all the various forms of resistance and relapse and the reappearance during treatment, for the most diverse reasons, of the symptoms, aggressivity, and polemical behaviour towards analysis.

We are dealing with cases, such as the one that follows, in which the patient seems to take "two steps forward and three back", sometimes unexpectedly but occasionally with disturbing regularity.

The Valley of Rabbi

In the case of S, a bright, sensitive young woman with significant wounds in the area of narcissism, the phenomenon was so regular and predictable that the analyst felt apprehensive and uneasy every time a "particularly good" session took place and contact was established with dependent and affective aspects, which were generally kept rigorously split. Indeed, the feeling of apprehension was directly proportional to the intensity of the contact reached. These sessions ended with a deep sense of emotional involvement. The following day, however, the patient would return with a livid expression and communicate in a metallic voice feelings of extraordinary solitude and desertification. S gave the icy impression that nothing positive had happened or might ever happen in that desolate land of analysis, or in the rest of her life. She gave vent to an intense rage towards the analyst, who was "as cold and indifferent as an SS officer", or towards her own ridiculous, useless attempts to give a more caring tone to existence. On one occasion this tendency towards the NTR expressed itself visually in a dream:

> S was with a colleague on a hike in the mountains. At first
> they made their way along a dangerous, tortuous path,
> then gradually the landscape became increasingly gentler

and more pleasant. They conversed happily, and S felt intensely moved, but at the peak of this feeling there suddenly appeared before S a gaping ravine, which opened up as far as the eye could see on the Valley of Rabbi [the Valley of Anger; the Valley of Rabbi actually exists—the name recalls the Italian *rabbia*: "anger"—and is familiar to both the analyst and the patient].

A few hypotheses with a view from the field (and a little history)

It is well known that these situations present difficulties in terms of countertransference. We find the work that we carry out with love and patience assailed before our eyes by a destructive, apparently unjustified anger. The analyst may then mount an accusatory counterattack, thus redoubling the negative therapeutic reaction with negative countertransferential reaction. It is evidently the patient's psychopathology (his masochism, guilt feelings, rejection of dependency, destructive narcissism) that keeps him from understanding just how good his analysis and his analyst have been for him! On the other hand, the analyst may feel hurt and become defensive, thus further encouraging the patient in his belief that his aggressive behaviour is effectively destructive. For quite some time, indeed, such situations were considered to be the results of a "disturbance" in the analytic relationship caused by the psychopathology of the patient. This was sometimes explained by a particularly sturdy grouping of "guilt feelings–expiation needs–masochism" (especially, in the wake of Freud, in North American psychoanalytic literature), but it was also interpreted as an expression of the "hidden and hypnotic power of destructive narcissism" (Rosenfeld, 1987a, p. 22) or of envy, which attack libidinal and dependent aspects. These moments have also been considered, on the other hand, as the consequence of a technical error on the part of the analyst (Reich, in *Character Analysis*, 1933, was, as far as we know, the first to speak of NTR as an excuse for poor technique) or as the product of some serious incomprehension on his part; they would not appear in an "ideal" well-conducted analysis. The problem was, then, still a sort of "who started first".

A step forward was surely marked by the EPF Congress held in 1979. The program was entirely devoted to NTR, and numerous papers began to view the question somewhat differently, seeking reasons for this phenomenon not only within the patient but also within the analytic relation. These points were taken up again by Limentani (1981), in an article with a significant title, "On Some Positive Aspects of the Negative Therapeutic Reaction", and in Italy by M. Arrigoni (1987). But it was above all the views put forward by Bion that contributed to the general change in perspective on analytic phenomena and provided several significant insights in NTR as well.

We are now proposing a number of hypotheses for discussion. It should be clear, however, that we are well aware of the role played in inducing NTR by the particular psychopathology of a patient or by the analyst's errors. There is no question that every patient enters the consulting room with his own particular psychopathology, with his own particular history, and his own particular disposition and constitutional set-up. We do not hold that the traditional explanations of NTR are not "true". We simply think that drawing a direct line from an analytic phenomenon such as NTR to a psychopathological characteristic of the patient (or to "technical errors" on the part of the analyst), while valid from a certain point of view, may cause us to run certain risks. We feel that such an approach may lead to the avoidance of problems that emerge from the analyst's attempt to understand what happens in other, more specifically analytic terms. Seen from this angle, the question of "cause" or "who started first" becomes decidedly secondary. [Pontalis observes: "When we derive our discouragement or our helplessness from a morphology of our patients' psychic reality, we behave like those among them who blame their inner suffering on a social or familial reality, which is supposed to be 'too this' or 'too that'. In all these cases we defend ourselves by means of reality." It matters little whether it is a psychic reality, a history, or an external situation; in every case we remain within that etiological, causalistic mode of thought that nourishes splits and simplifications, which has been a weary fellow traveller of psychoanalysis.]

Our hypotheses, then, are as follows:

1. Negative therapeutic reactions are sometimes not such a negative phenomenon after all. They do signal, however, the need to re-tune the analytic dialogue.

2. They may signal that certain functions of the analytic field that are indispensable for the development of the analytic relation have not been sufficiently activated.

3. They may indicate that transference–countertransference collusions have taken place ("bastions", as used by Baranger et al., 1988); that is, they may signal the existence of an unrecognized impasse of which they represent the point of crisis.

4. They may be channels for the communication, through action, of important emotional areas that have not yet had access to thinkability (in some cases, we feel, areas related to heavily traumatic experiences). They may represent, then, an initial, rudimentary orientation toward mental life and history for emotional nuclei up to that moment encapsulated in an ahistorical and purely repetitive dimension.

5. They may have an important defensive function with respect to the experience of an excessively abrupt impact with aspects of unbearable suffering or of blinding light (Bion). They signal the need, then, for a preliminary weaving together of the emotional conditions (filters) that make the experience possible.

6. The abrupt gesture of detachment and rejection represented by NTR may have a value of "vitality" that should be recognized and respected. It may be a way of "acting" in the transference dimension an acute problem of separation or differentiation that cannot be worked through otherwise due to nostalgia and/or anxiety for fusion (Asch, 1976; Grunert, 1981).

Far from being merely the symptom of a disturbance (the patient's or the analyst's), the negative therapeutic reaction may have an important communicative value and may represent an occurrence necessary for the development of a relationship in the analytic field.

A few clinical examples may throw light on some of these aspects.

A too clear-minded analyst, a too perfect patient, a misunderstood impasse

G had for a long time been the "consolation of his analyst" among many other difficult and desperate patients. He had asked for analysis due to his "difficulties in establishing deeper sentimental relations" (and the analyst remembers his initial hesitation in accepting to work with a person who appeared, at first sight, so well adapted and whose life was frankly enviable).

G was sensitive, intelligent, and punctual. He seemed to approach analysis with commitment, brought dreams regularly, associated, showed dedication and gratitude, improved symptomatically, indeed visibly. In a few years' time he married and proceeded brilliantly in his career. It turned out that he even had many of the same interests as his analyst.

For quite some time the analyst had the impression that he had a clear idea of the case and good intuitions. The patient seemed to understand the analyst's comments at once; indeed, detailed elaborations could be dispensed with in a collaborative construction, which appeared to proceed easily and to the satisfaction of both. Towards the third year, however, the analyst began to feel an annoying sense of boredom, restlessness, and slight "falseness". The analyst felt on occasion that he was more in contact with his other patients (with whom he would, perhaps, have to plod through periods of confusion) than with this one, who appeared so straightforward. But he tended to attribute the slight uneasiness he felt with this "good" and fortunate patient to his own weariness and the greater concentration required by the more serious and demanding cases. Towards the end of the third year, following a new, particularly productive period (in which the patient seemed to have responded to his perception of the analyst's decline in interest), the analyst praised his patient's "progress"—an uncommon sort of comment given his usual technique. Just as in a case reported by Limentani (1981), this unleashed a violent, unexpected negative therapeutic reaction: the analyst and the analysis were made the targets of demands, scorn, and disillusionment. The NTR was suddenly and dramatically interrupted by a car accident in which the patient was seriously injured. Analysis has recently resumed, but on a rather different plane.

G has now become a "difficult" patient like the others; the atmosphere of fictitious agreement has dissolved, and the analysis is filled with problems and fundamental anxieties. It is likely that nearly the entire course of the first three years of analysis can be considered as a vast acting out of false-self-type adaptive mode, forcing the analyst to collude in a narcissistic relation. But this collusion meant that the analyst had not received and answered the patient's true requests and needs, which had given rise to the request for analysis. It has been possible to reconstruct how the comment on "progress made" was experienced by the patient. It was perceived as a declaration that, for the analyst, as for everyone else, things "were fine as they were and could not be changed"; it was felt as a forewarning of the end of the analysis. The NTR, and, later, the accident, had served as outlets for the patient's anger and desperation and for aspects of his interior world, which had never before gained access to thinkability. [The issue of "traumaphilia" (this, too, a "classic") has frequently intertwined with our reflections and is worthy of our attention. The Barangers (Baranger et al., 1988) point out two aspects of the *après coup* changes in the stories of patients in analysis. On the one hand, situations initially presented as "traumatic" are put back into perspective, and on the other there emerge new traumatic memories or traumatic readings of previously neutral memories. This corresponds to a reopening of psychic temporality and to the possibility, offered by the analytic relation, of access to thinkability and to the history of areas of (traumatic) experiences that were previously dormant in a dimension of pure repetition. In our experience, however, we find that this is the "good" version of these moments of evolution. On other occasions, unfortunately, these nuclei are not (or cannot be) contained and elaborated in the new analytic relation but are "actings", often provoking real traumas or sequences of traumas that can be quite frightening. The real trauma can be considered, in this case, as the equivalent of an NTR, and both may be viewed as expressions of a "re-action", in the etymological sense, of dramatic experiences, of emotive–mental areas loaded with insufficiently bound death instinct, areas that have begun to resonate before becoming tolerable and thinkable. Similar considerations might be made concerning certain psychosomatic phenomena that appear during analysis (not necessarily and not exclusively on the part of the patient).]

Might the NTR be considered as an emergence point in an unrecognized impasse situation?

A blinding light

B is a patient in his second year of analysis who presents some "atypical" negative therapeutic reactions. Like the "Valley of Rabbi" patient, B's reaction often takes place after more intense sessions; but in this case it is not a reaction of anger or attack against the positive experience. B, to use his own words, "spaces out", "blacks out", or "short-circuits". These experiences are preceded by a sensation of uneasiness and followed by an impression of confusion, heaviness, the feeling "of not being able to remember anything, as if after electroshock treatment", a sensation that may extend over several sessions. These metaphors from electricity correspond to the analyst's impression that he is often handling live wires when he is together with his patient (and this is not a simple problem of timing). They are also rather worrying if we consider that on two occasions B risked being electrocuted by high-voltage electric shocks, which he had caused by handling electrical equipment at work "absentmindedly".

B is a photographer by profession. Recently, after one of the last "black-outs" and once contact was resumed, he began to talk about the question of light. Light is central to photography; a shot may be beautifully conceived, but if the light is wrong, the effect is destroyed. He described in detail complicated filter systems he was working on and a device intended for certain portrait pictures: in a dark room, a light source is made to pass through a pure crystal decanter full of water. The lighting device serves to obtain a light absolutely free from impurities. The idea was suggested to B by a refined friend of his, a homosexual aesthete who is always excited and sparkling with ideas, who had in turn, been given it by precious-stones setters. The system, however, had so far been a disaster . . . he had read a book recently, entitled "In Praise of Shadows" . . . (there followed a series of associations on Rembrandt's "The Night Watch", a painting on the "problem of light", damaged by a lunatic . . .).

There is clearly a meaningful and tempting chain of thought here: the night watch, the primal scene, excitement, destructive anger, and the negative therapeutic reaction—the analytic match, perhaps, as an intolerable primal scene to be attacked. But perhaps it is another level that is more pressing. It may indeed be a problem of light, and the analyst may not be providing the right light for a creative, fruitful mental match. There is a connection with the hyperstimulated and "over-exposed" boy, as the patient more than once described himself, on whom everyone was counting (including the analyst, initially) for his considerable perceptive abilities and quickness and his intelligence. And then there is his family background: everything was clear, out in the open, no secrets, parents who were intelligent, well-educated, open, and progressive, who understood everything and from whom nothing could be or should be hidden, clear and precise ideals and values . . . and the patient, who would occasionally run off into a secret corner of the house and fill his head with masturbatory phantasies until he was "dazed". . . . And the interior image of the mother is evoked, which B, for some reason, elaborated on: "sharp, precise woman, without shading"; and, above all, the memory of the glass eye, the precious artificial eye that his mother had had since she was a child: a highly sophisticated reflecting globe and at the same time an image of an experience with an inadequate containment and mirroring function; a recollection that is fundamental to B's professional vocation and to his interest in the problem of "visibility".

Perhaps, then, the problem is, indeed, one of achieving an experience of intimacy that is respectful and abstinent, moderate, not intrusive, not anguished by wounds, reasonably luminous, tolerant of shades and nuances, and, ultimately, one that does not require the elimination of "impure" aspects—an illumination, then, that is not narcissistic but sufficiently filtered, in a modulated way.

Might NTR be seen as a safety valve that signals excessive perturbation or an excess of tension or a distorted light, unbearable in the analytic field (and the need for reorganization so as to bring back an acceptable illumination)?

We have learned from Bion (1978) that the movement towards integration can become charged with anxiety and pain. And this is not merely because the activation of dependent aspects may unleash a destructive attack against envious and narcissistic aspects. It can have this effect entirely of itself: increasing insight capacity can throw an intolerable light on emotional areas that involve an intolerable pain: psychotic areas of the mind, or simply very traumatic areas, charged with tormenting pain; pain not yet worked through, not given mental shape and perhaps not open to being worked out; experiences too urgent to be mentally metabolized.

This is, in part, the case of the patient of the "Valley of Rabbi". For her, every experience of contact seemed paradoxically and dramatically to cause a short-circuit between an agonizingly intense, idealized phantasy of union and an equally radical and intolerable anxiety of separation/destruction—a narcissistic wound deep enough to unleash a preventative reprisal of analogous intensity and destructiveness. It should be noted that this reprisal certainly also served to make the analyst feel at least a trace of the feelings of desperation that resonated in the patient: after the patient's birth, her mother had suffered from a serious puerperal depression. [Arrigoni (1987) has drawn attention to the use of NTR as a mode of communicating, through projective identification, aspects of the interior world of the patient.]

Precursors of NTR and microfractures in analytic communication

There is another area of clinical phenomena to which we would like to draw attention. These are situations that we consider as possible precursors of NTR—that is, interruptions in communication, which, if not received by means of the patient's own signals, may lead to true negative therapeutic reactions (as an alternative to the patient's resigning himself to the loss of communicative contact).

This area is clearly different from what we have described previously. It is an area of elementary phenomena, which, if isolated from the relational field of which they are both expression and function, may suggest problems of timing, or of countertransferential modulation, or simply technical errors.

In many cases, moreover, there is no clear "paradoxical" pattern typical of the NTR—that is, a negative reaction to a "good moment". We have the impression, however, that the "good moment" often contains the problem that is expressed in NTR. The patient may follow us, accept our lead, try everything, so to speak, to make us understand something that we continue to refuse to understand, since we prefer to fall back on our own pre-formed ideas. This moment may even appear "good" until the NTR appears to signal the problem to us.

Problems of interpretative style

It is occasionally the "interpretative style" that can gradually lead to a negative transference. As Etchegoyen (1991) points out, if this is not understood as a precious indicator of the way in which the analyst/patient pair functions, it may gradually lead to a NTR.

Laura is a talented young woman, a psychologist with considerable experience of work with children. Analysis with her seems to proceed well, although the analyst occasionally feels that he is acting more the role of supervisor than that of analyst. Shortly after the analyst had considered this thought again, Laura recounts a visit she paid to a child who had a school phobia. The boy thought of packing his bags and running away from home, or of picking up a knife, because he was very angry with his older brother who would beat him up, hit him and hurt him . . . then she adds that she had come to the session angry herself, since she had had to leave her own new-born child at home in order to come. Then she notes that she had a dream in which Licia, a friend who spends her holidays at her mother's whenever possible, was travelling to the sixth floor in a lift. She could only see her feet; it was like something out of a horror film.

She associates with the dream the feeling of someone being taken by the shoulders and hoisted up like a dead weight, like a child pulled brusquely out of a swimming pool. . . .

If the analyst takes on the role of a supervisor (brother), addressing the more adult levels, he provokes anger, rivalry, jealousy, and persecution, and, above all, he blocks access to the child-like part of the patient, which must be "left at home" in the terror that otherwise she might be pulled up like a dead weight to a level that is too high for her, rather than find a mother on ground level who is truly ready and willing and who does not *know already* where to pull, but is able to *share the swimming pool*—not a mother who is worried about knowing and bringing up, but one who enjoys sharing discoveries and growth—processes that can be achieved only through living the experience of the immersion in the fluidity of meaning with the patient.

Respect for the patient's text

These considerations are connected to an issue of a more general character that concerns the respect for the "patient text"; the patient's need, that is, of an interlocutor who shares in his narratives, contributes to them, and thus participates in their evolution, rather than an analyst who draws out meaning and substitutes the patient's text with the "official version of the truth" (Bollas, 1987, p. 206). As Bollas reminds us, Winnicott said that we must be able "to play with the patient, to put forth an idea as an object that exists in the potential space between the patient and the analyst, an object that is meant to be passed back and forth between the two and, if it turns out to be of use to the patient, it will be stored away as that sort of objective object that has withstood a certain scrutiny" (Bollas, 1987, pp. 206–207).

We have the impression that many microfractures in analytic communication have roots in this problem. Clearly, it is not merely a question of the "form" of interpretation, whether "weak" or "strong", assertive or open to doubt (see Bezoari & Ferro, chapter three, this volume); the intervention of the analyst can also be decisive, factious, passionate—indeed, it is precisely in this that his ability to contain may lie; it may indicate the courage of new points of view, *contain (hopefully) an element of surprise as well as of contact and recognition.* But what is in question is the relationship the analyst genuinely feels he has with analytic truth—that is, as something that is established in the relationship and not as something that precedes it (being inscribed in the internal world or in history), and which he personally possesses. It happened to one of us that a girl, whose analysis had come to a halt in the face of unambiguous interpretations, signalled this problem quite directly through a dream in which she was not received after "her own intervention". "Intervention", here, referred both to the surgery she was about to undergo and to her own verbal discourse, which she feared was being interpretatively dissected rather than received in the richness of its textuality.

It is a matter, then, of interacting with the patient's text in an encounter that respects all the potential semantic richness of the text and sets in motion a process of transformation of beta into alpha elements, making possible the common experience of emotional areas that had previously been withheld from thinkability. This should gradually organize narratives that are or can become shared, and which should always be unsaturated, built up in the dialogue and the fruit of the relationship.

NTR, "characters" of the session, and functional aggregates

The "characters" of the session constitute an important signal that patients give us concerning the microfractures in the analytic dialogue.

> Marina, a young lawyer, expresses considerable concern, before leaving on Easter holiday, about the trip she is about to take with her new-born daughter Carla; for Carla it will mean moving, she won't have her own pillows, the crib will be in a different place . . . the analyst follows her as her text unfolds, until he is no longer able to resist the urge to interpret in rigid terms of transference. After a moment of silence, the patient says: "Carla likes to be held by everyone in the family, but she breaks out in tears if she is picked up by my uncle's trainee or a twelve-year-old girl". The analyst's immature and intemperate sides, though "activated" by the patient's narcissistic aspects, make babies cry. Then Marina wonders if analysts sometimes don't want to "work".

The analyst, who does not "transform" the unrestrained anxiety of the abandoned child, acts upon it by interpreting it; he does not "work", and evacuating interpretations are ultimately appropriate to "trainees" (Manfredi Turillazzi, 1978).

The characters of the session can be considered as the syncretic narrations of how the patient sees our functioning with him from vertices unknown to us but which we must share for a moment if we are to come into contact with him.

Considering the analytic situation as a bipersonal field, one of us has proposed the term "functional aggregate" (Bezoari & Ferro, chapter three, this volume) to describe a specific way of understanding stories, scenes, and characters as constantly changing precipitates of the pair's functioning. Initially, these precipitates belong neither to the patient nor to the analyst but are, as we have said, "functional aggregates" of their relation. We find this concept useful for following the text of the session as a living picture, which changes with the changes in the relationship.

This perspective enables a rapid mending of the field's emotional facts without resorting to interpretations that can freeze their meaning. The problem is, basically, to construct meaning together with the patient (Corrao, 1986; Gaburri, 1987) by "responding" to his nutritive needs without necessarily interpreting them. Our intervention should modulate the function of the particular "hologram" of the analytic pair's mental functioning, which, in turn, consists of the characters who appear in the patient's narration.

After a session in which the analyst had assigned correct but overly dense and premature "meanings", Luisa relates that she ate a *ciabatta* following the previous session [*ciabatta* is used to refer both to a kind of bread, similar to pitta, and to a slipper]. The analyst had shared this experience and, thinking of the cold, explicative climate of certain interpretations, draws a comparison with "the Italian soldiers retreating from Russia", who ate the soles of their shoes.

As if encouraged by this recovered narrative syntony, the patient tells of a friend who telephoned to ask about a baby girl who was born *prematurely* with a brain haemorrhage, which might have led to a hydrocephalus . . . her parents had placed considerable hopes in this birth. . . .

In the meantime the analyst intervenes to comment on the "parents' disappointment" . . . Luisa goes on to talk about a microcephalic boy with macroglossia, and the analyst intervenes to say how painful it is to accept a baby like that, not thinking of it as part of the patient or of oneself, considering it as a shared "thinking little" (microcephaly) and "talking much" (macroglossia) "prematurely" (hydrocephalus).

Then Luisa talks about parents of Downs syndrome children . . . that there is an association in Genoa that expects an enormous amount from these children, teaching them too many things too early—within the first 10 years, because then atrophy sets in. . . . The patient then asks herself why she is talking, in analysis, about situations that are so difficult; she wonders and suggests that maybe it is because . . . and raises a series of hypotheses that smack of theory.

The analyst answers that, perhaps, it is so that she can have someone near her that she can talk to and share these things with, doing without the suggested transference interpretation.

"Or maybe", she answers, "so that I can understand how lucky I am to have a daughter like Paola and not like that" (the analyst's narrative interventions transform the Downs/hydrocephalus/microcephaly/macroglossia into Paola). Then the analyst intervenes with further narrations on mothers who, if they overstimulate their children, make them feel Down. . . . Luisa speaks of her affectionate husband, who tells fairy-tales to their daughter, while she listens herself; the most beautiful one was the one about the little white wolf . . . that nobody wanted . . . when the snow came, the little black wolves couldn't catch anything because they were too visible . . . and the bears attacked them . . . but the little white wolf blended into the countryside and was able to catch enough to give to the others. . . .

The analyst comments that this is a *reversal of the more classic situation*. Luisa replies: "Yes, it's true. You've usually got the ugly duckling . . . (which is what the patient often feels like precisely in the more "classic" situation); my husband is very affectionate; . . . he reads *Orlando furioso* at home, . . . the *Divine Comedy*; that one he also reads to Paola, who doesn't understand the words, of course, but hears the sound, the musicality; I also appreciate the meaning; . . . we've got a Matriowska at home, made of a lot of little dolls that fit one inside the other but that also maintain their individual identity. . . ."

And on the way out: "Well, today I certainly won't need to go out and eat a *ciabatta* . . . !"

Unambiguous and excessively dense interpretations—"black wolves"—end up by generating persecution, flight, aggressivity, whereas narration and the use of the patient's text enable the white wolf to hunt for food for the entire pack without causing flight or persecution. Certain interpretations should remain with the analyst, others can be made explicit at all levels and their "semantic auras" find their appropriate place; thus "new" stories can be created and the terrible retreats of the freezing Russian campaign avoided.

CONCLUDING REMARKS

We shall limit ourselves to making a few notes on the conceptual frame that surrounds our observations.

Our first proposal, then, is that given situations that bear the characteristics of NTR (and, even more so, of impasse), the analyst should resist the sterile logic of "who started it?" (patient or analyst) and forego the systematic search for origins in a particular psychopathology of the patient or in events of his past history—that is, in aspects that lie beyond the analytic field (and concern, at best, the external conditions for its constitution). Instead, these situations should be treated as phenomena that signal that something important is happening *here*, something that concerns us directly. Blind spots, microfractures in analytic communication around which coagulate emotional areas that have not been thought and reclaimed: icebergs that suddenly surface in the analytic field and threaten navigation, perhaps caused to surface by the greater heat that broke the ice-cap (could this not be another way to think of the "paradoxical" course that characterizes NTR?). These are difficult waters in which the patient finds he must swim ballasted by weights that are often greater than his forces—waters that we must brave, as Bolognini put it (1990), by swimming together with him, not by describing the seascape from the porthole of the Nautilus or of Picard's bathysphere. The patient is trying in his own way or through these phenomena to say or propose something to us—something that is probably important, albeit from perspectives that are still new to us.

This is the first, clear move to make in order to prevent the "emotional turbulence" (Gaburri et al., 1990) that is expressed in the NTR and its precursors from becoming a genuine obstruction to possibilities of transformation and to guarantee that it may become a potential starting-point for the recovery of "missing" affective areas that have remained unexplored and untranscribed in an experiential–narrative order. The guideline, then, is to participate in the turbulence and to feel involved without blocking the way by "being the analyst" and carrying out premature translations of a meaning that has not yet been constituted and constructed in the encounter and in the relationship.

We have advanced a few hypotheses and sought to furnish a few illustrations of the meanings and value that the NTR can take on in the analytic relationship, once the more traditional points of view have been put in brackets.

The other general idea that inspires our observations is that of the analytic situation understood as a context in which the analyst and the patient participate not so much in the more-or-less truthful reconstruction of a scene from infancy but in the original construction, which takes place through new realizations, to use Bion's term, made possible by the analytic exchange; this takes place through a common merging in emotional and mental areas and in the construction of a transitional area, common to the patient and the analyst, which is largely unconscious (just as countertransference is largely unconscious) and which functions as a fly-wheel of transformability.

But it is clear that sharing, though certainly a necessary condition, is not sufficient to set a positive transformation in motion—a transformation that steers an ideal course (or oscillation) past the reception of emotive turbulence and towards the

constitution of shared affects and an initial level of symbolization analogous to an oneiric production in tandem (in which, as
Bezoari and Ferro state in chapter three of this volume with their
concept of "functional aggregate", the judgement as to whether
attribution of what emerges in the field should go to one member
or the other of the pair remains relatively suspended). Following
successive transformations, the journey finally ends with the
recognition of more *specific* affects and meanings, in which both
participants are better able to recognize and identify themselves. The journey is fraught with risks and difficulties. On the
other hand, as Bollas says: "Only by making a good object [the
analyst] go somewhat mad can such a patient believe in his
analysis and know that the analyst has been where he has been
and has survived and emerged intact with . . . an evolution in
the countertransference . . ." (Bollas 1987), to which there corresponds a potential evolution in the patient.

NTR and phenomena of impasse can bear witness, above
all, to the difficulties of this journey and signal to us how many
emotional pockets, which have never been worked out in meetings with another mind, can turn bitter and load themselves
with pain. They may also signal the strength of coercive power
and collusive grip in the pair's functioning of anti-evolutionary
ways of avoiding pain. But *they may also represent inevitable
and necessary events in the course of sharing.* One is reminded
here of Winnicott's words when he spoke of the *necessity* for
certain patients to be able to manipulate us in the use they
make of us in transference in order to achieve objective identity
and to be able to force their analysts to commit errors and
collusions "so that a certain play can be staged, already repeated innumerable times, it is true, but in a theatre without
spectators" (Bolognini, 1990).

As Bollas (1987) writes: "If our sense of identity is certain,
then its loss within the clinical space is essential to the
patient's discovery of himself".

The analytic relationship is, however, not a symmetrical one.
The analyst, together with the "openness to countertransference", must exercise a high level of vigilance and self-analytic
activity in order to prevent the anti-evolutionary and anti-oedi-
pal aspects of the field (his and his patient's) from prevailing,

and to keep the sharing from deteriorating into a *folie-à-deux*. This effort is essential if the question of "realization", a necessary precondition for any genuinely evolutionary aspect of analysis, with its significant dimension of "acting", is not to be limited to the simple orthopaedics of corrective emotional experience and of a traditional sense of "acting", with its evacuative connotations. It is the analyst's responsibility, then, to keep open the analysis-specific dialectics between the useful polarity of our discourse and the polarity formed by a series of other elements of the interior order and the formal setting: abstinence, separateness, privacy, tension towards thinkability and, also, towards that *fundamental element of psychoanalytic ethics that is constituted by the feeling of personal and individual responsibility towards one's own internal world.*

This polarity becomes an essential part of the analytic space and of the meeting that takes place in that space and keeps these two elements in a condition of non-saturation and non-coincidence of opening and oscillation "between O and K". It extends simultaneously towards the order of passion and sense, but also myth, to use Bion's language. In this polarity there co-exist and *continually enter into tension extraordinarily intense involvements and separateness, real exchanges between persons involving all their human qualities and an unavoidable aspect of "fiction", sharing and solitude.* It is the responsibility of the analyst, although involved in the field himself, to make sure that this dialectic is not obstructed.

From this perspective it is extremely useful, as we have stressed, to follow the session's characters as they enter the session, to pay attention to how they move, change, and leave the stage to make room for substitutes or additional characters (of an anecdote, a recollection, a story, a dream, etc.); but it is always something that gives shape and colour to what goes on in the mental functioning of the pair in that moment, thus making possible continual adjustments in the field. We consider it fundamental that the analyst should assume full responsibility for his own mental life as an element of the structuring of the emotional, affective, and narrative field that he shares with his patient, which gives life, among the many possible stories, to the unique, unrepeatable story derived from that one particular meeting with all the creative enrichments and limitations specific to it.

And if this is true for the entire course of an analysis, it is equally true for each individual sub-unit of analysis, whether this be a week or an hour.

This is a perspective that may involve moving into the background many considerations that are obvious and true (from other points of view) and, perhaps, more reassuring. But we must also ask ourselves when we face "disturbing" phenomena like negative therapeutic reactions: "What have I to do with what appears in the field?" Such phenomena are not to be understood only as repeated constraints or as the patient's transference or as phantasies projected by the patient, but more genuinely as signals we receive concerning what is happening in the present relationship, though from a perspective that is as yet unknown to us; and yet making that perspective our own often opens new roads of access to the patient.

CHAPTER EIGHT

On transference psychosis: clinical perspectives in work with borderline patients

Franco De Masi

A fundamental aspect of analytic work, in my opinion, is the capacity that patients have, and further develop in the course of analysis, to grasp and explore the way the analyst functions emotionally and perceptively, to introject this, and to interact with it. When we are deeply absorbed in our analytic task, we may find it difficult to determine whether the patient's introjection occurs on the basis of correct perceptions or under the influence of past experiences or of primitive internal objects. Internal objects may interfere with a good introjection and seriously distort the image of the analyst and the perception of the analytic relationship. Correct and distorted introjections frequently interact, and it is fundamental to help the patient to discriminate between adequate perceptions and possible conscious or unconscious distortions. Generally speaking, only when the analyst repeatedly gives distorted answers to the patient's communications (which often concern the analyst's way of interacting) can an impasse occur, and that may, unfortunately, lead to a premature termination. The patient is usually able to signal his difficulties, and it is there-

167

fore essential to pick up these indications, recognizing them as important contributions. In other words, I would like to emphasize how important it is that the analyst accept his share of responsibility and free himself of an immovable, idealized image of his role and of the analytic process. I argue that good receptivity on the analyst's part allows the patient to develop his capacity to explore and understand both his own psychic reality and that of others.

In his paper, "The Elasticity of the Psychoanalytic Technique", Ferenczi (1928) says that analysis "should be regarded as a process of fluid development unfolding itself before our eyes rather than a structure with a design pre-imposed upon it by an architect" (p. 90). I agree with Ferenczi and emphasize that the most important aspect of the analytic process is the possibility of triggering new developmental processes in the direction of improved relational capabilities and the acquisition of identity.

This concerns every analysis, but in particular those cases in which the earliest experiences of dependency have been impaired or distorted by the relationship with a pathological primal object. Such experiences create a traumatic nucleus, as it were, dense with pathogenic consequences. We are all aware that the complex relationship that joins patient and analyst is often silent and far removed from verbal expression. In some cases, the analyst must support the patient's vital functions over long periods of time, protecting him from the danger of physical or mental disintegration through his interpretative activity. The imbalance between the different aspects of this complex relationship plays an important role in producing the discontinuity in the developmental process that I mentioned above. The analyst's misunderstandings in the analytic relationship may pass almost unnoticed: the patient reacts to them with silence and with physical or mental withdrawal.

I will now attempt, through a clinical example, to illustrate this point and the difficulties related to it. The patient had come to analysis at the age of 24, for depression and a sense of emptiness following the premature death of her mother. In the third year of treatment she developed an almost total incapacity to understand what was going on between us, and this continued over a period of time. She became very quiet and unapproachable. Then, one day, she remembered a dream that indicated a state of confusion.

> She was in the kitchen and wanted to drink, but the only bottle left had a broken neck. She could not drink because there might be splinters of glass mixed up with water. At a certain point she had the impression that these splinters of glass might be all around her.

After a long silence, the patient said that she was trying to understand what was happening, but she could not. She wondered, for example, why she sometimes came late to analysis, even to the point of only arriving five minutes before the end of the session.

At the time, the patient's dream reports were only seldom followed by associations. I had felt the urge to understand, and on the material, which seemed very clear to me, I gave transference interpretations. But then I had to acknowledge that my interpretations had upset the patient. She admitted with difficulty that she had felt herself "torn away"; my words had made her feel "stretched from one side or the other, like a piece of chewing-gum". In other words, the patient admitted that she could not think, and that my attempts to help her further prevented her from thinking. This was the problem. I was forced to recognize that my interpretations, which according to the material seemed correct, were still unable to improve the situation or make it meaningful; it all remained meaningless until the patient produced another dream. In this dream a girlfriend gave her four ice-cream bowls back; but the bowls were dented, and the patient, seized by irrepressible anger, destroyed them completely. She associated the four bowls to the breast, and, at that very moment, she recalled a problem that had occurred with her mother in the past. This had always been a difficult point to clarify, and in the end it had been forgotten. After this dream she remembered that as a child there had been long periods in her relationship with her mother in which she had felt incapable of understanding and of being understood, and she had never been able to fathom whether this depended on her or on her mother. This situation was symmetrical to what we were now experiencing in analysis. With this dream, the patient had managed to clarify that she was living in a state of confusion due to the existence of "microscopic" splits (glass splinters mixed up with water). We could now realize that when my interpretations (the bowls) failed in their function of understanding and holding her adhesively, she could not but react with self-destructive anger. This dream also drew attention to the fact that the problem of her actual past with her mother, which had blocked her developmental experience and had made her confused, was still present and active and unconsciously affected the analytic situation.

The clinical example I have just described is a common, almost customary, event in analytic work. A temporary impasse in the process can occur, but this does not have dramatic or disruptive effects. The moment comes when the patient expresses, through the symbolic, clarifying language of a dream, the nature of his difficulties; the dream, once understood, marks a turning point, and the analytic process is resumed. This is not the case with more difficult patients, where a more serious reaction occurs, which may lead to the traumatic conclusion of the analysis. I am referring to the emergence in analysis of a psychotic process that centres on the analyst, a clinical condition, which is called *transference psychosis*. When the analyst finds himself at the centre of this psychotic process, his psychoanalytic attitude, which is essential for the analytic process to progress, is preserved with great difficulty whilst it is maintained with greater ease in cases like the one just described.

I come now to the central topic of this essay. In the analysis of one of my patients, a transference psychosis suddenly broke out, and it lasted for a few months. I felt bewildered and challenged by this situation, but also stimulated. I was forced to re-examine some aspects of my therapeutic attitude, and this experience improved my capacity to observe and think analytically. I found myself the target of his concentrated attacks in an extremely difficult situation where all collaboration and normal communication were interrupted and my interpretations were grossly distorted and thrown back at me with hatred and violence.

Transference psychosis is nowadays seen as the emergence of psychotic manifestations within the analytic relationship (Kernberg, 1975; H. Rosenfeld, 1978a, 1978b). In psychoanalytic studies of the past no clear distinction was made between transference psychosis and psychotic transference, and the two conditions were confused. The psychotic transference is a more exhaustive clinical manifestation, involving the figure of the analyst in the patient's delusional, magic omnipotent world, in the course of a psychotic episode that develops or has developed outside the analytic relationship. Transference psychosis, on the contrary, is a *psychosis in the transference.*

The borderline patient normally retains, at least for the most part, his capacity to distinguish between internal experiences and his perceptions of the external world. The psychotic nuclei remain limited and do not affect the figure of the analyst. In transference psychoses, however, the patient develops delusional ideas, psychotic behaviour, or even hallucinations only within the analytic situation, and these are essentially focused on the analyst's person.

The loss of the reality testing that comes about in the transference psychosis does not unduly interfere, however, with the patient's life, which remains apparently unchanged. The patient develops an enormous aggression and deadly hatred for the therapist and, at the same time, perceives him as a source of anxiety, dread, and persecution. The analyst is feared and attacked in a delusional way. The patient loses his capacity to distinguish between his self and the external objects, between phantasy and reality; he mixes up the past with the present, he confuses himself with the analyst. All interpretations are distorted and misunderstood, and all normal communicative work comes to a halt. The analyst feels impotent, overwhelmed by the violence of the psychotic process.

There are two approaches to transference psychosis, both from the theoretic and the technical point of view. The first is that of Kernberg (1975), who emphasizes the clinical importance of transference psychosis and advises us to observe it attentively so as to enrich our genetic point of view. Kernberg considers transference psychosis as the potentially inevitable development of the relationship that borderline patients tend to establish with the therapist. It satisfies primitive and aggressive drives that operate against the transference. Thus the patient repeats the unconscious pathogenic object relationships of the past, and confusion arises, due to the lack of boundaries of the ego.

> Ego boundaries fail only in those areas in which projective identification and fusion with idealized objects take place, which is the case especially in the transference developments of these patients. This appears to be a fundamental reason why these patients develop a transference psychosis rather than a transference neurosis. [Kernberg, 1975, p. 34]

For this reason, according to Kernberg, the transference psychosis should be actively blocked by establishing rules or limits on the patient's aggressive behaviour in the course of analysis.

The second hypothesis is that advanced with great conviction and substantiated clinically by Rosenfeld. He refers specifically to transference psychosis in his work, "Notes on the Psychopathology and Psychoanalytic Treatment of Some Borderline Patients" (1978a), where he describes traumatized borderline patients in detail and differentiates them from others. The latter, Rosenfeld argues, have idealized their destructive narcissism, whereas patients with traumatic infantile experiences are dominated by confusional anxieties and by psychological splitting processes. From the clinical point of view the most important element in these patients is the confusion between libidinal and aggressive aspects of the self and the inability to distinguish between the good and the bad aspects of the object. Also clinically relevant is the confusion deriving from the incapacity to distinguish between persecutory and depressive anxieties, between oral, anal, and genital impulses, between nipple and penis. In this last case, borderline patients present confusions of sexual identity.

The hypothesis formulated on transference psychosis by Rosenfeld is that these patients are unable to accept interpretations regarding the destructive aspects of their own self because of the presence of a very sadistic superego. I shall return later to this hypothesis and examine it in the light of my clinical material. When this kind of superego is projected into the analyst, a transference psychosis develops. The patient's anxiety has to do with the fear of disintegrating, of dying, of becoming completely mad, or of being driven mad by the analyst.

Rosenfeld's line of inquiry implies that the analyst should develop the ability to approach transference psychosis in a new way, not considering it merely as a threat of rupture. This outcome, which is certainly not desirable, need not be feared as inevitable, for, if understood on a deeper level, it may help to clarify the whole analytic process and provide a strong stimulus for a greater understanding of the patient and of his basic psychopathology.

I would now like to illustrate the development of transference psychosis in the case of my patient and to formulate some hypotheses on this evolution. I must first state that I am speaking of a patient who, from the very beginning, had been particularly difficult and, at the same time, highly stimulating. I had begun to see him in a new light when I was supervised by Dr Brenman in the course of a clinical seminar held at the Milanese Centre for Psychoanalysis. The transference psychosis, however, occurred some years after the end of the supervision and appeared as a total breakdown of our previous relationship. We were in the fifth year of analysis, when many of the difficulties and impasses seemed to me to have been overcome. The breakdown was particularly surprising because I believed that we were making satisfactory progress and that the patient's achievements, both in his external life and in analysis, had attained a certain stability.

I shall now report some data on the analysis preceding the psychotic episode and summarize the work carried out on the basis of the elements acquired during the supervision as well.

The patient, a man in his early thirties, was terrified by the idea that his homosexuality might become known and scorned, and this fear had made him avoid any homosexual experience. In fact, he had no sexual experiences at all. One of his greatest anxieties was connected with emotional, psychological, and physical contact or relations with women.

From the very beginning of analysis, he had been unable to provide sufficient information about his own childhood, and I reconstructed his history only gradually, in the course of the analysis, on the basis of the transference and inferentially from the analytic material. He was the third child, born when his mother was over 40, and there were already two elder sisters. As the patient was growing up, his mother became depressed and was increasingly absent from his life. When he was 12 years old, she committed suicide, but this fact had been concealed from him. The suicide had occurred away from home, in a little village near the patient's town; because of her depression the mother had been taken there to live with relatives. On a conscious level, the patient thought she had died suddenly, of natural causes.

During the analysis, he was for a long time quiet, unable to understand the nature of the psychic disturbances of his mother. In the first years of his life, he had developed an idealized, fusional relationship with her. He felt hostility, together with a real sense of disgust and physical repulsion for his father, who was often away from home and rather authoritarian.

He had never established any close relationship, particularly outside the family. Although he seemed to be a friendly person, his contacts with others were exclusively formal. His homosexual phantasies were far more secret and gratifying to him, and he held them essential for his very survival. His masturbation phantasies, centred on his own body or parts of it, induced in him an actual dreaming state, a special condition of pleasant withdrawal from the world.

I shall not dwell at length on the paternal transference, which developed with negative and persecutory aspects. Initially, I had assumed in the patient's eyes the characteristics of a sadistic, cold, indifferent homosexual, interested in the penis and in dominating him. I shall concentrate instead on his relationship with his mother; from a certain point onwards, and after the analytic work had made him fully conscious of her suicide, this was a source of psychotic experiences that were very difficult to navigate. This theme was to become central in the development of the transference psychosis.

At a certain point in the analysis he remembered that he, as a child, had withdrawn psychologically and also physically from his mother. He had refused, for long periods of time, to see her when, in her depressed condition, she would spend the whole day in her room. In analysis, the patient appeared lengthily involved in a struggle with superego accusations of having been unable to save his mother, and of being the only one responsible for her death. These accusations were often projected onto those around him, and this made the analysis of the situation more complicated. The trauma resulting from his mother's suicide had produced in him an image of a mother who had been unable to survive; this image was often confused with mine.

Just before any separation, the patient became domineering and intrusive, and as the analysis proceeded and developed, his anxiety focused on the fear that, when we were apart, I might have sexual intercourse—a thing he considered endangered my life. In these moments he was convinced that he must think of me constantly, as if to keep me alive, and that he was the only one who was looking after me. When, however, he realized that he was not the centre of the world or when the separations occurred, his experience of loneliness was total. His hatred for the frustrating aspects of the relationship was extremely violent, as were his persecution and guilt for the attacks he made on the absent object.

The oedipal experience manifested itself in these cases in crude and primitive forms, and identification with the depressed mother, who wished to die, was often his only reference model. The experience of the dead mother re-emerged again later, as a source of dread and persecution. The patient, in fact, would sometimes brusquely leave the session or become intensely frightened if I, in picking up or repeating his words, pronounced the word "mother". This same experience had occurred on other occasions, when I had pronounced the words "sexual intercourse".

I realize that, in my attempt to furnish a concise account of this analysis and in my occasional use of technical language, I am scarcely doing justice to the atmosphere, the complexity and involvement of the analytic relationship, or the fact that, despite my efforts and constant attention, the patient often seemed to end up by being more and more confused. But even in the most difficult moments, he manifested an intense attachment to me and to his analysis, based on the deep conviction and hope that in it lay his salvation.

This basic trust collapsed during the transference psychosis. The sessions were now dominated by his dread and deadly hatred for me. He became very hostile, critical, and verbally violent. After attacking me, he would order me to speak; but as soon as I intervened, he would interrupt and silence me, and his replies were extremely violent both in the expression he used and in his tone of voice. He told me that I was damaging him, that I was trying to change his mind, that I was a violent "communist" and he was frightened of me. When I pointed out the violence of his words, this only worsened the situation, as *it was not clear* in his mind *who was attacked and who was attacking.* However violent and terribly disturbing he was to me, it was also clear that he perceived me as a real threat for his physical and psychological integrity. At times, he would shout with exasperation that I had been tormenting him for 12 years (his mother had committed suicide when the patient was 12). I thus realized that he was actually experiencing me like an intruding mother who was trying to confuse him or drive him mad. It was clear that his aggression was a counter-reply towards an object felt to be destructive.

I tried to understand which past situation had been reactivated and thought it might be an infantile experience, which had been emerging in analysis for some time, and which must have been very traumatic. In his childhood, when his mother was distressed by her own fear of dying and of killing herself, and detached from reality and from the psychological experience of her child, she had used the patient to communicate to him her own death anxieties. She had often terrorized him with macabre stories about her death and about the wickedness of the step-mother who would take her place in the family, until the patient had refused point-blank to see her.

I also wondered what might have had a similar traumatizing and confusing effect on the patient in the analysis. I gradually began to refer, within myself, to a particular, fairly recent session in the course of which the patient, who worked in an office, had told me of his wish to help an elderly woman. There had been great contempt and challenge in his description of his colleagues, who had not been helpful to her and had laughed at her. I remembered that, in that session, I had taken up in words the patient's wish to help, but I had also emphasized his need to feel himself the only person able to offer help. On a deeper level, however, I had felt disturbed by what had appeared to me also—or, rather, merely—an exhibition of kindness on his part.

The patient now remembered the tone of my words in that session: he had felt frightened and threatened. He said that this had happened on other occasions, that I was a violent "communist". My calm was only superficial, like Czechoslovakia—apparently quiet, but with Russian tanks within.

I was aware that the patient was still speaking of his mother on this occasion: she was apparently calm and good, but then she had become violent and had committed suicide. From the patient's point of view, I had the cliché of the psychotic mother. I remembered that in one of my interpretations I had used the word "Nazi" with a negative meaning. "What do you have to say against Hitler?" he had shouted, "don't you know that he was maligned by Stalin about the business with the Jews?"

Sometimes he would be unable to come to his session and would write to me, saying that he would not return until I had changed my attitude towards him. Even when we succeeded in clarifying something in certain sessions, he would be confused when he returned, having drunk or taken drugs, and would refer to the previous sessions in delusional terms. On these occasions I felt powerless and, at the same time, very concerned about him.

At other times, however, he realized the delusional aspect of this dread of me and of his fear of dying. When he was calmer and more lucid, he could tell me how terrified he was at the thought of being unable to develop any personal life experience (in the patient's language, he would "never have any private property") and that he would be prevented in this by me, "a communist".

What distressed the patient was his inability to make use of destructive means against a threatening and devastating danger that terrified him. His fear of dying was expressed with the dread that the Russians, after invading Ethiopia and Afghanistan, would also invade America, and that the President of the United States could not use missiles to counterattack. Now I knew that something else, which had not been understood till then, had appeared in the transference. I began to think of "communism" as something that, in the patient's mind, belonged to his mother or to him and that it might be on this point that he was confused. There was something that frightened him, which he hated in himself and in me. This could explain his sense of dread and the fear of going mad and, consequently, the fury with which he fought against me and shouted at me.

At the same time, I became aware that in the session I referred to above I had not grasped the deeper aspect of the patient's communication. Now I realized how important it might be for him that I should grasp his ability to express, perhaps for the first time, feelings of solidarity and sympathy for the old, depressed woman (the elderly lady in his office). This should be extremely important, considering the contempt he had, so far, almost obstinately expressed for women (in particular for his mother) as "empty, needy, and whores". In his life he had always admired and, in fact, selected men who could possess and, at the same time, despise women. The desire to fuse with a man of this kind was another of the psychological aspects of his homosexuality. In the transference the attempt to set up this kind of perversion with me was one of the important aspects of the analytic relationship, on which I had been working. I had the impression that *my not having grasped this new aspect clearly might be devastating for the patient*, due to the difficulty he had had in reaching this position. He might have felt he was being thrown back, just as he was sorting out within himself the good aspect from the contemptuous one (the latter temporarily represented by his fellow employees, onto whom the contempt was projected). This might have been the reason I had turned into a totalitarian, dominating "communist", who prevented him from living and experiencing self-esteem. This, then, was the reason for the patient's bitter hatred. The same difficulty had probably arisen on other occasions as well, but till then he had been too afraid and unable to confront me with it. This made sense of the vindictive nature of his projections, his need to strike and beat me, to pay me back for all those times when he had felt picked on and attacked by me.

According to my hypothesis, therefore, any failures on my part in grasping his positive aspects, whenever they appeared, drove him violently towards a sado-masochistic relation: he became my masochistic victim, and I was put into the position of someone brought to account for his guilt and his sadism.

I worked with the patient in this direction and at this level, trying to reconnect and recognize these moments with him. The acknowledgement of these misunderstandings had a positive effect on him, and I must say that the patient felt progressively encouraged to re-examine *very far-off episodes* that had apparently passed by in silence.

I was, however, convinced that the situation was more complex and that we had to discover what made him so confused internally about his capabilities to live and experience self-esteem, and what it was that the patient hated so strongly in himself, or in his mother, and made him feel so persecuted. I directed my efforts towards *linking the pathological relationship with me to this area of internal confusion.*

As the patient regained his trust and as the atmosphere of tension and confusion relaxed, he gained more courage and began to speak to me of his "communism". In the patient's mind, a "communist" is someone who enters a house or a person to devastate or empty it. In these conditions, hunger and envy towards those who possess brings about an unbearable hatred; the state of deprivation feeds an irrepressible, destructive greed. The terrified patient was addressing this deprived and destructive self, confused with the depressed, suicidal mother, when he shouted at me: "You, De Masi, have you or haven't you two pennies to rub together?" He had a sadistic phantasy, which became progressively more conscious and available for working through: the "communist" entered the mother's body, removed her breasts, and attached them onto himself, confusing himself with her. He could only have for himself by killing; when he did this, Stalin immediately did the same with him. This seemed to be a key experience: the patient felt himself like the depressed mother and when the "communist" mother, depressed and hungry, addressed him, he felt threatened from inside. He would then draw the mother into a sexual relation and, during masturbatory excitement, he strangled her with his urethra (I mentioned earlier the importance of the body in the patient's phantasies).

Now we realized how unconsciously cruel was the relation with the internal depressed, sick mother, who turned to him, and why his sexuality had such terrifying, murderous connotations. The sadistic, murderous phantasies were, however, brought about by the terrible sensation of hunger or by the anxiety of being left to die. In the patient's mind, the internal depressed mother, empty and hungry, also kept herself alive with a voracious sexuality. In this state, the patient does not know whether the child or the mother, or both, are about to die, a prey to devastating voracities and impulses. The masturbation or homosexual fantasies (for example, of taking the penis to suck it or being penetrated anally), were based on intense oral anxieties and were a defence against his dread. It also became clearer that the patient had placed his own madness—the equivalent to the hated, avid, murderous self—in this external object he called "communism", which in the end contained and concealed very primitive and crude anxieties of mutual destruction.

The transference psychosis had brought out into the open how terrifying this object was for the patient, and I understood how terrible it must have been for him to be reached in this area. The patient feared that splitting and projection into the external object might no longer be possible for him and that this might result in a total confusion, with the risk that the destructive impulses be turned against himself and lead to suicide. The danger that the patient might commit suicide was very present and threatened him for the whole period when I was perceived as this wretched, envious, destructive mother, the "communist" who would not help him to live and who chose death, with whom he was confused. To fuse with this type of mother and commit suicide seemed the only solution. For reasons of space, however, I cannot here illustrate the emergence of this problem and its subsequent elaboration in the analytic relationship.

I would like to make some observations about this greedy, murderous self, which the patient defines as "communist". In the work I have already quoted, H. Rosenfeld (1979) describes in detail the basic anxieties of those borderline patients with traumatic infantile experiences. He observes that these patients are unable to accept interpretations on the destructive aspects of their own self because of the presence of a very sadistic superego. When this superego is projected into the analyst, a transference psychosis occurs.

I would like to observe that, in my experience, it is not so much the interpretation of the destructive aspects of the self that is intolerable and that triggers this process, as the interpretation that arises from a misunderstanding about the level and the position of the patient at that very moment. Until a murderous, guilty world—this sado-masochistic universe the patient considers and values as his only weapon for defence and survival—can be worked through and fully understood, the interpretation of the negative aspects of the self will be perceived by the patient as devastating or destructive. I fully agree with Rosenfeld on the character of the superego of these patients, and of my patient in particular, but I think that what is projected is not so much the superego as this greedy, murderous part, which, once projected, threatens the patient with madness and death from outside. This underlies the dread of dying or of being killed that these patients experience during transference psychosis.

I argue that projection is stimulated and acquires concreteness when the therapist fails to understand and distorts the meaning of a developmental experience. This may be equated with a destructive mother, who is envious of the well-being, mental growth, and generosity of the child. Furthermore—and this seems to me to be the most important element—projection becomes the only solution to free oneself of an intolerable guilt.

When we had succeeded in clarifying the situation, the patient addressed me in this way: "If you are a communist, De Masi, I will throw my communism at you and get free of it"—in other words, "if you don't recognize my good aspects, if you don't help me to distinguish them from the murderous parts, the guilt is intolerable. I free myself of this terrible, murderous relationship with my mother by throwing it inside you. You are the one who kills; you are Stalin, and Hitler is innocent!" What was really happening was that the projection had rid the patient of his guilt ("I'll throw communism back at you . . ."), but the relief was only momentary, and the patient was thrown back to greatest persecution and dread of dying. From this point of view, the transference psychosis appears to be a disastrous defence against guilt, which throws the patient into a confused, terrifying sadomasochistic relation, in which *he is totally identified with the sadistic superego and the analyst is identified with the murderous part*, which is feared, struck, and mercilessly beaten.

Once the transference psychosis had been overcome, the patient told me that when I had pointed out the aggression with which he addressed me, this had increased his confusion. Only now could he be aware that in reality he was not attacking me but was fighting against a part of himself that he hated, which was projected and confused with me. He continued, however, to hope to be helped to rid himself of the confusion and to take up contact with reality again. A healthy part of the patient had, in fact, remained alive, enabling him to continue to come to the sessions and to recognize the analyst as such; the same thing was possible for both of us. It was easier, after this, to work and to help him to separate himself from this intricate, confused experience of hunger and explosive hatred into which he was dragged.

As I said before, when the patient was seized by feelings of desperate hunger, he turned to the mother; at the same time, in his internal experience, the mother herself rushed towards him, threatening and voraciously taking him over. The confusion between himself and the depressed mother, between the mother and the analyst, the consequent hatred and the confusion between the voracious aspects and the desperate cries for help, had perhaps been the cause of misunderstandings in the attempts I made to help him clarify this problem. It was difficult, for example, to distinguish the relation of hatred and contempt for the depressed mother from the attacks made to defend himself, to separate and draw away from the danger of being taken over by the psychotic mother.

The attacks on the depressed, hungry mother expressed at the same time the hatred and contempt for the needy, hungry self (the "communist"). Internally, the patient did not know and was confused about what this overpowering, voracious request meant, as someone forced to intrude, empty, or steal in order to survive. An important moment in the analysis came when we could better understand this being forced to steal so as to survive by linking it to the fear of starving to death. This was the underlying factor in the confusion between the libidinal and aggressive aspects. For the patient, penetrating the object greedily seemed to be the only possibility, in phantasy, of receiving nourishment. The difficulty I had had in understanding his confused aspects at the right level had been experienced by the patient as a deliberate deprivation both by me and by a mother who makes him die because she wants everything for herself. At the same time, I also represented a depressed, resourceless mother, who did not understand him and was despised and attacked for this reason.

Rosenfeld (1978b) observed that borderline patients are all likely to have something in common—that is, disturbances relating to internal sources, but *more often to external sources*, which have impaired the normal elaboration of primitive anxieties, at the level of the paranoid–schizoid position. My experience with this patient bears out the importance of this observation. During this analysis, I became convinced that the original vicissitudes with his mother had been decisive for this patient and had constituted an impasse for a real working-through of his basic psychological experiences. I believe that before the transference psychosis and its elaboration, this nucleus could have been reactivated at any moment of particular difficulty, making the patient a prisoner of this experience. The transference psychosis, however, seemed to have occurred when the image of me, the analyst, overlapped with *the internal image of this pathological parent*, with which, up to that moment, *the patient himself had been confused.* Successively, the working-through consisted in recognizing what was the experience of confusion and hatred with the internal mother that had led to confusion about the external and internal reality in the relationship with me, and in understanding what had been the specific area of the pathological relationship with me.

It is also likely that a certain haste on my part in helping him may, at times, have activated the patient's anxieties about my ability to understand him and to accept his means of communicating the problem. This might also explain why he asked me, when he silenced me or did not come to the session, to give him the chance to have an analyst who would think things over properly before talking to him, one who was capable of assessing in greater depth the situation he was in. Bion has said that if a mother cannot tolerate the projection of suffering and confusion, the child will resort to continuous, increasingly violent projections. The violence with which the projection takes place deprives it of meaning, and a re-introjection of equal violence also occurs. The child then introjects an object that deprives him of any understanding and risks starving him to death.

I think that this is the dramatic fact that is reproduced in the transference psychosis, and that this is all the patient allows us to observe, even though not exactly as privileged observers, since we are not completely screened from the drama that is going on before our eyes.

I would like to go back, lastly, to the intensity of the relationship the patient had developed with me, which had increasingly assumed features of a new, real experience. I felt that the patient was turning to me to help him fill the empty spaces in the past. It also seemed that, for the first time, he was going through fundamental stages in his psychological evolution.

Related to this point is an episode of transference psychosis that reappeared, though in a milder form, in the very last period of analysis, when I once again became the "communist" to him. It was a brief episode, lasting only a few days, which the patient himself was able to understand and resolve. He had asked insistently to have the opportunity of meeting me and had begged me to dedicate part of my time outside analysis to him, to prove that I was like a friend or a father to him. I confess that I was somewhat disturbed, inwardly, by the re-emergence of these voracious requests. I thought I had already given him sufficient proof of my attachment and sympathy for him; I had worked with him to the utmost, and I was amazed, within myself, at the patient's inability to keep this point firmly in mind. In his work on understanding why I had again become the "communist" for him, the patient recognized that with one part of himself he had perceived my resistance to his requests, and this has meant that I was depriving him of the possibility of "thinking of me" as a parent. This was extremely important to him, in order to be hopeful about his possibility of psychological evolution even after the end of analysis. My partial refusal, he said, risked leading him back yet again to being forced to devour so as to survive, incapable of introjecting my image without the fear of being accused of stealing.

As I have said above, the patient I am describing, like other traumatized borderline patients, asks *the analyst to be that totally new experience*, with which he can live a new, real, and thus unknown experience, without which it is not possible to develop a symbolic experience. What he is continually exploring is the analyst's actual capacity to accept and keep him alive within himself, and this experience is the prerequisite for his personal growth and ability to symbolize. As long as the patient's mind had been dominated by greedy and destructive phantasies, any introjection of me or of the experience of the session was unconsciously equated to having destroyed or having stolen, and that made him feel guilty and persecuted. For the patient, the internal object and the external object could not exist simultaneously. Introjecting meant eating and destroying the external object. The patient made great progress when he realized that drinking milk did not imply destruction of the breast.

I am convinced that only the internal experience of an analyst who keeps him alive and who remains, in his turn, alive and thinking lessens the patient's need for and recourse to greedy phantasies of theft or to the compulsion to intrude inside the object in order to survive.

I believe that the patient I have described had developed a traumatic sensitivity to failures, even if temporary ones, of the analyst's capacity for mental containment. He feared the lack of a stable experience of this kind, and this seemed to endanger his chance of going on on his own towards an autonomous development, after the conclusion of the analytic relationship. I believe that the enormous psychological dependence that traumatized borderline patients develop in the transference and their intense demand to be understood may be explained by the extreme need they feel to free themselves and emerge from areas of confusion, which are unconsciously perceived as dangerous sources of madness.

* * *

I shall now briefly re-examine the problem of development and change in analysis. This is, of course, a complicated question that I consider related to the possibility of promoting a new experience relative to the old objects of the past. It is widely accepted that changes in analysis largely depend on the possibility of introjecting new objects, even if, as Brenman (1980) points out in his work, "The Value of Reconstruction in Adult Psychoanalysis", the old objects continue to live alongside the new and may re-emerge in moments of crisis. In some more serious patients, such as the one in question, the introjection of new experiences is often particularly difficult. Dominant delusional objects have been constructed in the course of the primitive intolerable experiences of dependence. Only when the overall experience of the analysis makes it possible for the patient to meet and face the old terrifying objects will he become convinced of the existence, the capacity, and the good quality of the new object. For the above patient, the delusional object had been built up through the masturbatory relation with his own body and its products. Sexualization and the confusion between penis and nipple—in the patient's words, "this ferocious deception between external food and my own body"—led him into repeated, complicated states of confusion, which had, as we have seen, the effect of reducing the analytic relationship to a situation of total incomprehensibility.

In the last period of the analysis, when change occurred and confusion came to an end, "the breakthrough into reality" enabled the unconscious equation between the patient's own genitals and the breast to be overcome. Then he realized that he had to "resymbolize everything" and confessed that, in order to understand the difference between masturbation and feeding, he had had to masturbate and drink milk at the same time. I would like here to quote the patient's own words, which are particularly expressive in describing the mental state that prevented him from experiencing reality as something with a life of its own. After the conclusion of the analysis, the patient wrote to me:

> *"I realize now that, in the past, I was like a man who, having denied the existence of light, considered himself blind before objects, which the light nevertheless illuminated. I have had to realize, unfortunately, that almost all outside life was not experienced by me as such, but like a film or the mirror of that film, which my mind projected onto the screen of my unconscious."*

Then the patient concluded:

> *"Unfortunately, the unconscious only feels and does not see, as eyes only see and do not feel. And since the unconscious does not have eyes of its own to see inside itself, into his phantasies, but can only feel, it transforms its internal images into external delusions and sees through eyes that internally it lacks."*

In the course of the analytic treatment, oscillations can be observed between the capacity for living new experiences and the re-emergence of the old delusional objects, which confuse the patient about the nature of his experience and lead him to lose contact with reality. These areas of confusion are likely to be projected into the analyst, and if the latter works through them incorrectly, this may generate a transference psychosis. In the case I have described, this was facilitated by temporary, but perhaps repeated, moments of non-receptivity on my part towards these psychopathological areas, while the patient was aware that his problems in these areas had to be overcome for his own psychological development to continue.

I fully agree with Rosenfeld that only the detailed analysis of psychotic transference makes it possible to re-establish the continuity of the analytic process. It is fundamental that the analyst live this experience together with his patient. Equally relevant is the analyst's ability to recognize and make good use of his own misunderstandings. This process helps the patient to introject an object that is not omnipotent and increases his trust in dependency and realistic reliance on the external object. As I have said previously, I think that it is just as important to seek out, beyond the analysis of the pathological inter-relationship of the analytic couple, those areas of internal confusion that underlie this process, which have distorted the development of a normal infantile dependency.

In this case it seemed to me that the introjection, the internal relation, and the confusion with a pathological parent were definitively conditioning the whole psychic organization and making every stage reached in analysis precarious. It was also important to discover and clarify with the patient what could have been the past experience that had warped and distorted the development of a normal infantile dependence.

The analysis of these borderline patients probably differs in certain important aspects from that of others, where the analyst's attention to splitting and projective mechanisms usually makes the patient aware of the split-off destructive aspects of his own personality and consequently activates reparation. I think that in certain borderline patients the analysis of the processes that lead to the confusion (between the self and the object or between parts of the self) is of primary importance. I argue that when this is lacking, the analysis, in particular of destructive aspects, runs the risk of being completely distorted in the patient's inner experience.

CHAPTER NINE

Cassandra:
a myth for hypochondria

Andreina Robutti

> *. . . by friends turned enemies,*
> *mocked without doubt in vain.*

Aeschylus, Agamemnon

Myth is a great collective dream, a creation unfolding meanings, which, like individual dreams—our private myths—can turn out to be a precious tool in the search for knowledge. Through the words of some patients, Cassandra slid into my consulting room and prompted thoughts on hypochondria, a rather enigmatic event. The brief appearances of the unbelieved seer in the accounts of mythologists and poets, together with psychoanalytic literature, have supported me in working through my patients vicissitudes and my own experience with them.

I think that the hypochondriac, like Cassandra, speaks about a truth that is never believed. I also think that this myth, which represents a painful series of insurmountable misunderstandings, tells us not only about a relational failure, but also about an internal fracture, a loss of contact with knowledge and with meaning. I shall now illustrate this hypothesis.

In myth, Cassandra is not always the disbelieved prophetess. This is how Homer sketches her in the Iliad:

> Neither was any other aware of them, whether man or fair-girdled woman; but in truth Cassandra, peer of golden Aphrodite, marked her dear father . . . and she had sight of that other lying on the bier in the waggon drawn of the mules. Thereat she uttered a shrill cry, and called throughout all the town: "Come ye, men and women of Troy, and behold Hector. . . ."
>
> So spoke she, nor was any man left there within the city, neither any woman, for upon all had come grief that might not be borne.

Here Cassandra is not foreseeing the future but is the only one who beholds a tragic event, which is then witnessed by all the others, so that pain and mourning are shared by all alike. Her experience is painfully human. The myth of the disbelieved prophetess is, on the contrary, the story of a curse. There are various versions of how Cassandra receives the gift of prophecy. I refer here to the best-known. Apollo, wishing to gain her favours, teaches Cassandra to foretell the future; but once she has learned the art, she refuses to yield to him. The angered god seeks revenge, but he cannot take his gift away, because gifts of the gods are inalienable. So he asks her for at least a kiss and, to pay her back for thwarting him, spits into her mouth, thus depriving her of the power to persuade (Apollodorus, Servius).

According to Dodds' interpretation (1951), the Greeks, in the passage from a civilization of shame to one of guilt, sought in a relationship with the divine a supernatural guarantee.

> But Greece had neither a Bible nor a Church; that is why Apollo, vicar on earth of the heavenly Father, came to fill the gap. . . . The crushing sense of human ignorance and human insecurity . . . would have been unendurable without the assurance that such an omniscient divine counsellor

could give, the assurance that behind the seeming chaos there was knowledge and purpose."(p. 75)

The prophetesses are the voice of the god, and Cassandra represents the fracture between man and god, the source of his meaning, of his knowledge, of his purpose.

Cassandra and the chorus

In the course of an analysis that has been going on for several years, a patient whose main symptom is hypochondriacal anxiety comes to a session in a state of hostile irritation. After a few comments on the insensitivity of his mother who does not have an empathic relationship with him and torments him with her own worries, he tells me that at this point he is at death's door. A whole combination of physical symptoms concerning circulation, kidneys, and intestines is definitely taking him to his grave. In fact. . . . and here there is a long and sententious description of how these symptoms are connected to others that he has been suffering from for some time. His explanations appear to me acrobatic, fantastic, and "unbelievable". I am particularly struck by the tone of the whole account. The patient appears to be saying that, as usual, I haven't understood a thing, and that I quite certainly won't give any credence to what he is saying. He suffers from a physical illness, which, although it is as clear as daylight, is disbelieved.

At this stage I lose track and find myself trying to show, in a placid and civil tone of voice, how the explanations that the patient has put forward have no anatomical basis. Under the impact of the implicit accusations I assume what I intend to be a reassuring attitude aimed at bringing him back to reason, and the patient, a bit perplexed, comments: "I don't know . . . of course my knowledge of medicine isn't up to yours, but . . . I am like Cassandra, who tells the truth and is never believed."

I follow Cassandra, and in my search for the sources of her myth I come across a dialogue that, born in the mind of a great poet, illustrates the unfolding of an incredible misunderstanding in a way that I certainly wouldn't be able to.

Cassandra, prisoner of the Greeks, reaches the palace of Agamemnon, where she "knows" she is going to be killed, together with the king.

CASSANDRA: *Apollo, Apollo!*
You of the roadside, my destroyer!
Ah, where have you brought me? To what house?

CHORUS: *To that of the Atreidae; if you do not understand this,*
I tell it you; and you shall not say that it is false.

CASSANDRA: *No, to a house that hates the gods, one that knows*
many sad tales of kindred murder, . . .
a slaughter-place for men, a place where the ground is
sprinkled.

CHORUS: *The stranger seems to have keen scent, like a hound,*
and she is on the track of those whose blood she will discover.

CASSANDRA: *Yes, for here are the witnesses that I believe.*
These are children weeping for their slaughter,
and for the roasted flesh their father ate.

CHORUS: *Indeed we had heard of your prophetic fame;*
but we seek no interpreters of the gods.

CASSANDRA: *O horror, what a plot is this?*
What is this great new agony?
A great evil is being plotted in this house,
unbearable for its friends, hard to remedy;
and protection stands far off.

CHORUS: *These prophecies I know not;*
but the others I recognized; for it is the talk of all the city.

CASSANDRA: *Ah, wretched one, will you accomplish this?*
The husband who shares your bed
you have washed in the bath, and . . . how shall I tell the
end?
For soon this shall be; and she stretches forth hand after
hand, reaching out.

CHORUS: *I do not yet understand; for now the riddles*
leave me perplexed at her obscure oracles.

The Chorus continues not to understand, while Cassandra describes with metaphoric images the "dream" in which she 'sees" Clytaemnestra kill Agamemnon. She foresees her own death and hints at Aegisthus' revenge of the house of Thyestes. Then she warns:

CASSANDRA: . . .
And if I fail to convince you of this, all is one; how can it be
otherwise?
The future will come; and soon you shall stand here
to pronounce me, in pity, a prophet who spoke all too true.

CHORUS: *Thyestes' feast upon his children's flesh*
I understand and shudder at, and fear possesses me
as I hear it truly told and not in images.
But when I hear the rest I lose the track and run off the path.

CASSANDRA: *I say you shall look on Agamemnon's end.*

CHORUS: *Unhappy one, lull your voice to utter no ill-omened*
word!

CASSANDRA: *But no healer stands by while this word is uttered!*

CHORUS: *No, if indeed it must be so; but may it not happen!*

CASSANDRA: *You utter prayers, but others are about the business*
of killing.

CHORUS: *Who is the man by whom this woeful deed is being*
brought about?

CASSANDRA: *Far, indeed, you have been thrown from the track of*
my oracles.

[Aeschylus, *Agamemnon*, 1085–95; 1239–52]

In the obtuseness of the Chorus I recognize myself and my resistance to understanding. Cassandra wonders in anguish: where has the god brought me? And the Chorus replies to the letter with "geographical" information and seems to be saying:

"Trust in me, in my adherence to reality." Cassandra replies that she trusts her dreams and her visions, but the Chorus refuses to listen: "We seek no interpreters of the gods." Cassandra quite clearly predicts the disasters that are about to occur there, in that house, and the Chorus replies that it does not understand the prophecy about the present danger, while it does recognize the allusion to the tragedy of Thyestes, tricked into eating his own murdered children. This often happens to us too. The tragedies that the patient has experienced in his past are easier to understand, while recent dramas, those that occur in the transference, can cloud our ability to understand. Is this the reason why I, too, do not understand, and I, too, seek no interpreters of the gods?

In a following session the patient brings the subject up again, and this time I manage to find a meaning for the symptoms he describes. I can see how they may represent a fracture in our communication, a lack of circulation of ideas between us, that may bring about "death" in the sense of emotional abandonment.

From what I have said so far, it may seem that the problem is to succeed in giving the symptom that is expressed somatically its symbolic and transference meaning. But I do not believe that this is enough. I believe, on the contrary, that the hypochondriacal symptom that appears in the transference is a warning and that it is not enough simply to interpret it. The important thing, in my opinion, is to stop and ask oneself *what happened earlier* (Nissim Momigliano, chapter one, this volume). I suspect that hypochondria situates itself on the thin edge between the possibility of making sense of one's own suffering and a total loss of sense. The somatic symptom, whether it be present or only predicted, is an indication that the mind cannot give a meaning to what is happening and is passing its suffering into the body. The hypochondriacal symptom that appears in the transference is, in other words, a warning that something is getting out of hand, that a communicational fracture has occurred and that the patient is getting lost. With his symptom he seems to be telling us: "You are no longer the one who can cure me. My body is ill, I need another doctor."

Another doctor

I imagine we all know how difficult it is to bear with a person who continually complains about so-called imaginary illnesses. It is difficult for the doctor, who continues to investigate the possibility of an organic illness that in fact does not exist and is continually confronted with the same problem. It is difficult for the analyst, who sees the patient "eluding" him, as it were. The hypochondriacal symptom interrupts communication. The patient says: "It's useless to go on with analysis. I've got cancer, and I'll soon die of it." Or: "You just go on interpreting, but can't you understand that I really am physically ill! You don't care, and I suppose that is logical. In fact, you can't do anything about it, it's not your business!" We feel stabbed in the back, powerless to act. Some patients leave us an opening. Leave your armchair, they say, and come here: look at me, touch me, get me to do some tests, give me some treatment. Or else, speak to my doctor, come to some agreement between you, consult each other, do something!

And I must, unfortunately, abandon my armchair and pay attention to what the patient is saying. However, listening is one thing, and understanding is another. Ideas, hypotheses, and unfortunately sometimes certainties, all to a large extent unconscious, are the very substance of that armchair the patient is asking me to leave. I have to abandon my interpretative stance and try to find out the point in time where something began not to work properly. I am obliged to find another point of view, and I do not always succeed, on looking back, in seeing where my thought and that of my patient have begun to diverge. All I can do is to place my trust in what the patient will go on presenting in the here and now of the session. But this is rather a challenge, as, I think, we all know.

The hypochondriac lives under the threat of a terrible reality that is always on the point of revealing itself. I suspect that this reality is a missing or defective encounter. This issue passes unnoticed at a conscious level but is dimly perceived unconsciously as a pervasive loss of sense. Such a reality is reactivated in analysis every time there is a lack of understanding within the analytic couple. Involving both parties at an unconscious level, this causes the patient to relive archaic experiences of breakdown, such as those so well described by Winnicott (1974) and by Green (1980) in his description of an early relationship with an object that goes on living and dying.

My hypothesis is that the hypochondriac suffers from the localization at body level of this hurtful relationship, of a misunderstanding that cannot be worked through. It is not so much a question of lack of communication on the part of the patient, as of the introjection of something that is unconsciously felt to be wrong or bad, and that is not available to be worked through. The harmful relationship locates itself in the body, and the "Other", the one who disappoints, soon disappears. His place is taken by a threatened and threatening body, which assumes the role of both the suffering subject—the threatened ego—and of the object that is causing pain and threatening death. Death, in the case of "imaginary illness", is what derives from lack of understanding: a loss of sense.

Psychoanalytic literature concerning hypochondria is extremely vast. I must limit myself here to a brief synthesis in which I will follow the particular train of thought that I have chosen: the oscillation between the absence and the giving of meaning in interpreting this symptom.

There is no meaning

In the course of his monumental work, Freud speaks relatively little about hypochondria, but the little he does say is a basis, albeit incomplete, for developments that were to take place long after him. He deals with the subject in his earliest writings (1895b [1894], 1895d [1893–95]), at a time when, as we learn from his letters to Fliess, he himself was experiencing this problem, which was causing him great anxiety. "It is painful for a medical man, who spends all the hours of the day struggling to gain understanding of the neuroses, not to know whether he is himself suffering from a reasonable or hypochondriacal depression. In such a situation one needs help" (Freud, 1887–1902, p. 82).

For Freud, hypochondria is an actual neurosis, and the hypochondriacal symptom cannot be interpreted symbolically; it has no hidden meaning but is, rather, the sign of something physical that is happening (the damming up of libido) that evades psychical working through. Therefore it cannot be analysed (1911c [1910], 1912f, 1918b [1914]). Freud always remained faithful to this idea, and many authors successively queried this stance. Richards (1981) believes that the structural theory, a later development relative to the last Freudian formulations on hypochondria, cannot fail to modify them, and that Freud himself would have agreed with this. Trying to find in Freud's work some backing—which, in fact, is non-existent—Richards recalls that Freud declared himself dissatisfied with his theories on hypochondria, as, for example, when he wrote to Ferenczi, saying, "I have always felt the obscurity in the question of hypochondria to be a disgraceful gap in our work" (Jones, 1953–57, p. 502). Evidently, however, Freud, who is often so exhaustive, bent on finding examples and explanations, continued to put up with this regrettable gap in the following years (and they were many). His concept of actual neurosis, which seemed at first so strange to me as to be almost incomprehensible, is nevertheless very interesting and has recently been taken up by those researchers who deal with psychosomatics (Barale, 1984).

The inner drama and the search for a meaning

Psychoanalysts feel lost without their symbols. Is this the reason why many later authors have not followed Freud along the path of actual neuroses? Many analysts interpret the hypochondriacal symptom according to the structural theory as the manifest result of a hidden conflict between the ego and other agencies (see Arlow & Brenner, 1964; Fenichel, 1945; Jones, 1923; Mack Brunswick, 1928; to mention only a few).

I think I can include Klein in this chapter on the search for a meaning, and it is, in fact, to her that I refer when I speak about "the inner drama", because Klein (1935) saw the hypochondriacal symptom as linked to the battle between the ego and its objects. It is the bad internal object that attacks the ego, in the persecutory variant, or attacks the good internal object, in the depressive variant. This Kleinian concept, which introduces us into a very humane and "meaningful" world of battling for someone or something is, I believe, at the root of a good deal of research (I could mention among the many: Munro, 1949, Bychowsky, 1953, Thorner, 1955) in which hypochondriacal symptoms are linked to the conflict between the individual and his internal objects. However, from this Kleinian concept there branched off, starting with H. Rosenfeld, another line of research that was to lead farther afield, even geographically.

Confusion and ambiguity

H. Rosenfeld (1950, 1958, 1963, 1964) follows up the idea of a battle between the individual and his objects, but holds that the most important term of the question is confusion. He describes patients who are not able to distinguish between libidinal and aggressive drives and between good and bad objects, patients who do not know whether these objects are damaged or hostile, whether they are to be treated or eliminated. In these conditions, the battle is too difficult. This confusion is situated in the body, where it is controlled by an attentive and desperate self-observation that Rosenfeld describes with extremely intelligent empathy.

After his first articles of the 1950s and 1960s, Rosenfeld takes the subject up again in his most recent book (1987b), where he identifies in hypochondria a battle between destructive and libidinal parts of the personality. In his latest works he underlines how important it is that the analyst should know how to face up to the destructive feelings that the patient projects into him.

A very interesting development of these ideas occurred in the 1960s in South America, where many authors, sometimes I think unknown one to another, worked on the concept of confusion in hypochondria. Carneiro Leão (1967, 1968, 1977) attempts to make a distinction between hypochondriacal and schizophrenic confusion. In the latter she sees a lack of distinction between the ego and the object, while in the former she identifies an "undifferentiated object"—that is, an object that is not recognizable as either good or bad. I shall return further to this idea, which seems particularly interesting to me. Other authors describe the impossibility to mourn where the relationship is that with an internal object that is neither alive nor dead (W. Baranger, 1961–62; Garbarino, 1963). Still more study the particular defence set up in hypochondria and describe, with the aid of clinical examples, the fantasy of a "cyst", a concrete expression of confusion. The cyst functions as a container for split parts of the self and the objects, variously intermingled. It is a locus of confused and painful material, confined to the body where it is controlled (Baranger et al., 1961–62; Freire de Garbarino, 1961–62; Nieto Grove, 1963, 1964; Muñoz & Baranger, 1964; Mendilaharsu, 1965).

In a paper of the same period, often quoted by South American colleagues, Meltzer (1964) speaks of the relationships between somatic delusions and the reintegration of split-off parts of the self. This paper ends with an important open question about the possible relationships between hypochondria, somatic delusions, psychosomatic illnesses, tics, stuttering, and so on.

The theme of confusion is developed in a particularly original way by another Argentinean, José Bleger (1963, 1966, 1970). I was initially struck by his description of a series of symptoms that I, too, had come across and found difficult to interpret. Bleger says that the surfacing of the "agglutinated nucleus" at levels that are dangerously close to consciousness is the cause of some of these phenomena. He holds that there is a primitive confusion between the self and the object, from which the individual only gradually differentiates himself, albeit incompletely; a smaller or larger part of the primitive indistinction is retained by each and everyone of us, and this is the psychotic part of ourselves that we all try to keep under control. This is the agglutinated nucleus that the hypochondriac

situates in his body, but by which he feels constantly threatened.

At this point, we can no longer speak about interior drama,
we are near to senselessness. Bleger recognizes his debt to
Klein and holds that his work is a continuation of hers. He
singles out a third position, in addition to the paranoid–schizoid and the depressive ones, which he calls "*glischro-carica*"
(from the Greek = gluey). This position concerns the primitive
indistinction I mentioned above. Therefore from this work there
emerges this "mysterious object", confused and confusing, the
source of unspeakable anxiety. When the agglutinated nucleus
threatens the sound part of the personality, strange phenomena are evoked: the subject starts, shudders, has sudden and
unaccountable illuminations, fears falling asleep, presents epi-
leptoid symptoms, and so on. Hypochondriacal anxiety attacks
very often appear as a sudden illumination, and in my experience the former symptoms are not unusual either. The Chorus'
words come to my mind again: *"Thyestes' feast upon his children's flesh I understand and shudder at. . . ."* Was this shudder the fleeting contact with something that is awesomely incomprehensible?

I think I can agree with Bleger that such an undiscrim-
inated and confused area exists within us all. I am not so sure,
however, that it is the "residue" of a more extensive situation of
primitive confusion; I am more prone to believe, on the contrary, that it might be the end-product of those amongst our
earliest relationships in which the search for clear and differen-
tiating answers was not adequately met (Di Chiara et al., 1985).

The search for the Other

Ferenczi (1919) takes up the Freudian discourse on hypochondria as an actual neurosis, but he does not stop at this. In the
complex fabric of psychoanalytic literature his work appears to
me as the beginning of a thread that runs through such authors as Anna Freud, Kohut, Winnicott, and others. In fact,

Ferenczi does not propose a different meta-psychological interpretation, but a different standpoint from which to observe things. He does not try to search for the hidden meaning of the hypochondriacal symptom, but looks for its origins. He sees hypochondria as the indication of a failure in the earliest relationships between the baby and his environment. In 1931, speaking about the particular trauma that is provoked by the loss of a significant relationship with parents, he says that "to be left deserted results in a split of personality. Part of the person adopts the role of father or mother in relation to the rest, thereby undoing, as it were, the fact of being deserted" (p. 406). And again: ". . . under the stress of imminent danger, part of the self splits off and becomes a psychical instance self-observing. . . ." This can become a tendency to help others or "remain arrested in self-observation and hypochondria" (p. 138). Further on Ferenczi points out that the worst situation occurs when the child is aware of a trauma and tries to let adults know about it, but they "assert that nothing has happened" (p. 138). Cassandra, to my mind, becomes the "mythical Cassandra" not when she shares the grief for Hector's death with the Trojans, but when she reveals misfortunes and is not believed. These theories of Ferenczi's introduce the problem of a *negative and unshared experience* as a traumatic factor that is particularly meaningless and destructive.

This idea is again to be found in that lovely short paper by Anna Freud (1952) in which she describes the drama of the so-called "narcissistic" child who is over-attentive to his own health only because there is no one else to take care of it for him. These are all ideas that will later tie up both with the fundamental work of Bion (1963) and the concept of a mother lending, as it were, the baby her alpha function, and with Winnicott's (1971) thoughts on the transitional area, which are too well known to us all for me to go over them here. I will instead recall a paper by Castets and Van der Stegen (1981), who consider the hypochondriac's spasmodic request for medical tests as an attempt to catch the other person's eye as a substitute for other eyes that have not seen him and therefore have been of no help towards the integration of his personality.

These authors say more or less the same thing, often in very different ways. If the Other, who understands and confirms our being with his care, his attention, and his intelligence, is missing, then we cannot build up a reliable image of ourselves, and our relationship with our body, the first party of the mind and interface with the world, will show the signs of a defective experience.

Missing encounters and loss of meaning

The presence of the Other is a fundamental element in Kohut's theories. As with Bleger, there is no specific work on hypochondria, but Kohut mentions it in several instances in his writings. He dealt with that particular area of human relations in which the first relationships between the individual and his objects are characterized by absolute dependence and, at the same time, by the need to recognize and tolerate separation. I think that this paradoxical need is well represented by Kohut's term "selfobject": the need for unity and dependence and at the same time for discrimination and detachment.

Kohut locates hypochondria at a precise moment in the history of relationships between the self and its objects. A series of experiences with selfobjects that are insufficiently empathic and therefore too often traumatic and destructuring produce a defective self, which tends to go to pieces when it loses its narcissistic unity with the idealized selfobject (in analysis with total understanding on the part of the analyst). Hypochondria makes its appearance at this point as a sign that something terrible is happening: the loss of self-cohesion and, consequently, the loss of one's own meaning—moreover, of one's own existence as an individual (1971, 1977, 1984). Therefore Kohut places hypochondria at a precise point of narcissistic regression: the point where the self is going to pieces under the impact of traumatic factors. According to him, the next step will be psychosomatic illness.

Falling back into the body:
Cassandra and the Wooden Horse

For many authors psychosomatic illness is tied up with a lack of symbolization. The ability to create symbolic structures is the fundamental human means by which we face up to absence and loss. Probably this is a potentially inborn capability, but it needs to be reactivated, and for this to occur it is indispensable that there be another human being and a human environment prepared to accept the loss of an ideal, magic unity.

Psychosomatic illness can be seen as a kind of adaptation to life's difficulties that is adopted when a more creative symbolic adaptation is not available. It is, however, one of the least efficient forms of adaptation inasmuch as it is often detrimental to the body—the least suitable means for satisfying a desire for life (McDougall, 1974).

I cannot venture into the vast field of psychoanalytic research on psychosomatics. However, I would just like to underline how all those responses to difficulties that include the use of phantasy, the creation of monsters, or the production of some sort of mental pain are more humane that the somatic choice. McDougall says wittily that "in the long run it is better to be mad than dead" (1974, p. 450). I think that on the whole she is quite right.

In hypochondria the appearance of somatic anxiety, incorrectly considered as "imaginary illness", tends to obliterate, in the patient as well as in the analyst, the space for imagination. Hypochondria is situated where the "mysterious leap from the mind to the body" takes place, and in my opinion it can be taken to be *the moment in which the search for a shared meaning is interrupted and fear of illness intervenes to signal that what cannot be understood is falling back into the body.* A clinical vignette may help to illustrate what I have been saying, though it is just an example, certainly not a proof.

We are going through a period in which work between the patient and myself is proceeding quite peacefully. During a session two people of opposite characteristics appear: one represents the arrogance of success, the other depressed and destructive marginalization. The patient feels that he is "between the two", with the task of making peace or at least of creating a link. Following him up, in my interpretations I try to analyse these contrasting aspects of his, but I re-propose things that have already been said. I feel calm, but I should not be, because this division between the strong and the weak, between the sadistic and the masochistic, is a worrying element in someone who, like this patient, tends to be disparaging towards anyone who expresses dependence. The fact that he now feels that he is "between the two" is something new, to which I do not pay sufficient attention.

The following day the patient tells me that in the previous session he had felt me a bit like "someone who is explaining" and tells me a dream in which a very ferocious animal abruptly kills another animal defined as "normal", which cannot defend itself. I do not take the comment about "someone who is explaining" very seriously, while the dream does not seem clear and triggers off in me only rather generic thoughts, which the patient confirms. The atmosphere of the session continues to appear as one of collaboration and friendliness. Suddenly, however, as if by chance, the following association emerges: "I was at home, with my wife and my children; we were playing. I was thinking how my life had changed for the better. And then I suddenly thought, I don't know why: well, here I am, I might get cancer and that would be the end of all this." I fail to understand at that precise moment, but this hypochondriacal apprehension puts me on the alert.

The patient comes to the following session with a headache. He feels confused and tells me about his difficulties in preparing for an examination. He recalls a similar situation in the past, when he had passed another exam by cheating, and he thinks about his mother who had helped him to cheat, and was even in favour of it since she believed that the fact that he might have to face up to any difficulty was "unthinkable". Then it occurs to me that behind my "explanations" there may have been an inability or refusal to accept something new, and that the patient could have felt that I was not sufficiently on his side at a time when he was about to face up to the more mature, new, and difficult situation of placing himself between two opposing tendencies. A mother who was too affectionately overbearing was ambushing him, ready to deny his capability to grow up and colluding with his boundless arrogance, thus giving rise to an ambiguous and confused situation in which, in fact, the "normal" child is devoured and killed.

What is cancer here? In my opinion it is a danger *signal*, which may signify destructive "glutination" or weakness of a self that is breaking down, or whatever else, but to which, in my mind, it is wiser *not* to attribute a meaning. What *should* be sought and interpreted is what happened earlier. The meaning had appeared in the account of an experience of life, it had been re-proposed and inadequately understood in the dream, and therefore it had become a hypochondriacal anxiety (cancer) and a psychosomatic symptom (headache).

I think that it would be an excessive generalization to hold that every hypochondriacal symptom that appears during the course of analysis has its origin in a failure of communication between patient and analyst. The patient is also living out his own life, and there will be many events that may be traumatic for him. Nevertheless it seems to me useful to bear in mind that there can be a defective understanding, since this is a delicate moment, a challenge for analytic working-through.

When faced with a patient who says: "That's it, this time I know I have such-and-such an illness, even my doctor is worried . . ." and so on, my reaction can be bored ("Here we go again") or scared ("This time it's true")—that is, I can take on one or the other of the two roles of the myth. The Trojans see a fine wooden horse outside the walls of their city. They do not suspect any danger. Cassandra warns them: be careful, the enemy is inside. But nobody believes her. Both the patient and the analyst can be either Cassandra or the Trojans, who demonstrate an incredible lack of imagination. Somatic anxiety, when it appears, is something concrete that impedes imaginative thinking. In the first clinical example in this chapter, I am the one who loses the ability to phantasize and sticks to anatomy. In the second case, the idea of cancer interrupts the patient's game. Once entangled in the myth, the roles become fixed. Symbolic interpretations of the symptom are rarely helpful; moreover, patients often refuse them. I do not agree with those who hold with the metaphoric value of hypochondriacal imagery and compare it to what is generated in dreams (Hillmann, 1975). Dreaming is something else, and first of all it involves sleeping (and therefore being able to feel trust). On the other hand, I believe that when the "Cassandra situation" occurs it is better to stop and think and try to return to the point of fracture.

Friends turned enemies

Cassandra, as we have seen, is condemned by her refusal to have intercourse with the god. She is the one who refuses—the myth does not tell us why. It does, however, tell us about Apollo's reaction: he is enraged, vindictive, and violent. I hope that I have not given the impression so far that it is only the analyst who "errs", does not understand, and has to correct his mistakes. Cassandra refuses a relationship, and our patients do the same, introducing the somatic symptom as something that no longer has anything to do either with our interpretative ability or with theirs. I should like to pause a while at this initial part of Cassandra's story, because it is important. At the origin of what happens there is something that is not clear—a "why?" without an answer.

The idea that our troubles all stem from defects in interpersonal communication is very popular in psychoanalysis today, but in itself it does not explain a specific symptom, or, rather, a particular way of expressing mental pain. It is an interpretation of events that may serve as an approach to all mental pathologies, from neurosis to psychosis, psychosomatic illness, and so forth. It is an all-embracing "explanation" that runs the risk of being far too general. On the other hand, the most difficult thing of all is to succeed in understanding why someone reacts in one way rather than in another.

I am convinced that *there is* a particular emotional pattern in the hypochondriacal patient, and what I have to do now is to make clear what type of patient I have in mind. So far, I have spoken about the hypochondriacal symptom that appears in the transference, but now I wish to explain that I am referring to the so-called chronic hypochondriac and leaving aside, for the moment, other hypochondriacal symptoms, those that accompany more explicitly neurotic situations (and tend to become manifest during periods of change) and those that are characteristic of the beginning of a psychosis.

If it is true, as I suggest, that the conviction of having a physical illness that cannot be demonstrated is a symptom that reveals a very vast and profound communication breakdown, then it is also true that this breakdown is expressed in chronic hypochondria in this and in no other way. I would like to know why this is so, but I have not reached this stage yet, although psychoanalytic literature has given me some useful hints.

H. Rosenfeld (1964) describes what seems to happen more or less like this: the patient has a confusion within him that, in analysis, is projected into the analyst and then *rapidly* reprojected into his own body. A similar mechanism is described by D. Rosenfeld (1983, 1984) and by Mancia (1985, 1987). The latter speaks in clear terms about a defect in projective identification. Therefore we are supposed to have here a basic communication defect, in which the patient's relationship with the other person is immediately abandoned and seems to be substituted by a "narcissistic" relationship with his own body.

Nevertheless, the hypochondriac is a person who never stops trying to communicate. We all know how insistent these persons are and how "unbearable" they become when they continually re-propose their anxieties about their health, not only to their analysts, but also to their friends and doctors. The defect is not, therefore, to be found in communication or in projective identification. To my mind the problem concerns *the moment of introjection*. In the analytic relationship the hypochondriacal symptom reappears unexpectedly, and I have suggested that the analyst should avoid trying to interpret its symbolic meaning, but should stop, turn back, and look to see where there has been a defective response on his part. So, my hypothesis is that a response that was not clear and was insufficiently worked through is taken in by the patient as it stands. The fact that the patient is unable to understand whether what he is taking in is good or bad for him should be added to this defective working-through. The patient's difficulty in working through occurs at the introjective level. All this goes on without the patient or the analyst being aware of it.

Carneiro Leão's idea that the hypochondriacal patient is dealing with an internal object whose goodness or badness he ignores seems very pertinent here. The patient's inner world probably already contains this type of object, and the responses that have not been sufficiently elaborated by the analyst are taken in as elements with the same confused and confusing quality. I recall a patient who spoke to me about a very well-known doctor with a strange name: in one language his name meant love, in another it meant death: two faces of the same coin with no space for nuances or differences between the two . . . friend turned enemy . . . !

Cassandra shuns a sexual act with the god. Why? We do not know. What is certain is that she shuns taking something into herself. This part of the myth might refer to the problem of introjection. What sort of past experience might make working through what is introjected so difficult? I admit that I cannot say; nevertheless, I think that a useful image may be the one described by Green (1980) in his fine paper, "The Dead Mother". The dead mother is the one who is subjected to unexpected depressions and suddenly and completely shuns emotional contact, even if, apparently, she remains alive in the external world: a living mother who becomes a dead mother; an inexplicable *volte-face*. It might be a relationship with an object of this type that the uncertainties and lack of understanding of the analyst reactivates in the transference.

I do not know whether this is really how things stand, but this image has often helped me in my work. And I think that it can be useful for these patients to be able to introject, and place alongside the object that inexplicably changes face, an analyst who *is trying to understand*, to discriminate and work through. For this reason I believe that an analysis of our misunderstandings can be of great help to the patient.

The Flesh is made Word

Cassandra refuses the god, and the patient, who, after years of reciprocal effort, misses a session because he absolutely *has* to have an urgent X-ray, without even considering the idea of giving his symptom a mental and relational meaning, does as Cassandra does. I can discuss this with him, and I think that it is important to do so, because this is the very intimate fracture that I remarked on at the beginning of this chapter. But there is something else I have to do, too. We feel betrayed by a patient who shuns us. What makes us feel most deeply frustrated is the almost disparaging refusal of what we have personally put into the relationship, be it right or wrong. Apollo spitting in the mouth of the chosen one who refuses him represents a particular type of revenge and seems to me to be a significant and crude representation of violent and non-communicating analyst-to-patient projective identification (Di Chiara, chapter four, this volume; Ferro, 1987), when the analyst imposes his ideas without even attempting to reconsider them and re-establish a "peace" that would make it easier for both parties to understand each other. This latter is the type of communication that can give birth to that shared meaning that allows the "Flesh to be made Word"—as a patient's amazing slip of the tongue suggested.

I think that the various ideas expressed in the literature on hypochondria basically all have something in common, even if they are at times in apparent contrast.

1. The patient defends himself from *a bad object*, as Klein and her followers put it. In this object we can see the result of the original defective relationship that is continually represented in the patient's internal world and reactivated in the transference.

2. The patient is *confused* within himself (H. Rosenfeld, Bleger) but this confusion, to my mind, may be the outcome of a relationship in which there is a lack of communication and where meaning is not made clearer.

3. The patient rapidly tries to free himself of this defective relationship by *limiting and controlling it within his body* (Mancia) and often tries to free himself of it in phantasy, and unfortunately sometimes in reality too, seeking diagnoses that "exclude" an illness or actually asking for operations or even attempting suicide (D. Rosenfeld). Personally, I believe that this "limiting within the body" is preceded by a defective introjection.

4. By falling back into the body, the defective relationship *loses all sense* and simply remains the non-evidenced and disbelieved sign of the relational fracture that occurred beforehand.

5. At this point the hypochondriacal situation comes close to a *psychosomatic* evolution (that real organic damage of which Freud speaks)—an eventuality at which some authors hint (Meotti, 1982; D. Rosenfeld, 1983, 1984; Meltzer, 1964), but on which it would be interesting to do some more specific follow-up research.

I admit that this synthesis may seem arbitrary. In fact, its main aim is to find the common thread that binds together a whole series of writings by authors to whom I feel indebted. They have provided invaluable material that, if studied directly by others, may lead to conclusions that are different from mine.

Protest and hope

The hypochondriac, like Cassandra, tortures himself, his relatives and friends, and also his analyst, with his continual predictions of death. I think that this should be considered as a positive sign and it reminds me of an excellent passage from Gide's "Philoctète".

During the voyage to Troy, Philoctetes, suffering from an incurable wound, is abandoned on a desert island because his lamenting and the stench of his wound disturbs his companions. Years later Ulysses goes back to look for him, because he wants to lay his hands on Philoctetes' infallible bow. He realizes that when Philoctetes is left on his own, he no longer laments. He asks him the reason for this, and Philoctetes says, "I stopped lamenting, on realizing that there were no ears to hear . . .". Then Ulysses says cynically: "Why did you not stop lamenting earlier, Philoctetes? We would have kept you with us." The hero replies: "I could not, Ulysses. In the midst of others, my silence would have been a lie."

So, for the patient his laments are a sign that the others are still there and that there still exists the possibility of making contact. They are, after all, a sign of hope, and this seems to me to be important. Hypochondria is a challenge, both for medicine and for psychoanalysis, since, by its very nature, it shuns both of them. However, it does not cut itself off completely; it goes on and on relentlessly protesting, it does not want to give in.

NOTE

1. I am grateful to Dina Vallino Macciò for having helped me to clarify this point.

REFERENCES

Abraham, K. (1919). A particular form of neurotic resistance against the psycho-analytic method. In: *Selected Papers on Psycho-Analysis*. London: Hogarth Press, 1973. [Reprinted London: Karnac Books, 1979.]

Accerboni, A. M. (Ed.) (1985). *Atti del convegno "La Cultura Psico-analitica": Trieste, 5–8 December 1985*. Porderone: Studio Tesi.

Aeschylus. *Agamemnon* (translated by H. Lloyd-Jones). Englewood Cliffs, NJ: Prentice Hall, 1970.

Albarella, C., & Donadio, M. (1986). *Il Controtransfert*. Naples: Liguori.

Alvarez, A. (1983). Problems in the use of counter-transference: Getting it across. *J. Child Psychother., 9*: 7–23.

_____ (1988). "Beyond the unpleasure principle: Some preconditions for thinking through play". Read at the Clinica Neuropsichiatrica Infantile, Turin.

Amati Mehler, J., Argentieri, S., Batini, M., Bellanova, P., Calvesi, A., Cargnelutti, E., De Lauro, L., Giannitelli, S., Giordanelli, L., Merendino, R., Paulin, P., Tappa, G., & Vergine, A. (1981). Formazione della coppia analitica e identità dello psicoanalista. *Rivista di Psicoanalisi, 27*: 99–121.

Ammanniti, M., & Dazzi, N. (Eds.) (1990). *Affetti. Natura e Sviluppo delle Relazioni Interpersonali.* Bari: Laterza.

Apollodorus. *The Library* (translated by J. G. Frazer). Chicago: Harvard University Press; London: W. Heineman, 1929.

Arlow, J. A., & Brenner C. (1964). The psychopathology of the psychoses. In: *Psychoanalytic Concepts and the Structural Theory.* New York: International Universities Press.

Arrigoni, M. (1987). La reazione terapeutica negativa. *Rivista di Psicoanalisi, 33*: 235–253.

Artoni Schlesinger, C. (1989). On *Metroide. Rivista di Psicoanalisi, 35*: 140–168.

Asch, S. (1976). Varieties of negative therapeutic reactions and problems of technique. *Journal of the American Psychoanalytical Association, 24*: 383–407.

Aulagnier, P. (1979). *Les destins du plaisir.* Paris: Presses Universitaires de France.

Bakan, D. (1958). *Sigmund Freud and the Jewish Mystical Tradition.* London: Bailey Bros. & Swinfen, 1965.

Balint, M. (1968). *The Basic Fault. Therapeutic Aspects of Regression.* London: Tavistock.

Barale, F. (1984). Teorie psicosomatiche e relazione terapeutica. Dalle "fantasie inconscie" e dagli "equivalenti di angoscia" al problema della integrazione psicosomatica. In: M. Sgarro (Ed.), *L'approccio e la diagnosi nella prospettiva psicosomatica.* Milan: Franco Angeli.

_____ (1990). Reflections on Freud's *Moses.* (Trauma and history from the last Freud). *Rivista di Psicoanalisi, 36*: 896–920.

Barale, F., & Ferro A. (1987). Sofferenza mentale dell'analista e sogni di controtransfert. *Rivista di Psicoanalisi, 33*: 219–233.

Baranger, M., & Baranger W. (1961–62). La situación analitica como campo dinamico. *Revista Uruguaya de Psicoanálisis, 4* (3–54). Also in: M. Baranger & W. Baranger, *Problemas del Campo Psicoanalitico.* Buenos Aires: Kargieman, 1969.

_____ (1969). *Problemas del Campo Psicoanalitico.* Buenos Aires: Kargieman.

Baranger, M., Baranger, W., Fernandes, A., de Garbarino, M. F., de Mondilaharsu, S. A., & Nieto, M. (1961–62). Mecanismos hipocondriacos "normales" en el desarrollo femenino. *Revista Uruguaya de Psicoanálisis, 3*: 3–54.

Baranger, M., Baranger, W., & Mom, J. M. (1983). Process and non-process in analytic work. *International Journal of Psycho-Analysis, 64*: 1–15.

Baranger, M., Baranger, W., & Mom, J. M. (1988). The infantile psychic trauma from us to Freud: Pure trauma, retroactivity and reconstruction. *International Journal of Psycho-Analysis, 69*: 113–128.

Baranger, W. (1961–62). El muerto-vivo: Estructura de los objetos en el duelo y en los estados depresivos. *Revista de Psicoanálisis, 4*: 586–603.

Berry, N. (1978). "De l'interprétation au narcissisme du psychanalyste." Second EPF Congress, Estoril.

Bettelheim, B. (1982). *Freud and Man's Soul.* New York: Alfred A. Knopf.

Bezoari, M., & Ferro, A. (1989). Listening, interpretations and transformative functions in the analytic dialogue. *Rivista di Psicoanalisi, 35*: 1014–1050.

Bick, E. (1968). The experience of the skin in early object-relations. *International Journal of Psycho-Analysis, 49*: 484–486.

Bion, F. (Ed.) (1980). *Bion in New York and São Paulo.* Perthshire: Clunie Press.

Bion, W. R. (1962a). *Learning from Experience.* London: Heinemann. [Reprinted London: Karnac Books, 1984.]

_____ (1962b). A theory of thinking. In: W. R. Bion, *Second Thoughts.* London: Heinemann, 1967. [Reprinted London: Karnac Books, 1984.]

_____ (1963). *Elements of Psychoanalysis.* London: Heinemann. [Reprinted London: Karnac Books, 1984.]

_____ (1967a). *Second Thoughts.* London: Heinemann. [Reprinted London: Karnac Books, 1984.]

_____ (1967b). Memory and desire. *The Psychoanalytic Forum, II, 3.*

_____ (1970). *Attention and Interpretation.* London: Tavistock. [Reprinted London: Karnac Books, 1984.]

_____ (1973). *Bion's Brazilian Lectures, 1.* Rio de Janeiro: Imago. Also in: W. R. Bion, *Brazilian Lectures. 1973 São Paulo; 1974 Rio de Janeiro/São Paulo.* London: Karnac Books, 1990.

_____ (1978). *Four Discussions with W. R. Bion.* Perthshire: Clunie Press.

_____ (1987). *Clinical Seminars and Four Papers.* Abingdon: Fleetwood Press.

Bion Talamo, P. (1989). Commento a "Cogitations" di W. R. Bion. *Gruppo e Funzione Analitica, 3*: 7–14.

Bleger, J. (1958). *Psicoanálisis y Dialectica Materialista.* Buenos Aires: Paidós.

_____ (1963). *Psicologia de la Conducta.* Buenos Aires: Paidós.

_____ (1966). *Psicohigiene y Psicologia Istitucional.* Buenos Aires: Paidós.

_____ (1967). *Simbiosis y Ambigüedad.* Buenos Aires: Paidós.

_____ (1970). El concepto de psicosis. *Revista de Psicoanálisis, 28*: 5–23.

Bollas, C. (1987). *The Shadow of the Object: Psychoanalysis of the Unthought.* London: Free Association Books.

Bolognini, S. (1990). Typical ways of functioning psychoanalytically. *Rivista di Psicoanalisi, 36*: 606–635.

Bonasia, E. (1988). Death instinct or fear of death: Research into the problem of death in psychoanalysis. *Rivista di Psicoanalisi, 34*: 272–314.

Bonfiglio, B. (1986). Sul dialogo analitico (note sulla comunicazione paziente–analista). *Rivista di Psicoanalisi, 32*: 231–247.

_____ (1987). Dall'essere "in uno" all'essere "uno" come percorso verso il contatto con le emozioni. *Rivista di Psicoanalisi, 33*: 463–481.

Bordi, S. (1978). Le basi intenzionali della coscienza morale. In: M. Mancia (Ed.), *Superio e Ideale dell'Io.* Milan: Il Formichiere.

_____ (1980). Relazione analitica e sviluppo cognitivo. *Rivista di Psicoanalisi, 26*: 161–181.

_____ (1985). Le prospettive teoriche della psicoanalisi contemporanea. *Rivista di Psicoanalisi, 31*: 437–450.

_____ (1989). Psychoanalytic technique: An historical survey of its development. *Rivista di Psicoanalisi, 35*: 546–614.

Bordi, S., Mattogno, M., & Muscetta, S. (1982). "Nuove conoscenze sulla prima infanzia: Implicazioni per la psicoanalisi" [[New findings on early infancy and their implications for psychoanalysis]. Read at the Fifth Congress of the Italian Psychoanalytical Society, Rome.

Brenman Pick, I. (1985). Working through in the countertransference. *International Journal of Psycho-Analysis, 66*: 157–167.

Brenman, E. (1978). "The narcissism of the analyst: Its effects in clinical practice." Second EPF Congress, Estoril.

_____ (1980). The value of reconstruction in adult psychoanalysis. *International Journal of Psycho-Analysis, 61*: 53–60.

Bychowski, G. (1953). The problem of latent psychosis. *Journal of the American Psychoanalytical Association, 1*: 484–503.

Calvesi, A., Cargnelutti, E., De Lauro, L., Giannitelli, S., & Paulin, P. (1981). La formazione della coppia analitica nelle analisi interrotte. In: J. Amati Mehler et al., "Formazione della coppia analitica e identità dello psicoanalista." *Rivista di Psicoanalisi, 27*: 99–121.

Carloni, G. (1979). Sofferenza psichica e vocazione terapeutica. In: G. Di Chiara (Ed.), *Itinerari della Psicoanalisi*, Turin: Loescher.

_____ (1984). Tatto, contatto e tattica. *Rivista di Psicoanalisi, 30*: 191–205.

Carloni, G., Meotti, A., Nobili, D., & Mantovani, M. C. (1981). Identità personale e professionale dello psicoanalista. *Rivista di Psicoanalisi, 27*: 123–164.

Carneiro Leão, I. (1967). Os processos de "splitting" do "self" e do objeto na hipocondría cronica. *Jornal Brasileiro de Psiquiatria, 16*: 17–61.

_____ (1968). Differenciação entre estado confusional hipocondríaco e estado confusional esquizofrênico. *Revista Brasileira de Psicanálise, 2*: 518–541.

_____ (1977). "Chronic hypochondria and hypochondriacal confusional state." Read at the Thirtieth IPA Congress, Jerusalem.

Castets, B., & Van der Stegen, J. (1981). Le déstin tragique de l'hypochondriaque. *Evolution Psychiatrique, 46*: 931–956.

Coltart, N. (1986). "Slouching towards Bethlehem" . . . or thinking the unthinkable in psychoanalysis. In: G. Kohn (Ed.), *The British School of Psychoanalysis: The Independent Tradition*. London: Free Association Books.

Cooper, A. M. (1985). Changes in psychoanalytic ideas: Transference interpretations. *Journal of the American Psychoanalytical Association, 35* (1986): 77–88.

Corrao, F. (1986a). Il concetto di campo come modello teorico. *Gruppo e Funzione Analitica, 7*: 9–21.

_____ (1986b). L'interpretazione psicoanalitica come fondazione di un campo ermeneutico e dei suoi funtori. In: *L'Interpretazione Psicoanalitica* (edited by the Società Italiana di Psicoanalisi di Gruppo). Rome: Bulzoni, 1987.

_____ (1986c). Il narrativo come categoria psicoanalitica. In: E. Morpurgo & V. Egidi (Eds.), *Psicoanalisi e Narrazione*. Ancona: Il Lavoro Editoriale, 1987.

218 REFERENCES

_____ (1989). Morphology and transformations of psychoanalytic models. *Rivista di Psicoanalisi, 35*: 512–544.

David, M. (1966). *La Psicoanalisi nella Cultura Italiana.* [Reprinted Turin: Bollati Boringhieri, 1990.]

De Simone Gaburri, G. (1982a). Il tempo dell'analisi fra sintomo e conoscenza. *Rivista di Psicoanalisi, 28*: 540–547.

_____ (1982b). Fantasmi di interminabilità e formazione del progetto nel processo psicoanalitico. In: G. Di Chiara (Ed.), *Itinerari della Psicoanalisi.* Turin: Loescher.

_____ (1985). On termination of analysis. *International Journal of Psycho-Analysis, 66*: 461–468.

_____ (1990). Further considerations on the conclusion of analysis. *Rivista di Psicoanalisi, 36*: 340–368.

Di Benedetto, A. (1985). Psicoanalisi e conoscenza estetica. In: A. M. Accerboni (Ed.), *Atti del Convegno "La Cultura Psicoanalitica": Trieste 5–8 December 1985.* Pordenone: Studio Tesi.

_____ (1991). Listening to the pre-verbal: The beginning of the affects. *Rivista di Psicoanalisi, 37*: 401–426.

Di Chiara, G. (1975). Narcisismo, onnipotenza, creatività. *Rivista di Psicoanalisi, 21*: 161–178.

_____ (1978). La separazione. *Rivista di Psicoanalisi, 24*: 258–269.

_____ (1985). Una prospettiva psicoanalitica del dopo Freud: Un posto per l'altro. *Rivista di Psicoanalisi, 31*: 451–461.

_____ (1990). Awe, autism and the defensive competence. *Rivista di Psicoanalisi, 36*: 440–456.

Di Chiara, G., Bogani, A., Bravi, G., Robutti, A., Viola, M., & Zanette, M. (1985). Preconcezione edipica e funzione psicoanalitica della mente. *Rivista di Psicoanalisi, 31*: 327–341.

Di Chiara, G., & Flegenheimer, F. (1985). Identificazione proiettiva. *Rivista di Psicoanalisi, 31*: 233–243.

Di Chiara, G., Meotti, F., De Simone Gaburri, G., Fusini Doddoli, M., Ciprandi, F., & Gaburri, E. (1981). Panel su "momenti perversi nel transfert". *Rivista di Psicoanalisi, 27*: 193–238.

Dodds, E. R. (1951). *The Greeks and the Irrational.* Berkeley & Los Angeles: University of California Press.

Etchegoyen, H. (1991). *The Fundamentals of Psychoanalytic Technique.* London: Karnac Books.

Fachinelli, E. (1983). *Claustrofilia.* Milan: Adelphi.

Fairbairn, W. R. D. (1952). *Psychoanalytic Studies of the Personality.* London: Routledge & Kegan Paul.

Fenichel, O. (1926). Identification. In: *Collected Papers of Otto Fenichel*. New York: Norton, 1953.

_____ (1945). *The Psycho-Analytic Theory of Neuroses*. New York: Norton.

Ferenczi, S. (1919). The psycho-analysis of a case of hysterical hypochondria. In: S. Ferenczi, *Further Contributions to the Theory and Technique of Psycho-Analysis*. London: Hogarth Press & The Institute of Psychoanalysis, 1969. [Reprinted London: Karnac Books, 1980.]

_____ (1928). The elasticity of psycho-analytic technique. In: S. Ferenczi, *Final Contributions to the Problems and Methods of Psycho-Analysis*. London: Hogarth Press, 1955. [Reprinted London: Karnac Books, 1980.]

_____ (1931). Child-analysis in the analysis of adults. In: *Final Contributions to the Problems and Methods of Psycho-Analysis*. London: Hogarth Press, 1955. [Reprinted London: Karnac Books, 1980.]

Ferro, A. (1985). Psicoanalisi e favole. *Rivista di Psicoanalisi, 31*: 216–230.

_____ (1987). "Il mondo alla rovescia". L'inversione del flusso delle identificazioni proiettive. *Rivista di Psicoanalisi, 23*: 59–77.

Fossi, G. (1985). Le narrative psicoanalitiche. In: A. M. Accerboni (Ed.), *Atti del Convegno "La Cultura Psicoanalitica": Trieste, 5–8 December, 1985*. Pordenone: Studio Tesi.

Freire de Garbarino, M. (1961–62). Disociación y confusión. Evolución del mecanismo disociativo y surgimiento de estados confusionales en el momento de la reientroyectión. *Revista Uruguaya de Psicoanálisis, 4*: 417–452.

Freud, A. (1952). The role of bodily illness in the mental life of children. *Psychoanalytic Study of the Child, 7*: 69–81. New York: International Universities Press.

Freud, S. (1887–1902). *The Origins of Psychoanalysis. Letters to Wilhem Fliess, Drafts and Notes*. London: Imago, 1954.

_____ (1895b [1894]). On the grounds for detaching a particular syndrome from neurasthenia under the description "anxiety neurosis". In: *S.E., 3*.

_____ (1895d [1893–95]) (with J. Breuer). *Studies on Hysteria*. In: *S.E., 2*.

_____ (1904a [1903]). Freud's psycho-analytic procedure. In: *S.E., 7*.

_____ (1905c). *Jokes and their Relation to the Unconscious.* In: *S.E., 8.*

_____ (1909d). Notes upon a case of obsessional neurosis. In: *S.E., 10.*

_____ (1910d). The future prospects of psycho-analytic therapy. In: *S.E., 11.*

_____ (1911c [1910]). Psycho-analytic notes on an autobiographical account of a case of paranoia (Dementia paranoides). In: *S.E., 12.*

_____ (1912b). The dynamics of transference. In: *S.E., 12.*

_____ (1912e). Recommendations to physicians practising psychoanalysis. In: *S.E., 12.*

_____ (1912f). Contributions to a discussion on masturbation. In: *S.E., 12.*

_____ (1913c). On beginning the treatment. In: *S.E., 12.*

_____ (1913j). The claims of psycho-analysis to scientific interest. In: *S.E., 13.*

_____ (1914c). On narcissism: An introduction. In: *S.E., 14.*

_____ (1914g). Remembering, repeating and working-through. In: *S.E., 12.*

_____ (1917e [1915]). Mourning and melancholia. In: *S.E., 14.*

_____ (1918b [1914]). From the history of an infantile neurosis. In: *S.E., 17.*

_____ (1921c). *Group Psychology and the Analysis of the Ego.* In: *S.E., 18.*

_____ (1923b). *The Ego and the Id.* In: *S.E., 19.*

_____ (1924c). The economic problem of masochism. In: *S.E., 19.*

_____ (1926d [1925]). *Inhibitions, Symptoms and Anxiety.* In: *S.E., 20.*

_____ (1930a). *Civilization and its Discontents.* In: *S.E., 21.*

_____ (1937c). Analysis terminable and interminable. In: *S.E., 23.*

_____ (1937d). Constructions in analysis. In: *S.E., 23.*

_____ (1951–1974). *The Standard Edition of the Complete Psychological Works of Sigmund Freud.* Translated from the German by James Strachey. London: Hogarth.

_____ (1955c [1920]). Memorandum on the electrical treatment of war neurotics. In: *S.E., 17.*

Gaburri, E. (1985). Narrazione e interpretazione: In: A. M. Accerboni (Ed.), *Atti del Convegno "La Cultura Psicoanalitica": Trieste, 5–8 December 1985.* Pordenone: Studio Tesi.

_____ (1986). Dal gemello immaginario al compagno segreto. *Rivista di Psicoanalisi, 32*: 509–520.

_____ (1987). Narrazione e interpretazione. In: E. Morpurgo, & V. Egidi (Eds.), *Psicoanalisi e Narrazione*. Ancona: Il Lavoro Editoriale.

_____ (1990). Coinvolgimento, personificazione, investimento affettivo [unpublished paper].

Gaburri, E., & De Simone Gaburri, G. (1976). Realtà psichica e setting psicoanalitico. *Rivista di Psicoanalisi, 22*: 191–205.

Gaburri, E., & Ferro, A. (1988). Gli sviluppi kleiniani e Bion. In: A. A. Semi (Ed.), *Trattato di Psicoanalisi*. Milan: Cortina.

Garbarino, H. (1963). Nacimiento, confusion y fobias. *Revista Uruguaya de Psicoanálisis, 5*: 251–266.

Generali Clements, L. (1982). Introduzione. Panel: "Gruppo di studio sulla relazione analitica: Tre anni di lavoro". *Rivista di Psicoanalisi, 28*: 193–206.

Generali Clements, L., & Mori Ferrara, G. (1980). "Correlazione fra la relazione analitica e la relazione madre-bambino" [Correlation between the analytical relationship and the mother–infant relation]. Read at the Fourth Congress of the Italian Psychoanalytical Society, Taormina.

Giannotti, A., & Grimaldi, S. (1987). Reazione terapeutica negativa. *Rivista di Psicoanalisi, 33*: 415–425.

Gide, A. (1912). Phyloctète–ou le traité des trois morales. In: A. Gide, *Le Retour de l'Enfant Prodigue*. Paris: Gallimard.

Gitelson, M. (1962). The curative factors in psychoanalysis. The first phase of psychoanalysis. *International Journal of Psycho-Analysis, 43*: 194–205.

Goethe, J. W. von, *Faust* (translated by Ph. Wayne). London: Penguin Books, 1949.

Green, A. (1977). Conceptions of affect. *International Journal of Psycho-Analysis, 58*: 129–156.

_____ (1980). The dead mother. In: *On Private Madness*. London: Hogarth Press, 1986.

Greenacre, P. (1950). General problems in acting-out. In: Ph. Greenacre, *Trauma, Growth and Personality*. London: Hogarth Press. [Reprinted London: Karnac Books, 1987.]

Grinberg, L. (1962). On a specific aspect of countertransference due to the patient's projective identification. *International Journal of Psycho-Analysis, 43*: 436–440.

_____ (1976). *Teoria de la Identificación*. Buenos Aires: Paidós.

_____ (1987). Il dolore mentale nella situazione analitica e nella clinica. *Rivista di Psicoanalisi*, *33*: 197–218.

_____ (1990). *The Goals of Psychoanalysis. Identification, Identity and Supervision*. London: Karnac Books.

Grinberg, L., Langer, M., & Rodrigué, E. (1968). *Psicoanálisis en las Americas*. Buenos Aires: Paidós.

Grunberger, B., & Chasseguet-Smirgel, J. (1978). "Le narcissisme de l'analyste. Une introduction" [The narcissism of the analyst: An introduction]. Second EPF Congress, Estoril.

Grunert, U. (1981). The negative therapeutic reaction as a reactivation of a disturbed process of separation in the transference. *Psycho-Analysis in Europe*, *16*: 5–19.

Guillaumin, J. (1989). La pulsion de mort, prothèse thèorique de l'impensé du contre-transfert dans la psychanalise? *Revue Française de Psychanalyse*, *2*: 592–618.

Harris, M. (1975). *Thinking About Infants and Young Children*. Perthshire: Clunie Press.

Hautmann, G. (1987a). Pensiero e sofferenza. *Rivista di Psicoanalisi*, *33*: 43–57.

Heimann, P. (1950). On counter-transference. *International Journal of Psycho-Analysis*, *31*: 81–84.

Heisenberg, W. (1930). *Physical Principles of Quantum Theory*. London: Dover.

Hillmann, J. (1975). *Re-Visioning Psychology*. New York: Harper & Row.

Homer. *The Iliad* (translated by A. T. Murray). Cambridge, MA: Harvard University Press, 1957.

Horkheimer, M. (1934). *Dämmerung. Notizen 1950 bis 1969*. Frankfurt am Main: S. Fisher Verlag, 1974.

Horney, K. (1936). The problem of the negative therapeutic reaction. *Psychoanalytc Quarterly*, *5*: 29–44.

Ibsen, H. (1867). *Peer Gynt* (translated by M. Meyer). London: Rupert Hart-Davis, 1963.

Jones, E. (1923). The nature of auto-suggestion. *International Journal of Psycho-Analysis*, *4*: 293–312.

_____ (1953–57). *Sigmund Freud: Life and Work. Vol. 2: The Years of Maturity 1901–1919*. London: Hogarth Press.

Joseph, B. (1978). Different types of anxiety and their handling in the analytic situation. *International Journal of Psycho-Analysis, 59*: 223–228.

Kafka, F. (1910–1923). *The Diaries of Franz Kafka* (edited by Max Brod; translated by J. Kresh, M. Greenberg, & H. Arent). London: Penguin Books, 1972.

Kernberg, O. (1975). *Borderline Conditions and Pathological Narcissism*. New York: Jason Aronson.

Klauber, J. (1980). Formulating interpretations in clinical psychoanalysis. In: J. Klauber, *Difficulties in the Analytic Encounter*. New York, London: Jason Aronson, 1982. [Reprinted London: Karnac Books, 1986.]

Klein, M. (1929). Personification in the play of children. *International Journal of Psycho-Analysis, 10*: 193–204. Also in: *Love, Guilt and Reparation and Other Works*. London: Hogarth Press, 1975.

_____ (1935). A contribution to the psychogenesis of manic-depressive states. *International Journal of Psycho-Analysis, 16*: 145–174.

_____ (1946). Notes on some schizoid mechanisms. *International Journal of Psycho-Analysis, 27*: 99–110. Also in: M. Klein, P. Heimann, S. Isaacs, & J. Riviere, *Developments in Psychoanalysis*. London: Hogarth Press, 1952. [Reprinted London: Karnac Books, 1989.]

_____ (1955a). *The Psychoanalytic Play Technique: Its History and Significance*. London: Hogarth Press.

_____ (1955b). On Identification. In: M. Klein, P. Heimann, & R. E. Money-Kyrle (Eds.), *New Directions in Psychoanalysis. The Significance of Infant Conflict in the Pattern of Adult Behaviour*. London: Tavistock. [Reprinted London: Karnac Books, 1985.]

_____ (1957). *Envy and Gratitude. A Study of Unconscious Sources*. London: Tavistock.

Kluzer, G. (1988). Latent foundational elements in the beginning of the psychoanalytic relationship. *Rivista di Psicoanalisi, 34*: 316–345.

Kohut, H. (1971). *The Analysis of the Self*. London: Hogarth Press.

_____ (1977). *The Restoration of the Self*. New York: International Universities Press.

_____ (1984). *How Does Analysis Cure?* Chicago: University of Chicago Press.

Langs, R. (1975). The patient's unconscious perception of the therapist's errors. In: P. L. Giovacchini (Ed.), *Tactics and Techniques in Psychoanalytic Therapy, Vol. II.* New York: Jason Aronson.

_____ (1980). The misalliance dimension in the case of the Rat Man. In: M. Kanzer & J. Glenn (Eds.), *Freud and His Patients.* New York: Jason Aronson.

_____ (1981). Modes of "cure" in psychoanalysis and psychoanalytic psychotherapy. *International Journal of Psycho-Analysis, 62:* 199–214.

_____ (1986). Diventare uno psicoanalista comunicativo. *Psicoterapia e Scienze Umane, 20:* 273–277.

Langs, R., & Stone, L. (1980). *The Therapeutic Experience and Its Setting: A Clinical Dialogue.* New York: Jason Aronson.

Laplanche, J., & Pontalis, J. B. (1967). *The Language of Psychoanalysis.* London: Hogarth Press. [Reprinted London: Karnac Books, 1988.]

Leonardi, P. (1976). Relazioni perverse tra gli oggetti interni e sessualità adulta. *Rivista di Psicoanalisi, 22:* 226–239.

_____ (1987). Pensiero, specificità degli oggetti e onniscienza. *Rivista di Psicoanalisi, 33:* 321–330.

Levi, D. L., & Sharff, D. E. (Issue Eds.) (1988). "The Intrapsychic and Interpersonal Dimension: An Unresolved Dilemma." *Psychoanalytic Inquiry, 8* (4).

Limentani, A. (1981). On some positive aspects of the negative therapeutic reaction. *International Journal of Psycho-Analysis, 62:* 379–390.

Lipton, S. D. (1977). The advantage of Freud's technique as shown in his analysis of the Rat Man. *International Journal of Psycho-Analysis, 58:* 255–273.

Little, M. (1951). Counter-transference and the patient's response to it. *International Journal of Psycho-Analysis, 32:* 32–40.

Lussana, P. A. (1984). Con Mrs. Bick discutendo la "mother-infant observation" accanto alle varianti dell'interazione analista-analizzato. *Rivista di Psicoanalisi, 30:* 356–367.

Mack Brunswick, R. (1928). A supplement to Freud's "History of an Infantile Neurosis". *International Journal of Psycho-Analysis, 9:* 439–476. Also in: R. Fliess (Ed.), *The Psycho-Analytic Reader.* New York: International Universities Press, 1948.

Mancia, M. (Ed.) (1979). *Super-Io e Ideale dell'Io*. Milan: Il Formichiere.

_____ (1981). On the beginning of mental life in the foetus. *International Journal of Psycho-Analysis, 62*: 351–357.

_____ (1985). "Stati psicosomatici e ipocondriaci: Loro relazione con la scissione e la identificazione proiettiva" [Psychosomatic and hypochondriacal states: Their relation to splitting and projective identification]. Read at the Milanese Center for Psychoanalysis.

_____ (1987). *Il sogno come religione della mente*. Bari: Laterza.

Manfredi Turillazzi, S. (1974). Dall'interpretazione mutativa di Strachey all'interpretazione delle relazioni tra gli oggetti interni. *Rivista di Psicoanalisi, 20*: 127–143.

_____ (1978a). Super-Io e Ideale dell'Io come funzioni degli oggetti interni. In: M. Mancia (Ed.), *Super-Io e Ideale dell'Io*. Milan: Il Formichiere, 1979.

_____ (1978b). Interpretazione dell'agire e interpretazione come agire. *Rivista di Psicoanalisi, 24*: 223–240.

_____ (1985). L'unicorno. Saggio sulla fantasia e l'oggetto nel concetto di identificazione proiettiva. *Rivista di Psicoanalisi, 31*: 462–477.

McDougall, J. (1974). The psychosoma and the psychoanalytic process. *International Review of Psycho-Analysis, 1*: 437–459.

Meltzer, D. (1964). The differentiation of somatic delusions from hypochondria. *International Journal of Psycho-Analysis, 45*: 246–250.

_____ (1966). The relation of anal masturbation to projective identification. *International Journal of Psycho-Analysis, 47*: 335–342. .

_____ (1967). *The Psychoanalytic Process*. London: W. Heinemann.

_____ (1973). *Sexual States of the Mind*. Perthshire: Clunie Press.

_____ (1976). Temperature and distance as technical dimensions of interpretation. *EPF Bulletin, 9*: 39–45.

_____ (1986a). *Studies in Extended Metapsychology*. Perthshire. Clunie Press.

_____ (1986b). Riflessione sui mutamenti nel mio metodo psicoanalitico. *Psicoterapia e Scienze Umane, 20*: 260–269.

Meltzer, D., Bremner, J., Hoxter, S., Wedell, D., & Wittenberg, I. (1975). *Exploration in Autism*. Perthshire: Clunie Press.

Mendilaharsu (de), S. A. (1965). La hypocondría. Algunos consideraciones a propósito del análisis de un paciente hipocondríaco. *Revista Uruguaya de Psicoanálisis, 7*: 307–323.

Meotti, A. (1981). L'identità dello psicoanalista e il carattere scientifico del processo psicoanalitico. *Rivista di Psicoanalisi, 27*: 127–136.

_____ (1982). Alcune considerazioni sul simbolo nella relazione analitica. *Gli Argonauti, 13*: 131–140.

Meotti, A., & Meotti, F. (1988). "Colpa e responsabilità: Un altro problema per il controtransfert e l'interpretazione" [Guilt and responsibility: Two problems in countertransference and interpretation]. Read at the Eighth Congress of the Italian Psychoanalytical Society, Sorrento.

Merleau-Ponty, M. (1964). Les relations avec autrui chez l'enfant. *Bulletin de Psychologie, 18*: 295–336.

Micati Zecca, L. (1982). La comunicazione pre-verbale nella relazione analitica tra fusione e individuazione. *Rivista di Psicoanalisi, 28*: 171–189.

Milner, M. (1952). *On Not Being Able to Paint.* London: Heinemann.

_____ (1969). *The Hands of the Living God.* London: Hogarth Press.

Mitchell, S. A. (1988). The intrapsychic and the interpersonal: Different theories, different domains, or historical artifacts. *Psychoanalytic Inquiry, 8/4*: 472–495.

Money-Kyrle, R. E. (1956). Normal counter-transference and some of its deviations. *International Journal of Psycho-Analysis, 37*: 360–366. Also in *Collected Papers.* Perthshire, Clunie Press, 1978.

Morpurgo, E. (1985a). Le strategie nascoste della parola. In: E. Morpurgo & V. Egidi (Eds.), *Psicoanalisi e Narrazione.* Ancona: Il Lavoro Editoriale, 1987.

_____ (1985b). Parola letteraria e parola analitica. In: A. M. Accerboni (Ed.), *Atti del Convegno "La Cultura Psicoanalitica", Trieste, 5–8 December 1985.* Pordenone: Studio Tesi.

Morpurgo, E., & Egidi, V. (Eds.) (1987). *Psicoanalisi e Narrazione,* Ancona: Il Lavoro Editoriale.

Muñoz, J. G., & Baranger, W. (1964). Aparición de un "quiste" hipocondríaco en el curso de un análisis. *Revista Uruguaya de Psicoanálisis, 6*: 39–45.

Munro, L. (1949). Analysis of a cartoon in a case of hypochondriasis. *International Journal of Psycho-Analysis, 29*: 53–57.

Musatti, C. (1976). La psicoanalisi nella cultura italiana. *Rivista di Psicoanalisi, 22*: 154–161.

Muscetta, S. (1990). Gli affetti nella teoria e nella pratica psico-analitica. In: M. Ammanniti & N. Dazzi (Eds.), *Affetti. Natura e Sviluppo delle Relazioni Interpersonali.* Bari: Laterza.

Nachman di Breslav (1981). *La Principessa Smarrita.* Milan: Adelphi.

Neri, C. (1985). Contenimento fusionale e oscillazione contenitore-contenuto. *Rivista di Psicoanalisi, 31*: 316–325. Also in: C. Neri et al., *Fusionalità.* Rome: Borla, 1990.

Neri, C., Pallier, L., Petacchi, G., Soavi, G. C., & Tagliacozzo, R. (1990). *Fusionalità.* Rome: Borla.

Nieto Grove, M. (1963). De la histeria a la hypocondría. *Revista Uruguaya de Psicoanálisis, 5*: 367–389.

_____ (1964). Mecanismos obsesivos y defensa hypocondríaca. *Revista Uruguaya de Psicoanálisis, 6*: 429–451.

Nissim Momigliano, L. (1974). Come si originano le interpretazioni dell'analista. *Rivista di Psicoanalisi, 20*: 144–165.

_____ (1975). "Una vicenda analitica esemplare: L'uomo dei lupi e le sue vicissitudini" [An exemplary analytical event: The Wolf Man and his vicissitudes]. Read at the Milanese Centre for Psychoanalysis.

_____ (1979). Taccuino d'appunti. *Rivista di Psicoanalisi, 25*: 178–198.

_____ (1981). Memory and desire. *Rivista di Psicoanalisi, 27*: 546–557.

_____ (1982). Note in margine a un testo: La supervisione analitica. In: G. Di Chiara (Ed.), *Itinerari della Psicoanalisi,* Turin: Loescher.

_____ (1987). A spell in Vienna: But was Freud a Freudian? *International Review of Psycho-Analysis, 14*: 373–389. Also in: L. Nissim Momigliano, *Letters from Milan: On Being a Psychoanalyst Today.* London: Karnac Books, 1992.

_____ (1990). Preface to C. Neri et al., *Fusionalità.* Rome: Borla, 1990.

_____ (1991). The psychoanalyst in the mirror: Doubts galore but few certainties. *International Journal of Psycho-Analysis, 72*: 287–296.

_____ (1992). *Letters from Milan: On Being a Psychoanalyst Today.* London: Karnac Books.

Ogden, T. H. (1979). On projective identification. *International Journal of Psycho-Analysis, 60*: 357–373.

_____ (1986). *The Matrix of the Mind.* Northvale, NJ, London: Jason Aronson.

Olinick, S. L. (1964). The negative therapeutic reaction. *International Journal of Psycho-Analysis, 45*: 540–548.

_____ (1970). Negative therapeutic reaction. *Journal of the American Psychoanalytical Association, 18*: 655–672.

Oliverio, A. (1984). *Storia Naturale della Mente. L'Evoluzione del Comportamento.* Turin: Boringhieri.

Pallier, L. (1984). Fusionalità, agora e claustrofobia e processi schizo-paranoidi. *Rivista di Psicoanalisi, 31*: 299–306. Also in: C. Neri et al., *Fusionalità.* Rome: Borla, 1990.

Petacchi, G. (1984). Fantasie fusionali. In: C. Neri et al., *Fusionalità.* Rome: Borla, 1990.

Petrella, F. (1988). Il modello freudiano. In: A. A. Semi (Ed.), *Trattato di Psicoanalisi,* Milan: Cortina.

Pitré, G. (1875). *Fiabe, Novelle e Racconti Popolari Siciliani, Vol. I.* Palermo: Pedone Lauriel.

Pontalis, J. B. (1981). Non, deux fois non. *Nouvelle Revue de Psychanalyse, 24*: 53–71.

Reich, W. (1933). *Character Analysis.* New York: Farrar, Straus & Giroux, 1970. [Reprinted London: Karnac Books, 1987.]

Ricci Bitti, P. E., & Caterina, R. (1990). La comunicazione delle emozioni. In: M. Ammanniti & N. Dazzi (Eds.), *Affetti. Natura e Sviluppo delle Relazioni Interpersonali.* Bari: Laterza.

Richards, A. D. (1981). Self theory, conflict theory and the problem of hypochondriasis. *Psychoanalytic Study of the Child, 36*: 319–337.

Rilke, R. M. (1923). *Duineser Elegien.* [*Duino's Elegies* (translated by C. F. Mac Intyre). Berkeley, Los Angeles, London: University of California Press.]

Riolo, F. (1983). Sogno e teoria della conoscenza in psicoanalisi. *Rivista di Psicoanalisi, 29*: 279–295.

_____ (1987). "Proton pseudos". Dal pensiero isterico al pensiero analitico. *Rivista di Psicoanalisi, 33*: 397–412.

Riviere, J. (1936). A contribution to the analysis of the negative therapeutic reaction. *International Journal of Psycho-Analysis, 17*: 304–320. Also in: A. Hughes (Ed.), *The Inner World and*

Joan Riviere: Collected Papers 1920–1958. London: Karnac Books, 1991.

Rosenfeld, D. (1983). Hypochondrías, delirio somatico y esquema corporal en la pratica psicoanalitica. *Revista de Psicoanálisis, 40*: 175–198.

_____ (1984). Hypochondriasis, somatic delusions and body scheme in psychoanalytic practice. *International Journal of Psycho-Analysis, 65*: 337–387. Also in: D. Rosenfeld, *The Psychotic: Aspects of the Personality.* London: Karnac Books, 1991.

Rosenfeld, H. (1950). Note on the psychopathology of confusional states in chronic schizophrenia. *International Journal of Psycho-Analysis, 31*: 132–137.

_____ (1958). Some observations on the psychopathology of hypochondriacal states. *International Journal of Psycho-Analysis, 39*: 121–124.

_____ (1963). Notes on the psychopathology and psychoanalytical treatment of schizophrenia. *Psychotic States.* London: Hogarth Press and the Institute of Psycho-Analysis, 1965. [Reprinted London: Karnac Books, 1985.]

_____ (1964). The psychopathology of hypochondriasis. In: *Psychotic States.* London: Hogarth Press and the Institute of Psycho-Analysis, 1965. [Reprinted London: Karnac Books, 1985.]

_____ (1968). "Notes on the negative therapeutic reaction". Read to the British Psycho-Analytical Society.

_____ (1969). Sull'identificazione proiettiva. *Rivista di Psicoanalisi, 26* (1980): 118–139.

_____ (1971). A clinical approach to the psychoanalytic theory of the life and death instincts: An investigation into the aggressive aspects of narcissism. *International Journal of Psycho-Analysis, 52*: 169–178.

_____ (1975). Negative therapeutic reaction. In: P. L. Giovacchini (Ed.), *Tactics and Techniques in Psycho-Analytic Therapy.* New York: Jason Aronson.

_____ (1978a). Notes on the psychopathology and psychoanalytic treatment of some borderline patients. *International Journal of Psycho-Analysis, 58*: 215–239.

_____ (1978b). Some therapeutic factors in psychoanalysis. *International Journal of Psychoanalytic Psychotherapy, 4*: 152–164.

_____ (1987a). *Impasse and Interpretation*. London: Tavistock.

_____ (1987b). The narcissistic omnipotent character structure: A case of chronic hypochondriasis. In: H. Rosenfeld, *Impasse and Interpretation*. London: Tavistock.

_____ (1987c). Narcissistic patients with negative therapeutic reactions. In: H. Rosenfeld, *Impasse and Interpretation*. London: Tavistock.

_____ (1987d). Projective identification in clinical practice. In: H. Rosenfeld, *Impasse and Interpretation*. London: Tavistock.

Russo, L. (1990). "La doppia scena dell'affettività. In: G. Hautmann & A. Vergine (Eds.), *Gli affetti nella psicoanalisi*. Rome: Borla, 1991.

Rycroft, C. (1956). The nature and function of the analyst's communication to the patient. *International Journal of Psycho-Analysis, 37*: 469–472. Also in: C. Rycroft, *Imagination and Reality. Psycho-Analytical Essays 1951–1961*. London: Hogarth Press, 1968.

_____ (1958). An enquiry into the function of words in the psychoanalytical situation. *International Journal of Psycho-Analysis, 39*: 408–415.

_____ (1968a). *A Critical Dictionary of Psychoanalysis*. London: Thomas Nelson.

_____ (1968b). *Imagination and Reality. Psycho-Analytical Essays 1951–1961*. London: Hogarth Press. [Reprinted London: Karnac Books, 1987.]

Sacerdoti, G. (1977). Transfert, preconscio e "cliché" culturali. *Rivista di Psicoanalisi, 23*: 215–229.

Searles, H. F. (1975). The patient as a therapist of his analyst: In: P. L. Giovacchini (Ed.), *Tactics and Techniques in Psychoanalytic Therapy, Vol. II*. New York, Jason Aronson.

Servadio, E. (1976). Il movimento psicoanalitico in Italia. *Rivista di Psicoanalisi, 22*: 162–168.

Shengold, L. (1967). The effects of overstimulation: Rat people. *International Journal of Psycho-Analysis, 48*: 403–415.

Soavi, G. C. (1984). Fusionalità contro fusionalità e altri argomenti. *Rivista di Psicoanalisi, 31*: 307–315. Also in C. Neri et al., *Fusionalità*. Rome: Borla, 1990.

Spairani Aulagner, P. (1975). *La violence de l'interprétation*. Paris: Presses Universitaires de France.

Speziale Bagliacca, R. (1977). Tecniche dittatoriali esterne e dittatoriali interne. *Rivista di Psicoanalisi, 23*: 431–436.

_____ (1982a). *On the Shoulders of Freud. Freud, Lacan, and the Psychoanalysis of Phallic Ideology.* New Brunswick: Transaction Books, 1991.

_____ (1982b). L'interpretazione-comizio. *Rivista di Psicoanalisi, 28*: 245–251.

_____ (1982c). Nota in margine al libro "Teoria della Identificazione" di L. Grinberg. *Rivista di Psicoanalisi, 28*: 581–584.

Spotnitz, H. (1969). *Modern Psychoanalysis of the Schizophrenic Patient.* New York: Grune & Stratton.

Stern, D. (1977). *The First Relationship: Infant and Mother.* London: Fontana.

Svevo, I. (1923). *Confessions of Zeno* (translated by Beryl de Zoete). London: Penguin Books, 1964.

Tagliacozzo, R. (1976). Terminabilità e interminabilità della analisi personale a fini didattici. *Rivista di Psicoanalisi, 22*: 36–50.

_____ (1980). Psicoanalisi come droga: Nota sul progetto e sulla terminabilità dell'analisi. *Rivista di Psicoanalisi, 26*: 307–316.

_____ (1982). La pensabilità, una meta della psicoanalisi. In: G. Di Chiara (Ed.), *Itinerari della Psicoanalisi.* Turin: Loescher.

_____ (1984). Angoscie fusionali: Mondo concreto e mondo pensabile. *Rivista di Psicoanalisi, 31*: 290–298. Also in: C. Neri et al., *Fusionalità.* Rome: Borla, 1990.

Thorner, H. A. (1955). Three defences against inner persecution. Examination anxiety, depersonalization and hypochondria. In: M. Klein, P. Heimann, & R. E. Money-Kyrle (Eds.), *New Directions in Psychoanalysis. The Significance of Infant Conflict in the Pattern of Adult Behaviour.* London: Tavistock. [Reprinted London: Karnac Books, 1985.]

Tower, L. (1956). Countertransference. *Journal of the American Psychoanalytical Association, 4*: 224–255.

Trevarten, C. (1990). Le emozioni intuitive: L'evoluzione del loro ruolo nella comunicazione tra madre e bambino. In M. Ammanniti & N. Dazzi (Eds.), *Affetti. Natura e Sviluppo delle Relazioni Interpersonali.* Bari: Laterza.

Tustin, F. (1986). *Autistic Barriers in Neurotic Patients.* London: Karnac Books.

Tyszblat, J. (1990). L'analyse interrompue. . . . *Revue Française de Psychanalyse, 2*: 511–518.

Usuelli Kluzer, A. (1980). Transfert/Controtransfert: Una relazione asimmetrica. *Rivista di Psicoanalisi, 26*: 111–116.

Vallino Macciò, D. (1981). Ansie di separazione rilevate nella osservazione del neonato e nella psicoanalisi di adolescenti e adulti. *Giornale di Neuropsichiatria dell'Età Evolutiva, 1*: 173–184.

Vattimo, G., & Rovatti, P. A. (Eds.) (1983). *Il Pensiero Debole*. Milan: Feltrinelli.

Viderman, S. (1974). Interpretation in the analytic space. *International Review of Psycho-Analysis, 1*: 467–480.

Viviani, C. (1975). *Psicoanalisi Interrotte*. Milan: Sugarco.

Wangh, M. (1962). The "evocation of a proxy": A psychological maneuver, its use as a defense, its purposes and genesis. *Psychoanalytic Study of the Child, 27*: 451–469.

Winnicott, D. W. (1955). On Transference. *International Journal of Psycho-Analysis, 37* (1956): 386–388. Also in: D. W. Winnicott, *Through Pediatrics to Psycho-Analysis*. London: Hogarth Press, 1977. [Reprinted London: Karnac Books, 1991.]

_____ (1956). Primary maternal preoccupation. In: *Through Paediatrics to Psychoanalysis*. London: Hogarth Press, 1977. [Reprinted London: Karnac Books, 1991.]

_____ (1960). The theory of the parent-child relationship. *International Journal of Psycho-Analysis, 41*: 585–595. Also in: D. W. Winnicott, *The Maturational Process and the Facilitating Environment. Studies in the Theory of Emotional Development*. London: Hogarth Press, 1965. [Reprinted London: Karnac Books, 1990.]

_____ (1962). The aims of psycho-analytic treatment. In: D. W. Winnicott, *The Maturational Process and the Facilitating Environment. Studies in the Theory of Emotional Development*. London: Hogarth Press, 1965. [Reprinted London: Karnac Books, 1990.]

_____ (1963). The development of the capacity for concern. In: D. W. Winnicott, *The Maturational Process and the Facilitating Environment. Studies in the Theory of Emotional Development*. London: Hogarth Press, 1965. [Reprinted London: Karnac Books, 1990.]

_____ (1965). *The Maturational Process and the Facilitating Environment. Studies in the Theory of Emotional Development.* London: Hogarth Press. [Reprinted London: Karnac Books, 1990.]

_____ (1971). *Playing and Reality.* London: Tavistock.

_____ (1974). Fear of breakdown. *International Review of Psycho-Analysis, 1:* 103–107.

Wittenberg, I. (1988). "The emotional experience of learning and its roots in infancy". Read at the Clinica Neuropsichiatrica Infantile, Turin.

Zaccaria Gairinger, L. (1970). L'autoanalisi. *Psiche, 7:* 75–87.

Zanin, J. C. (1990). Crises de interrupção da análise e controtransferência. *Revista Brasileira de Psicanálise, 24:* 513–525.

INDEX

Abraham, K., 134
acting
  in, 10, 78
  interpretative, 135
  out, 10, 78, 94, 125, 129, 130, 135
    communicative value of, 17
actual neurosis, 197, 200
adhesiveness, 103, 104, 170
Aegisthus, 193
Aeschylus, 193
affect, 58, 59
affective communication, 24, 49
affective matrix, 22
affective thought, 49
affective–cognitive phenomenology, 49
affects, 23, 24, 25, 36, 37
Agamemnon, 192, 193
agglutinated nucleus, 199, 200
agglutinated part, 53
aggression, 100
Albarella, C., 132
alienated areas, xxiv
alienated residue, 141
alpha function, 135, 201
Alvarez, A., 58, 90
Amati Mehler, J., 126, 130
ambiguity, and confusion, 198–200
Ammanniti, M., 24
anal erotism, 71, 75, 76
anal masturbation, 71, 75, 76, 77, 83
anal sadism, 71
analysability, 63, 121, 125, 130
analysis
  interminability of, 127, 129, 139
  child, xxi, 6, 93
  contraindication for, 130

dangers of, 131
failure of, 128
indications for, xix, 31, 130
premature termination of, 125–141
analyst
  behaviour of, 13
  difficulties of, 121
  error of, 11, 19, 57, 123, 128, 148
    technical, 10, 60, 79, 147, 148, 155
  failure of, 128
  identity of, 68, 83, 126
  as internal object, 108
  intimate relationship with, 57
  intrapsychic world of, xxv
  introjection of, as good object, 137
  mental attitude of, 57
  mental functioning of, 44
  mental health of, 61
  mental make-up of, 20, 35, 68, 91
    anxiety in, 90
  mental survival of, 68
  mind of, xxiii, 12, 27, 43, 51, 56, 57, 65–120, 121
    risks and benefits for, 61–65
  narcissism of, 20, 131, 138
  naturalness of, 40
  neutrality of, 2, 44
  –patient
    collusion, 122
    communication, 19
    encounter, xiv
    interaction, 138
    reciprocity, 133
    relationship, xxiii, 24, 25, 91, 92, 130, 138
  personality of, 131

235